CIVIC CHALLENGES, DEMOCRACY AND MEDIA

CIVIC CHALLENGES, DEMOCRACY AND MEDIA

Editor
Dr. Neeraj Khattri

ISBN: 978-81-7835-993-9
Price: 880

First Published 2014

Published by

Kalpaz Publications
C-30, Satyawati Nagar,
Delhi - 110052
E-mail: kalpaz@hotmail.com Ph.: 9212142040
Laser Typesetting : Shah Computer Graphics
Printed at : G. Print Process, Delhi

Cataloging in Publication Data—DK
Courtesy: D.K. Agencies (P) Ltd. <docinfo@dkagencies.com>

International Conference on "Civic Challenges, Democracy and Media" (2012 : Mangalayatan University)
Civic challenges, democracy and media / editor, Neeraj Khattri.
p. cm.
Includes bibliographical references.
ISBN 9788178359939

1. Mass media—Political aspects—Congresses. 2. Mass media—Political aspects—India—Congresses. 3. Mass media—Social aspects—Congresses. 4. Mass media—Social aspects—India—Congresses. 5. Democracy—Congresses. 6. Democracy—India—Congresses. I. Khattri, Neeraj. II. Title.

DDC 302.23 23

Dedicated to my
Dearest sister Shikha

Contents

Patron

Shri Pawan Jain,
Chairman, Board of Governors
Mangalayatan University

Shri Mohan Lakhamraju
Vice-Chairman, Board of Governors
Mangalayatan University

Prof. S.C. Jain
Vice Chancellor
Mangalayatan University

Shri Karthik Gopalan
Vice-President, Operations
Mangalayatan University, Aligarh

Foreword

Democracy is the best political system in the whole world and this is the reason for the wider access to public rights. The soul of the democracy lies in the interests of the public at large. So the state cannot deny the public benefits in a democratic set up.

Media, in recent days, has been considered as the forth pillar of the democracy that plays a very crucial role in safeguarding the democratic rights of highest body, that is public. Latest media technologies increased the reach of the media at wider level, so it is necessary to analyse the role and responsibilities of the media with a newer perspective with changing time.

In recent days, the role of media has been exceedingly crucial in public perspective. The Institute of Journalism and Mass Communication, Mangalayatan University is organising two day International Conference on "Civic Challenges, Democracy and Media", first step taken towards providing awareness to the public about the role of media in the democratic set up.

This is a matter of great pride that the Institute of Journalism and Mass Communication is publishing an edited book of a compilation of important research works, which has been received from the different eminent writers across the globe for the presentation at the conference.

I congratulate the editor and editorial board for the publication of this book.

February 25, 2012

Prof. S.C. Jain
(Hon'ble Vice-Chancellor)

Acknowledgements

I feel extremly delighted and honored to present this book entitled "Civic Challenges, democracy and Media". This book is the mirror of India in the democratic set up and focuses on the role of the Media related to the challenges of social life in democracy. The book includes the papers written on the various sub-themes under "Civic Challenges, Democracy and Media". Papers are contributions of eminent scholars in the field of Communication and Journalism and other fields with an interdisciplinary approach.

The concept of this edited book is given by Prof. Girija Shankar Sharma and we are thankful for his valuable inspiration and suggestions received by us from time to time. I would like to convey my sincere thanks to all students, teachers, research scholars and other writers for their contributions in providing a valuable knowledge platform. I would also like to convey my deep sense of gratitude to Prof. Satish Chandra Jain, Hon'ble Vice-Chancellor, Mangalayatan University, for supporting the publication process.

I will always be thankful to Prof. Virbala Aggarwal for her inspiration, support and blessings, from the core of my heart. Further, I am also thankful to Prof. Devesh Kishore and Prof. Pradeep Mathur for their valuable suggestions. I convey my sincere thanks to all the members of the editorial Board for their continuous support during the course of editing of the book. I must thank to Pt. Amandeep and Shri Jai Prakash Rai for designing the book in a beautiful manner.

I would like to thank to my father Shri Rajkumar Khattri and Mother Smt. Shashi Khattri for being sources for necessary motivation in the making of this book. At the end, I express my deep sense of gratitute for my younger brother Shri Pankaj Khattri and wife Smt. Priya Khattri for their constant support.

February 25, 2012

Dr. Neeraj Khattri
Editor

List of Contributors

Devesh Kishore, Professor Emeritus, Department of Communication Research, Makhanlal Chaturvedi National of Journalism and Communication, Noida Campus, U.P.

Jon Silverman, Research Institute of Media, Art and Design University of Bedfordshire. United Kingdom.

Yahya Fozi, Associate Professor, Political Science, Imam Khomeini International University, Qazvin, Iran.

Abhijit Bora, Associate Professor, Department of Mass Journalism Tezpur University, Napaam, Assam.

Smita Vashishta, Assistant Professor, Department of Journalism and Mass Communication, Dev Sanskriti Vishwavidalaya, Haridwar, Uttrakhand.

Mandavi, Ashutosh, Head, Department of Advertising and Public relation Studies, Kushabhau Thakre University of Journalism and Mass Communication, Raipur, Chhattisgarh.

Bahareh Bakhshi, Professor, Department of Social Communication Sciences, Damavand Branch, Islamic Azad University, Tehran, Iran.

Arijit Ghosh, Assistant Professor (contractual), Department of Journalism and Mass Communication Netaji Subhas Open University, Kolkata.

Vinod Kumar Pandey, Head, Department of Journalism and Mass Communication, Gujarat Vidyapeeth, Ahmedabad, Gujarat.

Debila Mishra, Research Scientist (JRF), GJUS & T, Hisar, Haryana.

Deepshikha Saxena Lectures, IER, Mangalayatan University, Aligarh

Jyoti Sankar Pradhan, Lectures, IER, Mangalayatan University, Aligarh.

Naseem Ahmad Khan, Assistant Professor, Department of Sociology and Social Work, Faculty of Arts, A.M.U, Aligarh.

Nadia Bilgrami, Research Scholar, ELLLM university, Shilling.

Abdul Hakim, Professor Department of Commerce, Government Girls P.G. College, Rewa.

Ruksana Begam, Researcher Chemistry, A.P.S. University Rewa.

Rehana Begam, Researcher Microbiology, A.P.S University Rewa.

Uma Shankar Pandey, Assistant Professor, Department of Journalism and Mass Communication, Surendranath College for Women University of Calcutta Kolkata, India.

Nicholas S. Iwokwagh, Assistant Professor, Department of Information and Media Technology, Federal University of Technology, Minna, Nigeria.

Minal, Faculty member, Institute of Business Management Mangalayatan University, Aligarh.

Shahzad Alam, Lecturer IJMC, Mangalayatan University, Aligarh.

Ahanuddin Haider, Professor and Director R.V. Northland Institute of Management Greater Noida.

Venudhar Routiya, Research Assistant to Chhattisgarh Legislative Assembly, Raipur, Guest Lecturer (law), Govt. J.Y.C.G. College, Raipur (C.G.), Chief Editor, "Nav Pravah", International Research Journal.

Devdas Saket, Research Scholar, Department of Philosophy Govt. T.R.S (Auto). College Rewa (M.P).

Skay Lamb Toofan, Guest Faculty, Department of Commerce, Govt. P.G. College Tikamgarh (M.P.).

Sandhya Singh, Research Scholar (Sociology) Banasthli Vidhapeeth Jaipur Rajasthan.

Ambrish Saxena, GGSIP University (former) New Delhi.

Rajshree Chatterjee, Lecturer, IMS, Ghaziabad.

Umesh Kumar, Karmveer Vidyapeeth, Old R.T.O, 64 Anand Nagar Khandwa (M.P.)

Minu Sharma, Karmveer Vidyapeeth, Old R.T.O, 64 Anand`Nagar Khandwa (M.P.)

Pradeep Kumar, Mangalayatan University, Aligarh.

Priyanka Singh, Mangalayatan University, Aligarh.

Abid Rizvi, Department of Psychiatry, J.N Medical College, A.M.U, Aligarh.

Prashanta Kumar Pal, IBMER, Mangalayatan University, Aligarh.

Sukhnandan Singh, Associate Professor and Head, Department of Journalism and Mass Communication Devasanskrity Vishwavidyalaya, Gayatrikunj, Shantikunj, Haridwar (Uttrakhand).

K. Kulasekarn, Research Scholar, Madurai Kamaraj University, Madurai.

P. Rajendran, Head and Academic Co-ordinator, Department of Journalism and Mass Communication and Law, D.D.E., Madurai Kamaraj University, Madurai.

1

Role of Diverse Media Content in Democracy

Prof. (Dr.) Devesh Kishore

Marshall McLuhan envisaged a 'global village' where media within new democracies are encouraged as a tool of power to take over previously unexploited social domains via information, entertainment and new technology. Some find media as guardian of the public, or public relation officer of power elites. Some prejudice it as agent of participatory democracy, or seller of consumer capitalism.

The mass media can be the backbone of democracy if its functions include surveillance of sociopolitical developments, identifying the most relevant issues, providing a platform for debate across a diverse range of views, holding officials to account for the way they exercise power, provide incentives for citizens to learn, choose, and become involved in the political process, and resist efforts of forces outside the media to subvert their independence. Commercial mass media in India controlled by a few chasing TRP and cheap popularity have become an antidemocratic force. The news is more entertaining than informing, supplying mostly gossip, scandals, sex, and violence. Political news is more about personalities than about their ideologies. In the absence of serious debate, voters are left with paid political propaganda containing only meaningless slogans and paid news making them disinterested and pessimist about democratic development.

Communication is equally essential like food, shelter and health for people. Factors that are basic to democracy are freedom of expression, mutual respect, freedom of conscience etc. which are mediated by communication. It can be exclaimed that the prerequisite of democracy is democratisation of communication, which strongly requires the empowerment of individual.

The media is privileged to democratise the communication by providing a platform for public debate and reconstituting citizen as a public body in the form of public opinion. It is also necessary to make public communication an integral part of democracy. People should have free access to the knowledge and information they require, they should be able to discuss matters of public interest with other members of community in order to influence actions to be taken. Otherwise, there can be no genuine participation.

But, media is moving away from creating responsible citizenship and is busy in transforming citizens into spectators by serving them cheap entertainment instead of providing right type of education. Media inspite of being a vehicle for advancing freedom and democracy started becoming a means of minting money and propaganda for the new and powerful class. The deteriorating attitude of media towards the masses is also influenced by the globalisation and economic liberalisation. The money has ruled over the ethics of media. Profit motives have made the media to forget its social responsibility.

Diverse Media Content

The way the public looks at issues and whether or not the public is even aware of certain issues is directly related to the way these issues are covered by media. The way that media covers the issues is directly related to the thinking of media workers employed – the reporters, producers and anchors who design and develop the stories. Thinking and philosophy of the employed media workers is directly related to the owners of the media and the one who owns the media is directly related to his policies and philosophy.

In an effective democratic system media should be fully representative of the communities that it serves. Diverse media content means that various media covers different aspects of stories so that members of community can get information from various angles and analytical views of experts on the topic cover various aspects of the stories. Studies have indicated that diverse media content helps the audience, readers and viewers in developing their analytical capacity in accepting or rejecting the news content.

Research studies have also indicated that people who make development news if involved while developing media content makes the stories more reliable and valid. Diverse media content can be of great help in understanding all sides of stories and taking a final decision. The old Chinese proverb i.e. "If you give a fish everyday to a person, you are keeping him alive for few days. If you teach him the method of catching a fish, you are keeping him alive for life long." Hence, diverse media content can help them in understanding the real news by analysing diverse media content.

Media in India

The world's largest democracy and one of its fastest growing economies has implications for media and communication globally. With growing round-the-clock news channels, cyber-journalism unrivalled in any other country India can be said as the world's most linguistically diverse media landscape.

The World Association of Newspapers also highlights that the sale of newspapers in India between 2000 and 2008 grew by 46 per cent. Daily more than 99 million copies of newspapers are sold in India, at a time when newspapers are closing down in the West on a regular basis. Journalists are finding new ways to communicate with a demanding and fragmenting audience, including a young and vocal middle-class mass through FM and community radio.

The journalism education in India is also experiencing a massive expansion and proliferation of media outlets, offering vocationally oriented journalism courses. Media revolution in India offers exciting opportunities, as well as challenges to professional journalists. This raises some serious questions as has competition encouraged journalists to move away from public-service news

World's Largest Newspaper Circulating Countries

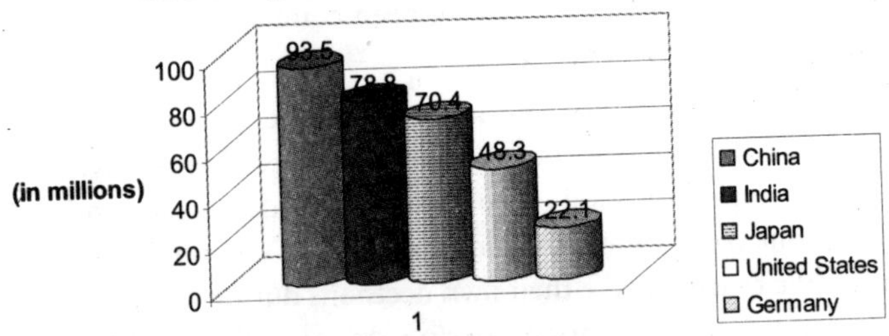

Source - World Association of Newspaper (WAN), 2005 Report

Communication and Media in India

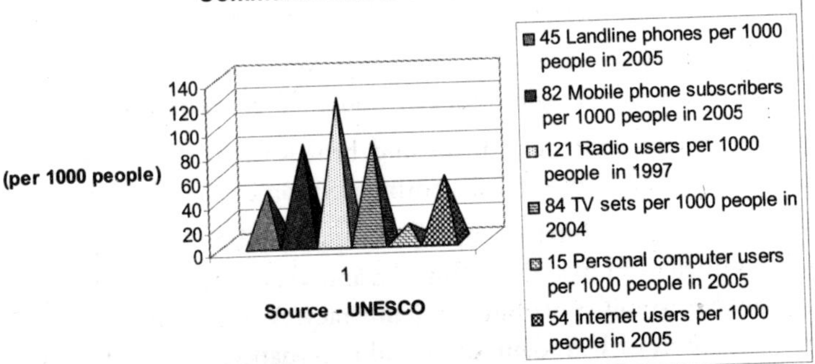

Source - UNESCO

agenda to a 'soft' version of news, with its emphasis on consumer journalism, sports and entertainment? Is the market-driven news media eroding the public sphere in a country where a majority of the people still lives in poverty? Given the scale and globalising tendencies of media in India, what are the international implications of these developments for journalism?

Democratisation of India

The concept of a "Free press" is well accepted to be the fundamental to the democratic process. Neighbouring country China in Worldwide Press Freedom Index 2007, Reporters Without Borders is ranked 163rd (or 7th from bottom) in terms of press freedom. Freedom House issued a report in 2006 claiming that the internet in China is still closely monitored by the state, with access to websites and publications critical of the government being restricted, as well as foreign satellite television and radio broadcasts being censored. Nevertheless, the Committee to Protect Journalists (CPJ) reported that China "continues to be the world's leading jailer of journalists," with 42 imprisoned journalists at the end of 2004, and accuses private companies, both foreign and domestic, of having been complacent toward or complicit with government censorship.

The Australian constitution does not include any guarantee of freedom of the press. The High Court of Australia has ruled that the right to freedom of "political communication" is fundamental to democracy and is therefore implied in our constitution. The idea of political communication is in order for the public to truly make their own decisions during an election campaign; they need access to information not directly controlled by the government.

Restrictive media laws in many post-communist countries curtail media freedoms guaranteed by these countries' constitutions or by international conventions that these countries have signed.

In state of Palestine a leading Palestinian journalist is jailed in the West Bank for broadcasting sessions of the Palestinian Legislative Council.

In Central America, a select group of powerful families control the media and threaten democratic gains realised through the peace processes of the 1990s.

Government control of print and broadcast media in many African countries leave little scope for dissenting opinion and public debate.

U.S. Agency for International Development (USAID) with its partners have attempted to address these obstacles and to develop media sectors around the globe that would contribute to democracy. As such, support for media is important aspect of U.S. democracy and governance.

In this context, the Indian media is fortunate to have uncensored press. Even the citizen journalism is very much supported and persuaded in local as well as national level media.

A view of the communication process, *i.e.* a two-way concept of sender and receiver, implies to the concept of "Free press". This is in recognition of the control that media organisations hold in choosing information to be published and not to be published. This system means that while a sender may be "free" from government censorship, (s) he is not guaranteed access to the media. If cross-media ownership laws are abandoned, it will mean a reduced number of "gates" for information to flow through, as large commercial interests will be able to own networks of different media. The danger is that large media corporations will be able to promote their own hidden agenda, to the exclusion of conflicting viewpoints. Regulation is therefore necessary to safeguard diversity.

The audience now has a much more diverse range of media available than it had earlier. If there is greater media diversity the threat of monopoly of news is reduced. The internet has opened up an unlimited world of communication, weakening the hold that major broadcasters once had over the audience. The internet has had a much all round effect on the media industry than any changes to cross-media ownership laws. The audience now has access to more "gates" than ever before, as well as an unprecedented opportunity to create their own "gates" of information. More than ever the audience is becoming the provider to media, rather than merely being a receiver of the media.

The Significance of Diverse Media Content in Democracy

Diverse media content can play a very significant role against increased corporate domination of mass media and the perceived diminishing of new and innovative ideas. It is necessary to scrutinise the option available with the media owners regarding what information is to be included or excluded.

The diverse media content ensures that citizens make responsible, informed choices rather than being ignorant and have misinformation about the happening in the nation and the world. It makes an individual wiser and effective decision maker and a rational thinker.

Assessing diverse media content serves as a checking function for the public to see that the elected representatives are holding their oaths of the office and fulfilling the promises made to their voters.

Alternative and citizen journalism may yield results in governance activities, particularly those related to decentralisation, anti-corruption, and citizen participation in the policy process.

According to article 19 (1) A of Indian Constitution, everyone has the right to freedom of speech and expression; this right includes freedom to hold opinions without interference and to seek, receive, and impart information and ideas through any media and regardless of boundaries. To support the democratic transitions, the goal behind promoting diverse media content is to move the media from one that is directed or controlled by government or private interests; to one that is more open and has a degree of editorial independence that serves the public interest.

If the media is to have any meaningful role in democracy, then the ultimate goal of media assistance should be to develop a range of diverse media content and voices that are credible, and to create and strengthen a sector that promotes such outlets. Credible outlets enable citizens to have access to information that they need to make informed decisions and to participate in society.

A media sector supportive of democracy would be one that has a degree of editorial independence, is financially viable, has diverse and plural voices, and serves the public interest. The public interest is defined as representing a plurality of voices both through a greater number of outlets and through the diversity of views and voices reflected within one outlet.

Concentration of Ownership Influence Media's Roles

Media is beyond delivering news and information. In the path to achieve a democratic media we need to look upon its amorphousness which encompasses everything from the universities that train future journalists to the courts that protect their rights? Media democracy remains an under-defined concept because of deliberate structural pressures that prevent individuals from questioning the connection between the press and democracy. Here are some suggestions that can be put forward to achieve democratic media content:

- Citizen participation should be considered as positive approach to freedom of the press. Access to diverse information can be helpful in having more informed, enlightened as well as responsible citizens of the country.
- Media ownership concentration should be examined critically because corporate ownership and commercial pressures influence media content, sharply limiting the range of news, opinions, and entertainment citizens receive.
- The ability to comprehend and scrutinise the connection between press and democracy is important because media has the power to tell various socio-economic, cultural and political stories etc. and thereby influence thinking, beliefs and behaviour.

- Existing laws should be further institutionalised to support for an independent media that keeps a track of judiciary, reports of the courts, and promotes a legal enabling environment suitable for press freedom.
- Free and fair elections conducted through transparent processes require a media sector which gives candidates equal access, and reports the relevant issues in a timely and objective manner.

As rightly said by Bernard Cohen (1963), that the press "may not be successful much of the time in telling people what to think, but it is stunningly successful in telling its readers what to think about". People need to be sensitised and alert in a media world full of complex issues and sensationalism. In the absence of other cues, people tend to judge the importance of issues from their salience in the media and to focus their attention on those presumably most important issues.

Bibliography

1. Research Papers and Articles

- Anger Fog, working paper 2005-05-20; The supposed and the real role of mass media in modern democracy.
- Patrick D. Murphy, 2007; Media and democracy in the age of Globalisation.
- LCCR Education Fund, Media Diversity Matters: A Media Justice Activist Toolkit.
- Centre for Democracy and Governance, June 1999; The Role of Media in Democracy: A strategic approach.
- B.A. Shridhara, Jan. 2003; Media Democracy and Citizenship.
- Solomen Wakeling, Media Diversity and Democracy.

2. Wikipedia

- Committee of Ministers of the Council of Europe.
- Media of the People's Republic of China.
- Communication and Information sector, UNESCO.
- Production of Diverse Media Content: Silk Road Radio Project – UNESCO.

2

Building Legitimacy : The West African Media's Role in Post-conflict Democracy

Prof. Jon Silverman

Context

In 2007, the *BBC World Service Trust* (BBCWST) launched a ground-breaking project to bring reliable daily reporting of the trial of the former Liberian president, Charles Taylor, to radio audiences in Liberia and Sierra Leone.[1] It was a solution to a straightforward problem. For reasons of regional security, the trial had been moved from the Sierra Leone capital, Freetown, to the Hague in the Netherlands. But how could the people of Sierra Leone and Liberia be provided with coverage of the proceedings on another continent and at a distance of thousands of miles? The answer was to fund, train and support a cohort of regional journalists to report directly from the courtroom in the Hague.[2] In the best traditions of cultural innovation, this was a pragmatic solution to a specific problem, but one whose longer-term legacy has the potential to foster democracy and stability in one of the most troubled regions of sub-Saharan Africa. Hence the title of this paper.

The indictment of Taylor by the Special Court for Sierra Leone (SCSL) in March 2003 and his eventual arrest three years later was regarded by proponents of international justice mechanism as a powerful symbolic statement about the end of 'impunity' for leaders who have maintained power through violence and oppression. "It is important for people to know that Charles Taylor is being held to account," said Tania Bermath, a researcher for Amnesty International in Sierra Leone (quoted in *Guardian Unlimited, 10.7.2007)*, echoing a consensus view amongst human rights NGOs and prosecutors that, following years of civil war, peace in both Sierra Leone and Liberia would be a fragile plant, without 'justice'.

Words such as 'justice' and 'accountability' ring round the chambers of international tribunals. But it is the job of academics (and, sometimes, reflective journalists and analysts) to interrogate and deconstruct such protean concepts. Can there be true 'accountability' without consistent, informed and independent oversight of the conduct of the tribunals themselves?[3] And how can this be achieved when the international media rapidly loses interest in the proceedings, and the local media has neither the resources nor the skills to scrutinise their work? The journalist and Nieman Fellow, Thierry Cruvellier, with unmatched experience of reporting extensively on three such tribunals – the International Criminal Tribunal for Rwanda, the SCSL and the Cambodian tribunal into the crimes of the Khmer Rouge – has written that two of them, the ICTR and SCSL, "show that these tribunals, like any bureaucratised and political institution, can become authoritarian, abusive, or corrupt once they realise that they have limited accountability."[4]

It is not the purpose of this paper to examine the structure and performance of the SCSL as an exercise in assessing whether, as a form of jurisprudence, it lives up the high standards it proclaims. Rather, it focuses on whether accountability can be measured through the impact on civil society of *reporting* of two of its trials, as well as the court's own outreach efforts in both Sierra Leone and Liberia. It is a dispatch, as it were, from the frontline of a three-year British Academy funded project,[5] which has been running for about fifteen months, and which is supporting a Ph.D. being undertaken by my student, Abou Bhakarr Mohammed Binneh-Kamara, who is based in Freetown. Understandably, any conclusions or judgments must be considered tentative.

Civil Society, Media and Democracy: Liberia

At a seminar for journalists from Eastern Europe, organised and chaired by the author in London in January 2012, a Ukrainian reporter pointed out that the freedom and independence of the media was invariably linked to the robustness of civil society.[6] In Ukraine, there is a direct correlation between a media, fearful of upsetting government, and a post-Soviet environment in which civil society organisations and NGOs lack the individual know-how and collective impact to make a difference. Thus, pressure for change tends to be exerted from outside the country, in the form of monitoring bodies such as Freedom House. This has consequences. As Paul Mitchell of the World Bank, puts it : '.....unless communication is seen as a "sector", it is not seen to have substance. Unless this happens,...the communication sector will not truly take its place in making governance and development work.[7]

In Liberia, after a faltering start during the first few years of the government of Ellen Johnson-Sirleaf (the first post-conflict president), the number of active civil society organisations has multiplied and so has the number of media bodies whose voice is heard regularly in national debates – the Press Union of Liberia, Liberia Media Center, Liberia's Publishers Association, Liberia's Broadcasters Association being the most prominent. As their titles suggest, these are chiefly advocacy bodies on behalf of the media. But of more relevance to this research is the newly-established Liberia Media for Democratic Initiatives (LMDI), which counts amongst its aims the building of a stable and peaceful democracy through the interaction of media and civil society. It organises regional forums, often attended by more than 300 people, in which the political and social issues of the moment are debated and broadcast on a network of 45 community radio outlets. The link with the BBCWST initiative described at the start of this paper is a linear one because the director of the LMDI, John Kollie, is one of the original cohort of six journalists chosen to deliver reports from The Hague on the Taylor trial.

It would be problematic to make the case that it was the BBCWST initiative in bringing the Taylor trial into people's homes through the medium of radio which is responsible for this nascent flowering of participative democracy. But, writing in 2009, the authors of *Liberia Media Assistance Strategy* declare : "…the media has become an important institution through which the country's democratic progress could be monitored or surveyed, assessed and analysed. Unlike in the early transition period [i.e. post-2003], there is greater media visibility and increased number of media engagement programmes in the country" (*op.cit* : 5). And, in a country with a high level of illiteracy, radio undoubtedly has primacy as a means of disseminating information and opinion.

In 2009, there were 22 radio stations in Liberia taking the Taylor trial reports from The Hague. Sixty-four per cent of the coverage of the trial was provided by the syndicated reports of the BBCWST team.[8] In order of reach/audience size, the three most important radio stations were *UN Radio, Star Radio and Radio Veritas* (associated with the Catholic church). Three stations in Nimba County – where Taylor draws much of his support – were taking the output. Most of the 22 stations do not have access to the Internet, which means that they took only the 30-minute weekly report. If they had had the means to do so, most, if not all, would have broadcast the daily reports (this is evidenced by the fact that some stations broadcast the weekly programme several times during the week to meet audience demand).

Without a formal ethnographic survey, it is difficult to gauge the impact of reporting of the trial on the population but those stations which encouraged listeners to text in comments, following a weekly broadcast, reported a high response. In terms of reaching Taylor's "constituency of support", two stations

(*Radio Ganta and Radio Gbarnga*) have Internet access and carried daily reports.

In addition, the radio reports have been a springboard for community discussions in a number of areas around the issues raised by the trial. Liberia's only law school, Louis Arthur Grimes School of Law [a partner in the British Academy-funded project], organised a number of discussions in Monrovia, at one of which another of the cohort of BBCWST journalists spoke in 2009. These events – and indeed, the work of the BBCWST project – were all the more important because outreach work by SCSL in Liberia has been patchy. In the early phase of the trial, this was because SCSL staff had genuine fears for their safety in Taylor-supporting areas up country. By 2009, the SCSL Outreach Office was distributing weekly video reports of the trial which were screened at community meetings, often in collaboration with activity by the *Coalition of Civil Society Organisations* (headquartered on Camp Johnson Rd in Monrovia). While it is true that some parts of Liberia have been better served than others – the south-east has fewer community and regional radio stations and Internet connectivity is poorer – there are encouraging signs of progress.

Sierra Leone

In Sierra Leone, the media picture is more mixed. Here, there has been more emphasis on training of journalists than on finding fresh ways of exploiting news, information and opinion as conduits for the spread of participative democracy. The country's post-conflict Truth and Reconciliation Commission recommended the establishment of an Independent Media Commission (IMC) to oversee and regulate media, and the IMC has been active in promoting reforms.[9] Its own structure has been decentralised, with offices opened in the regional cities of Bo, Makeni and Kenema. And on a wider strategic level, the Sierra Leone Broadcasting Corporation (SLBC) has been transformed from a government-owned and controlled service to a state broadcaster overseen by a board of trustees, along the lines of those created in Ghana and South Africa.

As stated earlier, at time of writing, the British Academy-funded research project is less than half way through its life-span (It began in October 2010). It will examine media coverage of two of the four trials conducted under the auspices of the SCSL. These are the Civil Defence Forces (CDF) trial, which ended in May 2008, and the Taylor trial, in which judgment is still awaited. In the former case, three alleged leaders of the CDF (also known as the Kamajors), Sam Hinga Norman (now dead), Moinina Fofana and Allieu Kondewa were found guilty of eight counts of war crimes, crimes against humanity and other serious violation of international humanitarian law.

The CDF was one of three organised groupings alleged to have committed atrocities during the conflict in Sierra Leone since November 1996. The other two were the Armed Forces Revolutionary Council (AFRC) and the Revolutionary United Front (RUF). The reason for selecting media reportage of the CDF trial for analysis was that, within Sierra Leone, it was the most contentious of the prosecutions. Many saw the CDF as a defence militia seeking to bolster the elected government when it first came under attack rather than undermine it and believed the prosecution to be politically motivated (because, by the time the remit of the SCSL was drawn up, the country's president, Ahmed Tejan Kabbah, was seeking to distance himself from his former ally, the CDF leader, Sam Hinga Norma). And some of this inherent distaste for the trial seems to be reflected in responses to the first ethnographic survey carried out as part of the research by Abou Binneh-Kamara in December 2011.

The Survey

To achieve a geographic spread, the research was carried out in all four regions of Sierra Leone. That is Freetown (the capital) in the West. Bo (South), Makeni (North) and Kenema (East). The methodology was to invite representatives of civil society groups to come to a central meeting place and respond to a set of agreed questions. Thus, the interviews can best be described as mainly structured. Eleven participants took part in the Kenema session ; eleven in the Bo one; and ten each in Makeni and Freetown. They were invited to respond to a set of twelve questions designed to test their awareness of the trials, whether they considered the reportage balanced and fair, and how relevant they thought the proceedings were to civil society. The responses were anonymised to preserve confidentiality.[10]

It would be impossible to give an exhaustive list of the responses in this paper (not least because some transcription work is still taking place). Moreover, there are factors which may skew the responses, such as ethnic origin and loyalty. The two largest ethnic groups in Sierra Leone, the Mende and Temne, have traditional differences, not only in language but in political allegiance - the former ruling party, the SLPP (Sierra Leone People's Party), has been largely Mende-dominated and stronger in the south and east, with its largely Mende population. Whereas, the Temne, who tend to support the APC (All People's Congress), come mainly from the north and west.

It is also worth pointing out that reports from the Taylor trial were delivered in English and Krio but there are plenty of Sierra Leoneans who speak neither and were probably reliant on second-hand accounts for information about the proceedings. So, the following is more of a snapshot – but no less interesting and revealing for that.

A Selection of Responses

To the question : *"How aware of the two trials were you?"*, none of the respondents rated their awareness at more than fifty per cent (meaning awareness of about half of the proceedings in the trials). A number put it at forty or even thirty per cent, though, on the whole, it was higher in towns than rural areas. One respondent said :

"The outreach programme embarked upon by the media (sic) did not take place at chiefdom and district levels. Media practitioners only stayed in Freetown, using difficult grammar, without informing the people in their own local dialects."

Other reasons put forward for low levels of awareness were lack of access to television (to see footage from the courtroom); lack of reliable radio access; and a failure of awareness-raising by SCSL outreach. One respondent put it like this :

"The video clips should have been marketed to the people to enable them to see how the trials were being conducted. All we knew was that people were tried but without much information dished out."

In the case of the CDF trial, it was suggested that this lack of awareness extended even to the families of the accused. And here it can be seen that there was a failure to educate and inform people about the legal process itself, and in particular, the decision to protect the identity of some witnesses by pixillating their on-screen image and/or distorting their voice. A respondent commented:

"The reporting was not balanced. The reason is that most of the issues discussed in the trials were not sent out to the people –specifically, the protection of witnesses. As people were of the opinion that they should have been given the opportunity of seeing those who served as witnesses against the accused".

It was clear that the limits of responsibility of the media's reporting was not fully understood either. One respondent said:

"For me, the reports were not totally balanced as we were not contacted in our villages to corroborate what the witnesses had testified in relation to the accused."

Another said :

"The media people failed to cross-check their reports with the grassroots, where the events occurred. In other words, information was not fact-checked. The reporting was not for people like me from the grassroots in the village of Kaikondu village but rather for those in the international community."

In the south and eastern regions, where the Kamajors were well represented, there was a fairly widespread view amongst the respondents that the Kamajor leader, Hinga Norman, should not have stood trial and that he was a "war hero" not a criminal. And an equally strong opinion that the long delay in the court delivering its judgment on Charles Taylor, is, in the words of one respondent :

"*Having a lot of effects on civil society, especially when so many Sierra Leoneans are highly dependent on members of civil society. We serve as the voice of the voiceless, speaking on their behalf, and, as such, they expect much from us. As the court has made no pronouncement, to date, on the Taylor trial, there is the possibility of this causing the people to think negatively about civil society.*"

The civil society representatives were asked how they would compare the reliability, balance and accuracy of reporting from the local and international media (i.e. BBC, Voice of America, Radio France International) and the international media scored consistently higher in their estimation. Though this raises an intriguing issue of terminology. The BBCWST daily reports from the Taylor trial in The Hague were singled out for their perceived fairness and were, in the main, considered to be examples of 'local' reporting. This is true in the sense that the reporters were either from Sierra Leone or Liberia but the project itself was an external initiative (in the early days, a co-production between BBCWST and the charity, Search for Common Ground), and the mentoring was in the hands of a foreign trainer (the present author).

Regarding the media's role in fostering reconciliation and thus strengthening civil society, opinion was divided but the following comment from a respondent in Makeni reflected a sizeable body of opinion :

"At the end of the war, many who had actively taken part in the war were afraid to go (back)to their people. It was the media who made it known over their radios that such people should be accepted by their own people into their communities as the war had come to an end. That brought about some form of reconciliation. The media also made it possible for our local justice to acknowledge the supremacy of the rule of law. So, the media helped in impacting the process and reconciliation in this country."

As for the delay in delivering judgment against Charles Taylor, there was widespread disappointment about the impact on the population. A typical view was :

"The civil society has great concern....if the final verdict on Taylor has not been pronounced, what will members of the civil society say to the people of Sierra Leone? ...In fact, if we do not get a verdict by early next year [i.e.2012], we shall embark on clamouring over the radios for the trials to be completed."

Conclusion

While radio is undoubtedly the principal means of communication in both Sierra Leone and Liberia, each country has a varied selection of newspapers too. The research will examine, in particular, three of the Sierra Leonean publications – *Awoko, Standard Times,* and *For di People.* These have some of the largest circulations (though, in a country with such a high degree of illiteracy, the term 'large' must be considered relative). In a survey carried out by the international ngo, Fondation Hirondelle, 4.5 per cent of those surveyed said they read *Awoko,* 3 per cent *For di People,* and 2.9 per cent *Standard Times.*[11] Their reportage and commentaries on the two trials will be the subject of discourse and framing analysis. And other factors, such as hostility amongst some editors who come from the south-east, to the trial of Hinga Norman, will be entered into the equation before any conclusions are reached.

As stated several times, this is ongoing research but preliminary indications support the view of a recent large-scale population survey in Liberia that, despite progress since the end of the conflicts, many people rely "predominantly on informal sources of information (e.g. friends, family) due to poor access to media".[12] But where there is community and regional radio, especially in Liberia, there is also active sponsorship of initiatives designed to bolster civil society and enable it to be more resistant to those latent forces which threaten to destabilise democratic governance in one of the most traditionally turbulent regions of Africa. Proponents of international justice usually cite the imperative of ending impunity as a reason for setting up war crimes tribunals. But it may be that the indirect promotion of democratic governance is the more achievable and durable long-term legacy.

Appendix

This is the full list of questions put to civil society repre-sentatives in Sierra Leone.

1. How aware of the two trials were you?
2. Did you follow them regularly, occasionally or not at all?
3. Can you say what you consider fair and balanced reporting to be?
4. Within your definition of those terms, do you consider that local media provided fair and balanced coverage of the Taylor and CDF trials?
5. If not, why not? Too biased in favour of the prosecution? Or the defence?
6. What about the international media – BBC, Voice of America, Radio France International? Did you hear any of it? If so, how did it compare in thoroughness, accuracy and balance with local media?
7. Did the media coverage change the people's views in any way?
8. How does coverage of the trials in both countries impact the process of reconciliation and justice?

9. Was the money spent on the trials worth it? Would you rather it had been spent on reconstruction/alleviating poverty?
10. How relevant were the CDF and Taylor trials to civil society in Sierra Leone and Liberia?
11. Did the media sufficiently explain the special nature of the SCSL trial (i.e. a hybrid trial) before it began?
12. What effects has the delay in pronouncing a judgment in the Taylor trial had on civil society?

References

1. In the interests of full disclosure, the author was the consultant/trainer on the project before taking up his present academic post.
2. The method used to send dispatches via email is FTP (File Transfer Protocol).
3. The last in-depth study of the SCSL was a report by the International Center for Transitional Justice entitled "The Special Court for Sierra Leone Under Scrutiny" in March 2006.
4. Cruvellier T., "War crimes tribunals in Africa and sleeping press watchdogs", Nieman Reports, 2004.
5. The British Academy is the national academy for the humanities and social science. This project is being funded under the International Partnership programme, which is designed to develop links between British institutions and those in Africa, as well as intra-regional partnerships. The three institutions 'partnered' in the project are the University of Bedfordshire (leading), the University of Sierra Leone, and the Louis Arthur Grimes School of Law in Liberia.
6. Seminar held at the London Jewish Cultural Centre and featuring journalists from Ukraine, Latvia, Poland and Hungary, 24-26th January, 2012.
7. Quoted in Liberia Media Assistance Strategy (2009), Arogundade L, and Randall L.
8. Source : "A review of media coverage of the transitional justice process in Liberia" (2008), The Liberia Media Center.
9. The former chair of the IMC, Bernadette Cole, Head of Dept.of Mass Communication at Fourah Bay College, University of Sierra Leone, is a partner in the British Academy research project.
10. The full list of questions is contained in an appendix to this paper.
11. The study (2008) was carried out on behalf of UNICEF.
12. "Talking Peace : a population-based survey on attitudes about security, dispute resolution and post-conflict reconstruction" (2011), Human Rights Center, University of California, Berkeley-School of Law.

3

Political Benefits and Inconveniences of Electronic Government

Yahya Fozi

Introduction

One of the concepts which is discussed so broadly in political and administrative fields in many countries of the world in recent decades is the concept of "Electronic overnment". This article examines the political benefits and damages of *e-Government* and also the strategies to reduce these damages will be studied.

3.1 The features of Electronic Government

There are different definitions for e-Government. We can conclude this meaning by considering all of them: Electronic Government (*e-gov*) is the use of information technology, internet, and other new technologies by the government and public organisations. This will provide necessary facilities for adequate access to the information and governmental services, improvement of the quality of services, and it grants broader opportunities for participation in the democratic processes (Hughes : 1998, p. 75). In brief, four kinds of implementation form the main pillars of e-Government (Davison: 2005, p. 24) which are:

1. The interaction between government and citizens (G2C, government to citizen). This interaction is the most important and the most extended implementation of *e-Gov*.
2. Relationship between governments (G2G, inter-agency relationship). This eases the relationship between governments.

3. Government and business enterprises relationship (G2B, government to business enterprises). It was the first relation which was developed; therefore the needs of the business community were paid attention to. These services are multi-faceted. Economic enterprises, supplier, and customers interact with each other.
4. The interaction between government and employees (G2E, government to employees). This type of relationship is to strengthen the internal governmental network and human resources information exchange is very important.

3.2. The Political Benefits of Electronic Government

The most important political benefits of electronic government can be summarised as preparing the grounds for integrated governance mechanism, as well as deepening good governance indicators. We are going to study these benefits:

3.2.1a Electronic Government paves the road to an integrated governance and strengthening the government authority

Integrated and network governance is one of the goals of *e-gov* that can be particularly important for the national security of the countries. Focus on strengthening internal relations between the concepts of e-government and integrated government is the infrastructure of new strategies of the e-gov in the countries. The ultimate goal of integrated governance is to improve collaboration between public servers on one hand and on the other hand is an impalpable but effective control of the citizens, and also strengthening the government authority in order to provide national security.

For this purpose the government reengineers the internal and inter-government processes through integrated governance with effort to meet the needs. This will lead to increased capability and capacity of the government's immediate and rapid response to information received from multiple servers. The increase in ability to respond to crisis is another advantage of integration. Moreover, the compatibility and information security will increase through the creation of common standards. It also improves the policy coordination between multiple public servers and the faster and more effective implementations of government decisions through data and information sharing.

3.2.1b Electronic Government paves the road to good governance

Including other political benefits of the *e-gov*, we can mention deepening the indicators of good governance.

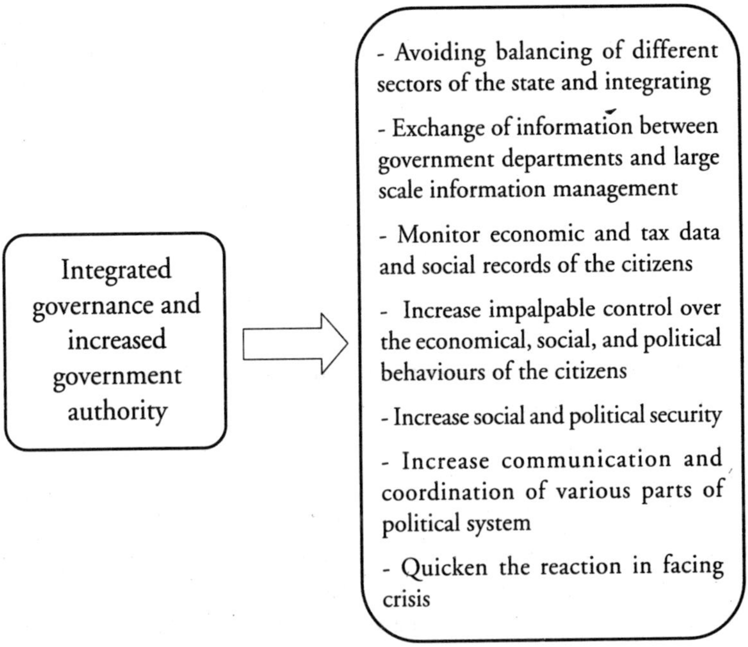

Theory of good governance is a paradigm for sustainable human development with the practical interaction of the three sectors of government, private sector, and the civil society. A fundamental basis for good governance features are the eight indicators which are discussed by the United Nation Development Program (UNDP) and the World Bank (World Bank).

These indicators are as following:

1. *Participation:* Participation means the presence of all the people in the various decisions both directly and through representatives legitimate institutions. Strengthening this civil partnership will have an important role in leading to the creation of public confidence in government.

E-Government has the potential to participate the citizens governing processes by putting them through interaction with policy makers throughout the policy cycle and at all levels of government.

To achieve this goal, ICT is necessary to create mutual and multi-sided communication channels, which allows users to announce their views on legislative or political projects.

Thus, this step of *e-government* can include advisor bodies established between citizens/governments. These bodies are online communities where individuals can exchange their ideas, so the public awareness of issues increases. In fact this phenomenon has bestowed one of the key tools for achieving the ideals of good governance by providing facilities so that citizens and civil society organizations could monitor the processes of various public sectors democratically. Electronic Government provides the condition that the politicians pay the same attention to the needs of citizens. And this is an example of maturity of democracy thanks to information technology.

2. *Rule of law*: Establishment of good governance system requires not only legal frameworks which are fair and impartial but also the ruling of those regulations in the society. In e-gov with the help of easy, fast, and cheap access of people to information and communications, related to laws, the rule of law is deepened with public scrutiny that results in the capability of individuals in questioning and being aware of their social rights and the rule of law in all affairs.

3. *Transparency*: Transparency means the free flow of information and easy accessibility to it for all relevant stake-holders. Information should be enough and understandably available and on the other hand making and implementing decisions should follow certain rules and regulations. One of the results of electronic government is transparency and access to the state information. Equal access of citizens to information and public resources would make the direct supervision of individuals and free criticism and suggestion to the non-governmental sectors and citizens happen (Finger and Picad, 2003).

4. *Responsiveness*: Good governance requires that institutions and decision-making processes provide the necessary services to all the stakeholders within a reasonable time frame. Achieving this goal is only possible if the decision maker organisations have a sense of responsibility towards supplying demands and desires of individuals. Electronic Government can improve this responsibility by reflecting demands and desires of the people in the community to the authorities.

5. *Consensus orientation*: Good governance requires leading the various tastes and interests in society to a widespread consensus which has the best and most benefit for the whole society. *E-gov* can make an enormous change in the traditional forms of ruling community affairs by the use of information technology and transform the relationship between government and citizens. Electronic Government leads to developing ways through which the information flows vertical and diagonal and therefore covers a wide section of society, and a greater volume of information between the government and the civil society members and also between the government agencies will flow.

6. *Inclusiveness*: Health and welfare occurs in a society when all its members feel that they are involved and effective in the society. This is not possible except by creating opportunities for the vulnerable levels of the society to improve their welfare. In good governance all the individuals should have equal opportunities. Welfare in a society is depended on ensuring that all members feel they are stakeholders in the community. To accomplish this all vulnerable groups should have necessary support to increase their capabilities. *E-Government*, with regards to its high capacity, can provide access to justice by creating equal opportunities.

7. *Efficiency and effectiveness*: Good governance means that decision maker institutions and organisations always have peoples' needs in mind and use the existing resources in an efficient way. *E-gov* is a tool that is trying to use the knowledge and the new technology of information and communication to reduce the gap between the state and the people, and help the citizens to receive the services they need with lower costs, more speed, and more desirable quality from governmental organisations.

Electronic government has increased the performance by turning the relation between government and citizens into citizen-oriented government from state-oriented government, renovating the state through the processes based on new technologies, enhancing the speed and quality of services, reducing unnecessary tasks, and the gradual changing of the government agencies dominant culture to focus on the customer and his needs.

8. *Accountability*: Accountability is vital for good governance. Not only governmental institutions but also private sector and civil society organisations should be accountable to the public and all the stake holders. It should be noted that accountability is not applicable without transparency and rule of law. Politicians would find out that countless eyes are watching their performance in e-gov and that hiding issues from the public would be difficult.

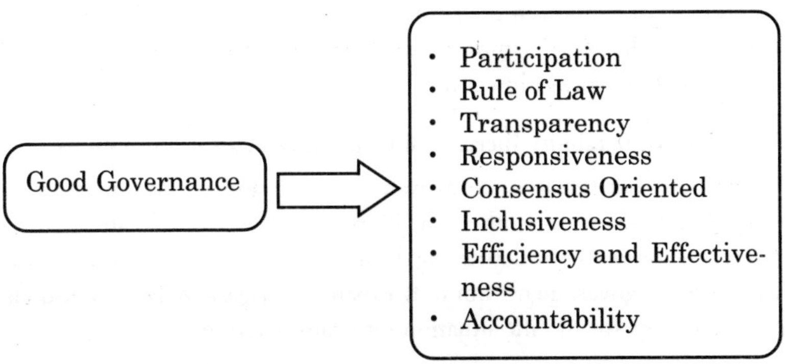

E-Government will pave the road to direct dialogue between citizens and public authorities and thus this type of communication is far more effective than the traditional relationship between citizens and government and this will help considerably to the realisation of accountability and responsiveness in public sector organisation (Tek Nath, 2002, pp. 25-36).

Therefore *e-government* provides extensive facilities to form ideals of good governance. It helps importantly to improve the processes of providing services in public sectors, to accelerate providing the services to citizens, to make the government officials more accountable, the transparency of information, to reduce the gap between individuals and politicians, more effective participation of citizens and members of civil society in the process of public decision making, to expand social justice through equal opportunities to access information, etc. It helps to create an accountable, legal, transparent, and modern government on one hand, and effective participation of all citizens in government activities on the other hand (Okut Yuma, 2003).

3.2.2 Inconveniences of Electronic Government

Despite the benefits of the *Electronic Government*, it also faces significant damages that can be pointed as following:

3.2.2.1 National Security threats

Electronic information faces more complex and more diverse threats. Therefore maintenance and security of information has achieved a specific position in the world of communication, science, and technology. The main purpose of information security is to use the set of policies, guidelines, tools, hardware and software to provide an environment free from threat in production, refining, transmission and distribution of information in all public and private sectors. These threats may include unauthorised copying or stealing information, manipulating information, and other threats in finance. Prevention of disruption in the country's information system and expansion of these threats doubles the importance of information security and specifically the security of networks (dpsecure).

3.2.2.2 The Vulnerability Increase of Courtiers in Critical Situations

The potential threats such as war, terrorism and natural disasters like earthquake and so on are another kind of inconveniences which can be a major threat for *e-governments* by destroying the infrastructures and communications. This makes the governments not only expand the *e-government* but also take the local strategy for specific situation into consideration.

3.3 Reduction of Inconveniences of e-Government

However the e-Government can facilitate the upheaval and create new and efficient administrative processes, but can't solve all frauds and inefficiencies and is not able to overcome all the barriers against civil partnership. Moreover, the achieving an *e-government* would not occur by purchasing more computers or creating more websites. But, *e-government* is a process which requires programming, permanent allocation of resources and political will. According to these issues, it is necessary to consider the following points:

3.3.1 Developing Local Strategies and the National Programme for Using New Technologies

The first step in developing *e-government's* strategy is to provide a definition. It means, the policy makers should know that what they are exactly looking for. Any government, according to its special condition, can define the sphere of influence of this phenomenon when tries to develop the e-Government strategy.

After this stage, the development of the strategy is required. This strategy is important in terms of guiding the scientific and engineering processes and approaches in a way that is in the line with e-Government.

This strategy should encompass the stages such as:

- defining the *e-government* structure and its key components and elements
- Identifying the audiences and users of *e-government* facilities and determining the required policies in order to support *e-government* objectives and recognising the condition of each country and its potential crisis.

3.3.2 Creating Digital Culture

All experts emphasize on the important role of creating culture and making public the use of IT in official and commercial affairs. Governments' overviews and their initial studies for implementing *e-government* plan has shown that the main problem in creation and development of *e-government* is not the technology, but the problem arises from this question that "if the society is ready to accept ongoing extensive changes?" It seems that the lack of technologic structure isn't the only challenge, but non-proliferation of culture of this kind of governance among the society and public organisations and their perceptions, especially the government attitude toward cyberspace is another major challenge which needs required attention to be taken.

3.3.3 Providing Local Experts in the Field of IT

A fundamental element in success of *e-government* is the existence of human experts in new Communication and Information Technologies. Also, the people should be able to use and understand (Information Communication Technology (ICT) and create local context. The governments can produce this human capital by their training policy. In the other words, people should be educated in the field of ICT which is of necessity for permanent localisation of e-Government.

3.3.4 Strengthening the Security Mechanism

Development of information security and transferring process should be properly taken into consideration more than ever. The *e-government* can't achieve its potential objectives without creating trust and security for the people and commercial units. People need to have trust in security of transfer, process and storage of information through networks.

3.3.5 Providing the Legal Infrastructures

Any *e-government* plan requires developing a legal framework for protecting the privacy, computer crimes persecutions, the creation and strengthening of credibility assessment authorities and legal digital signature. In other words, a legal infrastructure to support and implement *e-government* should be included as follows:

E-government Act: it allows the government to provide administrative procedures, functions and services in digital form.

Data Protection Act: it deals with protecting and maintaining the privacy of personal information.

Freedom of Information Act: it provides broad access to public information.

The Digital Signature and Electronic Authentication Act: it allocates electronic identity and recognises digital signatures and documents.

The Network Fraud and Abuse Act: it protects digital intellectual property rights.

Conclusion

In general, we can conclude that in current situation *e-government* is not an option, but it is a necessity to improve the political system performance and strengthen the government on the one hand and move in the direction of having efficient and well reign. Nowadays, many countries by compiling and implementing the *e-government* projects endeavor to adjust themselves for new facts and environment to benefit from its advantages. They attempt to reduce the *e-government* inconveniences, since if the *e-government* plans are designed and implemented in an efficient and targeted way, profound organisational reforms will be done in public section. But, it should be added that *e-government* will not occur by purchasing more computers or constructing more web sites rather *e-government* is a process which needs planning, sustainable resource allocation and political will. A stable and liable is formed on the basis of a precise strategy founded upon local needs and conditions of any country.

References

Davison, Robert M. Christian Wagner and Louis C.K. Ma (2005), from Government to E- Government Information Technology and People, Vol. 18, No. 3, pp. 280-299, Emerd Group Publishing Limited. http://www.worldbank. Org/wbi/governance/pdf/trowish.pdf

Dhakal, Tek Nath (2002): "Non-Government Organizations in Grassroots Development: Implications and Challenges" in *Public Administration Journal,* Vol. XVII, No. 1, July 2002, Kathmandu, pp. 25-36.

http://www.dpsecure.net/electronic.htm

Hughes, E. (2003), Public Management and Admin: An, third edition, Palgrave.

Hughes, own E. (1998), Public Management Administration: An Introduction, Second edition, Macmilan Press Ltd.

Information Communication Technology.

Nath, 2002.

Okut Yuma, 2003.

Research Center of Parliament of Islamic republic of Iran.

Tek Nath (2002) pp. 25-36.

The research Center of Parliament of Islamic republic of Iran.

United Nations Department of Economic and Social Affairs, 2009.

United Nations Department of Human Development.

United Nations Department of Human Development.

www/Uncgr.ch/development/governance.html.&. UINE SCA, 2007: 101.

4

Freedom of Expression in India–A Myth or Reality : Role of Government Versus Media

Dr. Abhijit Bora

Censorship : How Far and How Much

India – the largest functioning democracy in the world with a continental proportion has freedom of expression and choice guaranteed by none other than the Constitution itself in its Articles. But if we scratch the grounds a bit what do we find in reality.

Let us put the question in this way.

Are we free to watch any film that we would personally like to see ? Are we free to read any book or magazine that we would like to read from anywhere across the world. Can we launch a newspaper or magazine whenever we want to, without a licence. Can we start a TV / Radio station without a licence at our own will ? Hardly so.

So, we can't watch a movie we would like to, unless the central Board of Film Censorship (CBFC) clears it. But, how come a few persons (supposed to be learned people of the society) possess the power to decide what more than 120 crore people of the country would watch.

Why should the government hanker after banning a book or a film whenever there are protests against them only because they may not be conforming to the existing situation in each and every field of our society.

Sometime back, even reputed and old academic institutions like Delhi has succumbed to such pressure tactics by withdrawing the essay, 'The 300 Ramayanas…' By a noted scholar on the subject as it was vehemently protested by an organisation against its continuation.

It is highly ironical that in a country where we can decide about whom to vote and whom not to at a somewhat early age of 18, we have to be told by someone else which movie we should see and which not.

On the other hand one chairman of the CBFC a few years ago opined that even 'x' rated movies should also be allowed to be screened in public. However, the matter did not raise much enthusiasm and it died down before a storm could brew.

And now, the service providers of social networking sites are the latest targets of this information restriction campaign of the government. Only time will tell whether this is feasible in the long run of not.

As against this, the USA, armed with the First Amendment of its Constitution is really means business in this regard. There, a licence is not required for launching a newspaper or magazine, no penal action can be taken by the authorities before anything is published or broadcast. Action, if anything can be taken only after the contents are broadcast or published at all.

In contrast, what is the scenario we do experience here in our country.

Talking of censorship of media it is quite strange how the Peoples' Republic of China (PRC) has been managing to go scot free in the international platform by curbing freedom of expression of both the media and the common public. The system was in full swing just before and after the Beijing Olympics (2008) when the country even blacked out internet sites as well as restricting the activity of the foreign journalists staying there for coverage of the Games.

Interestingly, such an effort was further experienced even as late as in the third week of July, 2011, when two bullet trains of the country collided with fatal casualty of more than 30 passengers and injuries to many others. Soon after the mishap, PRC's Central Propaganda Department issued strict directives to the journalistic community not to try to investigate into the causes of the mishap on their own but rather sticking to whatever information the government was doling out. (*The Telegraph*, India, 2011).

"The major theme for the Wenzhou bullet train case from now on will be known as 'in the face of great tragedy, there is great love. Do not question, do not elaborate," the news report quoted this statement from the department.

This is important to note that even in this advanced age of the 21st century there are societies and countries around the world which still believe in such coercieve regimes trying to keep the freedom of expression of the people at bay under any circumstances.

But, why would somebody, specially a government try to gag freedom of expression in any country unless there must be something fishy and there is no transparency.

This also leads to an ironical situation in which gate-keeping does not have any meaning at all in this age of the internet as a means of information dissemination. Even if any country had any such mechanism in place how much of it would actually be effective in reality.

In the Indian context the year 2010 was a watershed on a few major counts. First of all – there was a major allegation against the print journalism of the country that huge amounts of money changed hands to the newspapers from the politicians and political parties for getting news items published favourable to a particular election contesting candidate or maybe a political party itself during nation-wide polls to the state-level assembly Houses or the parliament. The controversy gained such momentum that finally the Press Council of India (PCI - a quasi-judicial body) had to institute a committee to investigate this and the committee in its report acknowledged existence of such a nexus.

So, in addition to the commercial and technical challenges being faced, this is another aspect where there is a huge challenge of rising above such a state while discharging their duties by the media in India. Only when this would happen peoples' faith in the media (specially news media) would be reverted back in the near future.

For example, many of you may recall the incident in which there was major hue and cry from several countries when a Danish newspaper published a cartoon showing Hazarat Mohammad in a lighter mood. A huge public outcry spread across several nations of the world with a strong demand for intervention by the government concerned against that specific daily.

However, the stand taken up by the Danish government was highly encouraging and motivating for those in the media. The country's premier had apologised to those concerned expressing regrets over the issue. But, it was also said in no ambiguous terms that the country revered the media in high esteem and believed that the media was matured enough to take its own decision and there could be absolutely no interference with the latter's freedom at all.

Another sensitive aspect that needs discussion here is sourcing of news or information from social networking sites (SNSs) like Facebook, Twitter etc. Mr. Rusbridger further opines that in this regard the judgment of the journalists of a certain news media organisation would make all the difference. He says that these are also news sources like any other sources whereas these should not be taken as representatives of the public at large. "This is an interesting, extra dimension to information. We will use it as a source. It is an imperfect source like all others, but a very useful source and journalistic tool" (2010).

In India also from time to time incidents happen which undermine the freedom of expression of the media. About a decade ago, a new TV news channel *Tehelka.com* was launched with a big bang – a nicely-executed sting operation that exposed bribery charges for awarding of big ticket Defence contract deals by the president of the party which was holding power at the Union Government. When it was done, after the usual denials and other routine methods the government mounted pressure on the channel for changing its version – by registering almost a hundred different cases of violation of all possible legal provisions of country.

But the government failed to prove anything of substance in the courts of law and all those cases had to be withdrawn with a lot of humiliation.

ROLE OF GATE-KEEPING : SELF-REGULATION OR EXTERNAL IMPOSITION

At this we need to seriously look into what kind of 'gate-keeping' role this system is actually performing at all. At this point there also arises another very important question – whether we need the services of gate-keeping for dissemination of all of our information at all or not. This is because a gatekeeper is akin to that a 'censor' authority which is usually regarded as a nuisance to the globally-accepted norms of freedom of expression.

In my country – India there is a strange situation. That is – we have a gatekeeper for films called the Central Board of Film Censorship (CBFC) which is the body responsible for issuing certificates to feature films for public viewing.

In case of news media there is no such restriction as such yet except that private FM radio services still not allowed to air news and current affairs programmes produced independently.

Yet, there is no doubt that there is indeed en express need for 'self-regulation' which only can inculcate a good taste among the masses.

Let me recall another important incident that is an example of sheer negligence of one's responsibilities while discharging one's duties in the field of media, more so in the world of journalism.

During the infamous India Pakistan conflict in the Kargil region of Jammu and Kashmir in 1999, a team of journalists were taken to the field spot on the Indian side by the Defence Ministry officials for a better coverage of the happenings. The scribes' community was repeatedly requested specifically not to use 'satellite or cell phones' for calling back their offices for passing on the news. But a journalist from a prominent TV news channel ignored this and used her satellite phone to call her office back in New Delhi and report about the activities. The enemy forces managed to pick up the signals and almost in no time directed their howitzer firing at that specific spot resulting in serious wounds to several of Indian Army personnel.

Another pertinent question is whether we would be content with an 'external regulator' – either a college or a single person-keeping a tab on what we are doing and restricting our professional duties. Or we would practice self-regulation in such a manner that there won't be any need for such an arrangement at all.

Media is like an elephant which is not much aware of its own enormous powers to influence public opinion and the governments – more so in developing nations and thereby suffer silently in the hands of various stakeholders always working with a motive trying to manipulate the media in their own frame of things.

THE INFORMATION REVOLUTION

In today's age it is needless to reiterate the significance of the saying that - 'information is power'. It is the in thing that empowers the people from kings to commoners alike and thereby converting them into 'thinking human beings. So that it can effect a difference in their lives by acquiring and processing all information available to him or her all around the environment.

And whenever this world has experienced revolutions in the field of 'information and its dissemination' the human civilisation has also witnessed major developments as a result. In other words we can term this as a series of 'information revolution' since the *mediaeval age* which have brought in 'far-reaching' changes to the masses in each and every walk of life.

The first information revolution was initiated by the invention of the printing press by Johannes Gutenberg in 1487 in Germany. This has ushered in the unprecedented advantage of making books available – the eternal source of knowledge to many hundreds and thousands of people. This convenient availability of this source has created a situation in which masses also got ample opportunities to acquire knowledge which made them knowledgeable and be able to lead a better life.

This was one of the most important causes behind the happening of the great Reformation movement led by Martin Luther King which was an epoch-making revolution.

Then came the series of developments like the Radio, TV and in the latter part of the last century the 'internet' has assumed a similar role in empowering the masses by throwing open the floodgates of knowledge for common consumption.

This is also nothing but a highly successful information revolution that has created a never-before scenario of information dissemination that we could never even think of.

We also know how the internet has been instrumental in making the liberation struggle of the people in Middle-East and Africa a big success in the recent times. At this point it would be pertinent to look at a few questions concerning several important aspects related to this entire issue.

First of all – in this tremendous free flow of information of all kinds among the masses how and where do we keep a tab on the authenticity of the information being passed on or disseminated around through the net. Also, how do we ascertain whether these information that we are consuming day in and day out are worth it or not. This needs to be expressly tackled because circulation of specific information by people or groups having vested interests in mind could cause major havoc in the society.

Media is a magic multiplier. We speak or write one thing and it is transmitted innumerable times to the masses which do affect a lot of peoples' intellectual capacity.

Secondly, it is highly interesting to note that more the number of outlets of information dissemination more it is becoming quite difficult to disseminate information falsely to the masses anywhere across the world.

Let me refer to the incident when a photograph of the Israeli bombings of Palestine a few years ago published by a major daily in the United Kingdom supplied by Reuters had to be withdrawn when it was pointed out by a blogger that the photograph was actually a doctored one. Even the freelance photojournalist who clicked the photograph admitted that it was a common practice to touch up photographs to create a better effect in the minds of the audiences.

Further, how can we be sure that these disseminators are conforming to the basic tenets of journalism before disseminating information to the masses at all.

Many of you may remember that in November, 2008, several important landmarks in the city of Mumbai – India's financial capital was taken to ransom by a few fanatic suicide attackers which was later countered by military commando action. This entire development was captured by the electronic media in a minute-by-minute detail outside the Taj hotel – a prominent icon of the city.

In a way the commodity - information has become the liberating panacea of life, the equaliser of status for everyone in any society across the globe and nations are going to great lengths to maintain networks of free flow of information.

Many of you might definitely recall the immensely important role played by the network of community radios in Nepal during the turmoil times after power was usurped by a kin of the then King who tried his best to block all forms of communication with the outside the world even including the internet which of course could not succeed only because of mass media's efforts.

In the prevailing information technology scenario, is there any real meaning of those restrictions on freedom of information, choice and expression. Hardly any.

THE MOBILE CHALLENGE

"Outside of newspapers, there has been a real explosion in consumption of information, whether, it is mobile phones or iPads...So, it is wrong for newspapers to imagine that what applies to everyone else does not apply to us. There is an urgent message there, that we ought to be developing journalistic ideas that fit into the mobile", said Mr. Alan Rusbridger, Editor of *The Guardian* of London in an interview in the prominent daily from India–*The Hindu* (2010). The prominent mediaperson believes that his organization has just started thinking on the lines of how to look at what these incredible basic things of the mobile like location devices can do for us.

This is of special significance for India as the mobile phone subscribers' base is about 700 million by now which is big enough a number to do business with by any news media outlet.

If we can combine meaningful information including news and disseminate the same through the mobile or other communication modes this is going to usher in an unprecedented positive development in the days to come.

Another very important aspect in this regard is how journalism is playing the role of being a leader of the society. That is – as we all know journalism is expected to play the role of an able leader of the society by providing the right kind of information and news to the masses.

RELATIONSHIP BETWEEN JOURNALISM AND MASSES

In fact, the relationship between journalism and masses or its readership should be very complementary – it should be empowering for both the sides. Journalism is expected to create or inculcate a good taste among the people about everything in life and thereby lead the audiences towards a better world. On the other hand it is also the duty of the audiences to keep a check on the functioning of journalism and actively go for 'course correction' whenever needed.

Eminent New media researcher Dan Gilmore says that grassroots journalists are dismantling big media's monopoly on the news, transforming it from a lecture to a conversation (Subramani, MW, p. 43). He further opines that the blog has been becoming the standard news medium of the world and the old media through the new media, to we media, using the power and knowledge and the energy of people at the edges.

Today, the circumstances have transformed the situation to such an extent that blogging as well as SNSs are also providing news and information to the masses – at least to the participants and members of these virtual communities whoever might be interested in it at all. The days of conventional newspapers seems to be headed for a serious confrontation with the virtual ones.

With easy access to the technological tools at hand, an increasing number of people are starting to demand themselves to be heard and be considered as a part of the news and information dissemination system through the web.

And we all know that in mass media 'the switch is in our hands' and the moment someone does not like to listen to us or read us, he or she would switch it off. As this virtual media revolution is an inevitable part of our life nowadays it would be better for the conventional news organisations to go by the saying 'if you can't beat them, join them'. It would be in their own interests that the newspapers should integrate to this new and emerging phenomenon to keep their readership in good humour. Sooner the better.

Further, it is a greatly liberalizing aspect for all of us concerned – newspapers and the readership. This is because earlier everyone had to depend upon the journalistic skills of one or a few mediapersons for getting to know the facts. While it was a highly 'centralised' activity earlier, it has become a far more 'decentralised' one with so many possible participants in the process and thereby reducing the possibilities of follies in the news services.

SOCIAL RESPONSIBILITY VERSUS CORPORATE SOCIAL RESPONSIBILITY

It hardly needs mention that today media has become a highly 'commercialised industry' with everything aimed at garnering profits rather than anything else.

"The commercial endeavours have taken upper hand and thus media has acquired the status of an industry. It has changed the very characteristics of media and media's function to mould public opinion". (Ravi, p. 28)

This aspect brings in an important side of the media in the developing nations like India where 'literacy' has been a major problem plaguing the country even today, after almost seven decades of Independence. The 'official' Indian literacy rate is 75 per cent according to the latest India census carried out this year out of the total population of almost 110 crore. However, the official Indian definition of a literate person is 'someone who can just sign his or her name' nothing else. This means that in the practical sense, just about half of this percentage in actually literate in the real sense of the term.

Further, even today more than 70 per cent of the Indian population live in some six lakh villages. Under these two circumstances the media still has a sky high responsibility towards disseminating meaningful information to these masses who are devoid of the benefits of formal or informal educational system.

This is one of the most important challenges of the media in the current century as a successful execution of this activity would translate into an 'empowered' nation in the near as well as distant future.

This is important because of the fact that mass media today wields enormous power over the masses anywhere across the globe. They are increasingly playing the role once played by family, community, religion and formal education. The media is also a key agenda setter. Television in particular has been acknowledged as a powerful audio-visual medium which leaves long-lasting impressions on the minds of the public and is therefore a powerful tool to shape public opinion (Majumdar, 2011, AMITY, p. 59).

The challenge here is how to utilize this enormous power to reach out to the masses for passing on meaningful information to the people at grassroots level.

Media is a highly prolific interdisciplinary social science. This means that each and every walk of our life – whether it is something trivial to something highly scholarly – media is needed by everyone for making their presence felt.

In this regard it needs to be mentioned that our academic institutions, research institutions etc. which are carrying out research and development works anywhere across the world are being able to acquire a lot of knowledge and information which have vital significance for helping in the development of mankind.

Now, the challenge is how to carry these life-enhancing information-cum-knowledge to the masses who should be the ultimate beneficiaries of such endeavours in any society. This is because unless such knowledge are applied for the enhance-ment of human life's development what is the use of keeping them in laboratories. This challenge of becoming a suitable bridge between such storehouses of information and knowledge and the masses is a highly skillful job.

So because the challenge also lies in looking for and acquiring such information, translating them to a language understandable to the common people and presenting the same in an effective manner.

The modern day development of digitization of the information dissemination system has two sides to it. First – it is making the media somewhat sophisticated and thus seemingly out of reach for the masses at grassroots level. However, as more and more governments and societies around the globe are trying to expand the benefits of the 'broadband digital' system network to reach out to the maximum number of people, this acts as a 'liberating' factor by becoming a catalyst of delivering such knowledge which in turn can be utilized by the masses for improvement of their life under any circumstances.

Justice Markandey Katju, a senior and experienced Judge of the Supreme Court of India in a newspaper article (*The Hindu*) in June this year expressed lot of expectations from the media in the country as mentioned here. "To my mind, the media in our country today must be able to help the people in their struggle against poverty, unemployment and other social evils and to make India a modern, powerful, industrial state," said the *The Hindu* editorial page article.

However, our question here is can't we think of such responsibilities of the media as something akin to the 'Corporate Social Responsibility (CSR)' aspect of the established commercial entities across the world. In other words even if we consider media – specially journalism – as basically a commercial endeavour rather than a social service yet, it is expected to escape from the CSR obligation which ties it up to the issue of social developmental issues.

This is because even out and out commercial ventures do have at least some basic obligations for contributing to the society in kinds in addition to the responsibility of creating jobs and opportunities.

This aspect needs a thorough debate involving all the parties concerned.

NO NEWS AND CURRENT AFFAIRS FOR C.R. IN INDIA

Despite the big publicity over 'empowering' the community through CRs, the MIB till date does not allow this medium to air news and current affairs programmes. At the same time private satellite and cable TV channels are allowed to do the same without any hitch. There may be two sides to this aspect.

First of All, the GoI may be scared of the apprehension that if the masses are served news and current affairs programmes from sources independent of government control the true picture of the society would be reveled to them and it shall indirectly lead the people towards a 'rebellious path'. That too at a time when the Maoists and secessionists are already creating a lot of trouble in several hundred districts of the country.

Also, there might be a feeling on the parts of the MIB or for that matter the GoI that the masses at the grassroots level who are the main target audiences of CRs are 'not capable' listening to and absorbing news and current affairs programmes and these would be sheer waste. Ironically this happens at a time when they same citizens are considered responsible enough to exercise their voting rights.

Secondly, and More Importantly, all the important political parties irrespective of their ideology whenever they come to power at Delhi are never in favour of a complete decontrol of such a convenient and widespread true mass media which can be utilised for pushing through those parties' agenda to the masses in the name of government schemes and developmental programmes.

And in the name of allowing CRs to be set up the MIB is in reality encouraging setting up of such stations at schools, colleges and universities, hospitals among others.

CITIZEN JOURNALISM

Mr. Rusbridger (2010) is of the opinion that a far greater involvement of the readers is becoming extremely important for the newspapers to see them through the troubled times of the present era. This is because nowadays the readers have the facility to publish and link up. "The realm of newspapers is shrinking and all kinds of energy being created elsewhere and it is a life or death position for newspapers as to whether they essentially ignore all that or redefine their role."

This is a foregone conclusion that the new media has already made its presence felt in a rather very strong manner and is going to stay on track for the at least in the foreseeable future under any circumstances.

Noted communication scholar and researcher Professor Clay Shirky (2011) is of the opinion that ever since the rise of the internet in the early 1990s, the world's networked population has grown from the low millions to low billions and over the same time 'social media' have become a fact of life for civil society worldwide involving many stakeholders in the process – from individuals to governments.

Professor Shirky (2011) claims that social media have become the coordinating tools for nearly all of the world's political movements at a time when the world's authoritarian governments have been trying to limit access to it. Even though the powers of the social media have been brought to limelight in the recent times by the peoples' uprisings in Egypt, Tunisia among others, the roots can be traced back even to the days of impeachment trial of the Phillipines President Joseph Estrada in January, 2001.

So it is evident that the news media would definitely gain a lot of benefits from such a handy and available source of information of any kind anywhere across the world.

"Journalists believe that blogs are not significantly creating any impact on the mainstream journalism, but they believe that blogs are complimenting the profession. This is clear indication of the gradual penetration of the blogs in the mainstream media. Blogs are yet to reach the status of mass communication, but it is considered as forms of communication. Blogs are changing the agenda-setting function of the media and it has created notable changes in the process of communication and further we need to examine it" (Subramani, 2010).

The entire system has also been contributing towards the convergence of all media into one highly powerful integrated one capable of delivering the goods to the masses at their doorsteps. It would be a great mistake if we ignored this phenomenon and try to carry out the old and conventional system without concern.

Mr. N. Ram, Editor of the prominent Indian daily *The Hindu* once opined that the conventional newspaper in the Indian context was still safe to a big extent from the onslaught of the electronic media as majority of the population were not media savvy because of various factors. However, this would not hold ground to a far distance. This is because the Government of India has taken up several ambitious projects for providing broadband net connectivity to most of the country's villages across every nook and corner. Once this became a reality an unlimited potential would be opened up for the media to deliver the news and other meaningful information to the masses at the click of a mouse.

A combination of these two great forces with enormous powers would be able to achieve unlimited success in reaching out to more and more masses anywhere across the world at nominal costs.

Another very important challenge for the news media – whether in print or broadcast is how to maintain its social responsibility status and public welfare goals despite the commercial onslaught day in and day out.

We can also see that all kinds of media – specially the news media serving more and more commercial interests rather than focusing basically on providing news to the masses. We also understand that it is the commercial advertising revenue which keeps the media (news media included) going under any circumstances. Yet, where to draw the demarcating line between pure entertainment and news. As this line has been getting more and more blurred in the course of the functioning of the media in the name of survival it is high time we took a decision about where the stop and recapitulate. This is because even the commercial 'for profit' enterprises have at least some basic amount of social and professional commitments to the society to be fulfilled and carried out to the best of their knowledge and efforts.

CHALLENGE FROM CYBER MEDIA : NEED TO CONVERGE

Now the question is how do we strike a balance between this kind of individualistic journalism practices in comparison with the established proper format of journalistic practices with the conventional system.

Of course, there is a way out of this problem to a big extent. That is – as most of the established news media groups are finding it quite difficult to ignore the challenge of social networks and virtual communities via the net, their kind of information dissemination is expected to conform to at least some basic amount of journalistic principles rather than others.

"As a whole there is a silent revolution in the world of 21st century. For instance, the highly interactive convergence media is a major vehicle to transmit news and views. It has added new dimensions to the users by placing within easy reach, a mind-boggling range of information. Today, the receiver is even the sender and mass communicator. And as the numbers of people on it multiply, the opportunities are getting larger (Ravi, 2011).

It needs mention here that print journalism has been well adopting to this new situation of emerging challenges over the years and we strongly believe that it would be successful in doing it without much of a problem at all.

Then there is the important challenge of victimisation of the media persons across many nations of the world. Even in India – a prominent crime beat reporter of a daily published from Mumbai was shot dead in June, 2011 in broad daylight in the city allegedly by hitmen hired by mafia gangs with a remote control in a foreign country. This incident comes a few months after a prominent journalist was gunned down in Pakistan by unidentified killers.

CONCLUSION : SUPPORT FROM ACADEMIA AND SOCIETY

This is a battle in which the journalists' fraternity can't carry on their own and the society and the state must shoulder at least some responsibility in this regard. Else, it would lead to a chaotic situation in which no good-minded people would come forward to pursue this noble profession.

At this point the academic institutions offering courses in mass communication and media must also contribute their portion to the society by providing quality training to more and more interested people so that a trained manpower can be created over a period of time.

So because it is them to whom the society turns back always when faced with a crisis for solutions. Thus they must live up to the expectations and play a pro-active role in advancing the cause of the society to the greatest possible extent. They must also provide the right kind of leadership to the masses through the media.

These are a few of the major challenges that the media in the current century has to confront with on the road towards an all-round progress of all the stakeholders concerned – the news media, the audiences or readership, regulatory bodies among others. We strongly believe that despite all the roadblocks and hiccups journalism would be able to raise itself much above the normal circumstances and thereby prove it worth in the near as well as distant future.

Further, the relationship between the traditional or conventional news service system and the new media must be developed to such a standard that both of them may become highly complimentary to each other. As this phenomenon is becoming an integral part of our life we can ignore it only to our own detriment. And thus we must devise the best possible way to integrate both these two so that the masses can acquire the best possible advantage out of it.

References

China tries to censor cause of train crash. The Telegraph (Calcutta, July 26, 2011, p. 2),

Mobile phone can be a livelihood tool *: UNCTAD. The Hindu* (Chennai, October 6, 2010, p. 14).

Ravi, B.K. (2011), Dominance of Digital Media over Traditional Media : A critical study. *Amity Journal of Media and Communication Studies, Vol. 1, No. 1*, pp. 23-33, ISSN: 2231-1033.

Subramani, R. (2010), Emergence of Blog – impact on Mainstream Journalism. *Media Watch* (research and news feature journal in journalism and mass communication). *Vol. 1, no 2* (July-December, 2010). p. 43.

Ravi, B.K. (2011), Dominance of Digital Media over Traditional Media : A critical study, *Amity Journal of Media and Communication Studies,* Vol. 1, No. 1, pp. 23-33, ISSN: 2231-1033.

Majumdar, Pallavi. (2011), Media Regulation Vs Democratic Values in India, *Amity Journal of Media and Communication Studies*, Vol. 1, No. 1, p. 58 - 62, ISSN: 2231-1033.

Katju, Markandey. (2011), Freedom of the press and journalistic ethics, *The Hindu,* Chennai, June 3, 2011.

Rusbridger, Alan. (2010), We are going through a profound revolution, *The Hindu,* Chennai, September 20, 2010, p. 11).

Media [illegible]

5

Identification of the Problems Faced by the Print and Electronic Media Journalists

Dr. Smita Vashishta

The fourth pillar of democracy is a strong representative of the voice of people. Though the advancement has increased the tools to write and display, but somehow the lack of quality and research has raised many questions in Journalism. Thus on one side there is growing Journalism and on the other hand there are alarming issues on behalf of Journalist which needs attention for the better representation in the society.

Trikha (2007) Wage board in India has defined "working journalists" as a person whose principal avocation is that of a journalists and who is employed either whole time or part time in, or in relation to one or more newspaper establishment and includes an editor, a leader, writer, news editor, sub-editor, feature writer, copy tester, reporter, correspondent, cartoonist, news photographer and proof reader.

Parasarthy (1989) the most controversial law against the press and the freedom of journalists was the Vernacular press Act 1878, this law gagged their press and disarmed their person. Under the Vernacular Press Act, several newspapers were penalised, with their editors being sent off behind the bars.

Chakravarthy (2005) Panchcowire Baneerjee, editor of Nayak (Calcutta) said "more or less, we editors and printers are dummies in the hands of our proprietors I am not ashamed to confess that we are obliged at times to take to seditious writings at the behest of our proprietor because it sells."

Gupta (2000) Low wages and insecure employment often typified the conditions of Indian language journalists. A keen sense of lower status accompanied such conditions. They invariably showed keen eyes for cost but relish less for production standards, training or amenities.

The researcher is trying to explore the three major periods of Journalism and the role of Journalist in it. The first phase is the 'passion phase', the second phase as the 'makeover phase' and the present phase as 'cosmetic phase.' The passion phase is the period when Britishers were ruling Indians who were gradually realising the importance of freedom. There were no legal restrictions on the press except precensorship. Deportation was the most effective weapon used to eliminate troublesome and unwanted editors.

The makeover phase is the free India but growth of new Institutions of Journalism rather Sensational Journalism became a fashion with some of the countries interest ceased to be paramount. Bengali Editor confessed that he adopted a communal policy "because playing down riots and disturbances curbed his sales.

Sharma (1990) Television programming was initially kept tightly under the control of the government, which embarked on a self-conscious effort to construct and propagate a cultural idea of the Indian nation. The 1990s have brought a radical transformation of television in India.

India experienced the rise of more than 300 satellite networks. Satellite Television came to India as an agent of global Capitalism and complex forms of globalisation. As competition intensified, however economic pressures turned news producers into mediators.

Leading psychiatrist Dr. Sanjay Chug explains, "These days' news channels give greater focus on TRPs than the actual job. Also this has led to much competition which in turn has erased the concept of fixed working hours. Moreover, it should not be forgotten that, the nature of the work in journalism is stressful enough and all these factors have added to increase in stress."

Abdullah, conducted a research titled as *"Self-reported Stress Among Multi-professional Media Personnel and* Job Stress on Job Satisfaction among organisations" the objective of the study was to study self-reported stress and its association with work (work duty, working hours and shift work), sick leave and gender among multi-professional media personnel. A questionnaire was used on the sample of 1339 employees, between the age group of 30-55 years old. Sample included both T.V broadcasting employees and print media. Females reported stress and absence from work more often than males. Self-reported overtime and sick leave appear to be associated with higher level of self-reported stress, regardless of age, gender or work duty.

Joshi, (2006) Studied Women as a journalist, has always been talked with a stereotyped image. Keeping this view and to know the image of women a study was conducted. The title of the study is *"Images of women in Print Media— A Research Inquiry."* The sample included Journalists from English and Gujarati press of Baroda city. The objectives of the study were to study the opinions of male and female Journalists regarding: Journalism as a Profession and women's magazines. An interview was a research tool. And the results were that "The opportunities for women are there in journalism, but they have to grab the opportunities." Male journalists from vernacular press reported that population of female Journalists is less in the press due to un conducive work.

Khan (2005) studied *"The Influence of Personality Traits on journalists Work behaviour:* An Exploratory Study Examining a Bangladeshi Sample was conducted, an attempt is made here to provide a wider theoretical platform for analysis of news people's characteristic tendencies along the lines of their unusual occupational activities. The study aims at broadening the domain for psychology based research more closely related to the actual performance of Journalists. Eysenck's test of three personality dimensions was applied to a sample of 100 journalists from various media organisations in Bangladesh. A total of 100 journalists, 50 reporters and 50 desk workers, took part as respondents in this study. Among them, 87 respondents are male and 13 are female. The personality trait of extraversion was significantly related to engaging strongly with news sources. Neuroticism, another dimension of personality, was found to be significantly related to feelings of discomfort in noisy newsrooms and agonizing about errors. Neuroticism was also related to news-missing apprehension and being worried of deadline pressure.

Coleman (1976) studied, "The Moral Development of Journalists: A Comparison" was made with other profession and a moral development of journalists was studied comparison with other professions on the basis of high quality ethical reasoning was made. This study helps fill that void by gathering baseline data on a national sample of 249 journalists in order to compare journalists to other professionals. Two other variables—investigative reporting and civic journalism— have been linked to moral development in journalists in qualitative work.

This study attempts to test those ideas quantitatively. It has been shown that investigative reporters make moral decisions regarding wrong doing then abandon objectivity to push for the public good, 31 serve as moral judges, 32 and deal with ethical issues more than other types of reporters. The journalists in this study averaged 14 years in the profession, and were 38 years old on average. Twenty-eight percent said they had done civic journalism, 7.2% did Investigative reporting and 46% had done both. Thirty-one percent had management-level job titles. The ethical development scores of the journalists in this study were normally distributed. Data fell within a normal curve and rose in a straight line on a normal probability plot.

Miho Hatanka, Yutaka Matsui (2010); Job-related traumatic stress experienced by broadcast journalists in Japan was investigated. A questionnaire inquiring about the most traumatic event they faced when covering the news and the Impact of Event Scale-Revised (IES-R) were administered to 270 journalist participants working for Japanese news companies. Of these, 6% met the IES-R criterion for potential posttraumatic stress disorder (PTSD). Moreover, posttraumatic stress reactions at the time of the survey were strongly related to symptoms of stress experienced during the stressful assignment. The early assessment of stress symptoms in journalists that experience traumatic news coverage is important for preventing the development of PTSD symptoms.

Voakes (1997) studied the Social influences on Journalists' decision making in ethical situations, this study attempts to refine and test a theory of social influences on ethical decisions of journalists. The theoretical model proposes that several social factors influence any given decision, and that a hierarchy of influences assigns relative value to each: individual, small group, organisation, competition, occupation, extra media, and law. Print and broadcast journalists reacted to 3 hypothetical scenarios that raised ethical problems. The journalists then rated the salience of various reasoning statements, each representing 1 of the 7 social influences. No single source of ethical guidance appeared; in many cases different influences emerge as powerful under different circumstances. But of the 7 proposed influences, 5 showed consistent strength in predicting the decision the journalist makes. The individual influence was the weakest of the 7, despite its prominent strength in the literature.

METHOD

Participation: There are 100 Journalists from New Delhi, among them, 50 are from print media and 50 from electronic media. The same has been applied to Uttrakhand state. The sample of 50 is divided into 25 males and 25 females.

Materials: A survey method is applied and a Question-naire is developed considering all the dimensions of the study. A Questionnaire has been constructed. There are 36 item in it. The categorisation is as follows: The questions are closed-ended. Each item/question has five options to tick mark. Starting from strongly agrees, agree undecided, disagree, and strongly disagree. Each option is scored from 5-1 in order of the higher problems items.

OPERATIONAL DEFINATIONS

JOB SATISFACTION: Job satisfaction has been defined as "a pleasurable or positive emotional state resulting from the appraisal of one's job or job experiences" (Locke, 1976).

ORGANISATIONAL SATISFACTION: The interrelationships among employee trust in the organisation, and work is organisational satisfaction.

SUPERVISORY SATISFACTION: Donna Bjerregaard (1999), the interactive process in which the organisation goals and values are communicated and interpretated to employees, and they in turn are guided and supported to help reach those goals.

OCCUPATIONAL STRESS: *Occupational stress* is a term used to define ongoing stress that is related to the workplace. The stress may have to do with the responsibilities associated with the work itself, or be caused by conditions that are based in the corporate culture personality conflicts. As with other forms of tension, occupation stress can eventually affect both physical and emotional well being if not managed effectively.

JOB INSECURITY: Job insecurity is defined as the perceived stability and continuance of one's employment with an organisation. It is a condition wherein employees lack the assurance that their jobs will remain stable from day to day, week to week, or year to year

WORKING ENVIRONMENT: It represents the Environment which increases the efficiency of the employee.

COMPETENCIES: Boyatzis, Competency is the ability of an individual to perform a job properly.

DECISION MAKING: The thought process of select a logical choice from among the available options.

PROCEDURE: The newspapers and channels which easily agreed to fill the Questionnaire are considered for the study.

RESULT: The percentage tables were made for all the statements and for all the variables for two states and gender.

Thus the problems which were identified and needs a solution are as follows.

There are no fix policies on which organisations work.

There was no security from the company.

The nature of working sincerely is among the journalists of English Media in comparison to Hindi Media.

Promotion opportunities lies in the creativity and hard work, journalists lacked it.

The supervisors who have come due to the source do not have any knowledge on media management and working.

They have no honor for the organisation, thus lacking dedication to work.

There was no satisfaction with the salary.

Stress and work pressure is mainly due to the multiple tasking and lack of skills.

The working hours were satisfactory for Uttrakhand journalists but not for New Delhi journalists.

Their living style has changed. They have the habit of smoking and lack of exercise.

They were not taking medicines for stress.

There was the acceptance of fast food among New Delhi journalists then the Uttrakhand journalists.

Women have basic facilities at office but the night duties have created a problem for them.

Female's proposals of marriage were not accepted as they were journalists.

Journalists are influenced by the political parties, thus they take advantage of it.

There is no compassion among the journalist at workplace.

A woman is still not safe at media.

Print media has no threat from electronic media.

NEW DELHI AND UTTRAKHAND

NEW DELHI FEMALES (PRINT AND ELECTRONIC)

New Delhi electronic media females were satisfied with the job in comparison to the print media.

New Delhi print media journalists were satisfied by the organisation then electronic media.

Female journalists from print and electronic were not satisfied by the supervision.

Female New Delhi print media journalists had occupational stress in comparison to electronic media.

Female journalists from both print and electronic were insecure in the job.

Both were satisfied by the working environment.

Electronic media journalists lacked competencies then print media journalists.

Decision making powers were with electronic media journalists than print media.

NEW DELHI MALES (PRINT AND ELECTRONIC)

New Delhi print media journalists were more satisfied with the job than electronic media.

New Delhi electronic media journalists were dissatisfied by the organisation than print media.

New Delhi print media journalists were more satisfied with the supervision than electronic media.

Both complained occupational stress.

New Delhi electronic media journalists were more insecure in job than electronic media.

New Delhi electronic media journalists complained about working environment than print media.

New Delhi electronic media journalists were more competent than print media journalists.

New Delhi electronic media journalists had more decision making power than print media journalists.

UTTRAKHAND FEMALES (PRINT AND ELECTRONIC)

Both print and electronic media journalists were satisfied by the job, organisation and supervision.

Print media journalists had occupational stress than electronic media journalists.

Electronic media journalists were more insecure in job than print media journalists.

Electronic media journalists were satisfied with the working environment than print media journalists.

Both print and electronic media journalists were competent.

Electronic media journalists had decision making power than print media journalists.

UTTRAKHAND MALES (PRINT AND ELECTRONIC)

Both print and electronic media journalists were satisfied by the job, and organization but with not supervision.

Both print and electronic media journalists had occupational stress.

Both print and electronic media journalists had job insecurity.

Electronic media journalists had no working environment in comparison to print media.

Both print and electronic media journalists were incompetent.

Print media journalists had no decision making power than electronic media journalists.

DISCUSSION

The National Union of Journalists (India) was formed at a national convention of Journalists held in New Delhi on January 23 and 24, 1972. NUJ(I) has stood and fought for ameliorating the economic conditions of journalists, promoting their professional and trade union rights, freedom of the press, journalistic ethics, delinking of press ownership from other industries, and protecting and defending the journalists from all kinds of external and internal onslaughts on their independence.

Star News CEO Uday Shankar emphasises that the company had high volume of insurance coverage, which included casualties or permanent incapacities of any sort. "Journalists work in hostile environments and occupational hazards are always there."

Job and working environment today is a big problem for journalists. Psychologist Mike Anderson (2002) studied Working Unusual Hours and Its Relationship to Job Satisfaction. They found that stressful working conditions, such as working unsocial hours and irregular working patterns, create strains that together with intervening factors related to work, family, or the work environment ultimately reduce job satisfaction. Commenting on the contract system of Journalists PCI reports that "the uncertainty level of job security is really high."

"The journalists reported that sole right to discontinue the services of the employee concerned rest with the employee at any point of time", is the clause found in almost all the contracts. 362 employees were dismissed without prior notice in HT in 2004.

Journalism is considered as an art by some where one is there to create a vision, to show the world a way, to create an opinion. "Under the wage board act one had to work for six hours and rest of the time was given to the journalist to develop his personality, opinion and vision. Under contract it's more like a Yes Boss system.

There is a lack of training and skill among the journalist. Commenting on the young generation of journalists Gautier, commented on Indian journalists said "So what is needed is a new generation of Indian journalists who will be proud of their country without being chauvinists who will be brilliant without being superficial, who will take the best of the west without being western clones who will draw inspiration from the knowledge alive in the country, without being bigots."

Anurradha Prasad, senior Journalist covering parliamentary proceedings, PTI and DD said, "Female journalists work with motivation but media is always a business. The growth will happen not just with the induction of state-of-the-art equipment, but investing in the right people and ideas. People are all important. It is not just a financial investment; it is also an emotional investment. At media channels we expect to work like a family but things are in terms of contracts and business. It has given a long list of priorities.

Indiantelevision.com, journalist Ashwin Pinto said, "The changes that women want in their workplace include: Positions advertised and proper selection and interview procedures introduced."

Thus the need of the hour is that journalist should be provided with the environment where they could give a reliable and a valid approach to journalism.

References

Abdullah (2009), A Study of Job Stress on Job Satisfaction among organizations in Malaysia: Empirical Study; *European Journal of Social Sciences, Volume 8, No. 1.*

Chkravarthy (2005), Journalism changing society emerging trends, Author's press, New Delhi.

Coleman (2004), The Moral Development of Journalists, *Journalism and Mass Communication Quarterly: Vol. 81, No. 3,* 511-527, AEJMC.

Gupta (2000), Encyclopaedia of Journalism and Mass Communications (Vol. 5), ISHA Books, Delhi.

Hatanaka (2006), Traumatic Stress in Japanese Broadcast Journalists, *Journal of Traumatic Stress,* DOI. 10.1002.

Joshi Uma, Prof. (2006), Images of Women in Print Media—A Research Inquiry, *Indian Me.*

Khan, Zakaria (2005), The Influence of Personality Traits on Journalists Work Behaviour: An Exploratory Study, *Asian Journal of Communication,* Vol. 15, No. 1.

Rangaswamy Parasarthy (2007), Journalism in India, Sterling Publishers, New Delhi. *India Studies Journal,* Vol.1, No.1. July-Dec.

Sharma (2000), Development of Journalism: Anmol Publications Pvt.Ltd, New Delhi.

Suter, D.(1997), The protection of journalists in armed conflicts, *the RUSI journal, volume 142, Issue 5,* October 1997, pp 76-78.

Trikha(2008), Working journalists and others Newspapers Employees (condition) of services and miscellaneous Act, 1955, Media Law, University Publications, Varanasi.

Voakes, S. (1997), Social influences on journalists' decision making in ethical situations, *Journal of Mass Media Ethics, Vol.* 12, Issue 1, March 1997, pp. 18-35.

6

"Advertising is the Engine of The Growth for Mass Media"

Mandavi, Ashutosh

Communications comes from the Latin word *communis*, means 'common'. We deliberately communicate ideas, information etc. to establish a 'commonness' with others. The essence of communications is to bring about understanding between the receiver and the sender. The messsage bring about intended behaviours as well. Newspapers, films, radio, television etc. are used to convey messages to the general public. Communication makes the people understand each other and share joys and sorrows, problems and responsibilities. Communication is a planned and organised activity.

Wilber Schramm in his article, "How communication works" identified three elements of communication, namely, the source, the message and the destination. Today we are living in the world of communication. Nothing moves without communication. It makes human life very convenient. Communication is power. An eminent communication scientist Everett. M. Rogers observes: "Wherever change occurs, there flows communication." We cannot imagine our lives and society without communication. It helps people and society grow together and further. In reality communication should be perceived as "human communication". Therefore the phrase "mass communication" has been used by the communication scientists. Mass communication deals with the communication which is of the people, by the people and for the people in the democratic sense.

Advertising is a "Means of communicating information pertaining to product, services or ideas by other than direct personal contact and on an openly paid basis with an intent to sell or otherwise obtain favourable consideration." Informative advertising enables consumers to secure relevant and adequate information about all rival products and their relative merits. Thus, advertising helps consumers to exercise their right to choose and buy a product of service intelligently. Advertising enhances the decision making by providing information and by supporting brand names. It provides an efficient means to communicate. By generating various product association, advertising can add to the utility a buyer receives from product. Advertisement increases sales and consumption of product by either introducing new articles in the market or by familiarising people with the new uses of the old articles. It attracts attention, creates interest and awareness and arises and maintains consumers demand. It influences the buying behaviour of the prospective customers. It widens the market for a product. It encourages mass production and enables a businessman to enjoy the large scale economics. It reduces per unit production and distribution costs. Optimum utilisation of resources reduces costs and increases profits.

Advertising is a form of commercial mass communication designed to promote the sale of a product or services. Advertising in the sense of communication link between a buyer and a seller or a producer and a consumer is really as old as civilisation itself. As we know from the beginning in India. It was also known that the Bengal gazette or hickey's gazette was the first newspaper in India published on 29 january 1780 after its founder editor, james Augustus Hickey and it carried advertisements. As an organised Profession in India, advertising is relatively young. The first advertising agency was set up in 1907. Within the brief span of years advertising in India has made rapid progress. During the last two decades, and particularly since the beginning of the nineties, it has reached a fairly high level of maturity in the advanced industrialised countries. Not only has its progress been very fast in few years but its character has also undergone a radical change.

In recent years various big and notable changes have been witnessed in the field of communication and media. Many new concepts popped up and new media advertising is one of them. India is new to new media advertising but this concept has been around for quite a long time now. By the latest trend we come to know that new media advertising is the emerging and hottest medium of advertisement. New media advertising is synonym of online advertising and has taken web media with a stride. Now people instead of going for traditional advertising trend to give more weightage to online advertising. This is mainly due to fact that it is more targeted maximum exposure. New media advertising has got a bright future. The advantage of new media advertising is that it is relatively cheaper in comparison to other media and can also be done in an attractive manner. Moreover, various small and upcoming businesses can easily go for new media advertising because it has emerged as one of the most convenient way to promote any product and services.

In this communication age, advertisement bloomed to its full form with the liberalisation policy, technological advancements and introduction of various modern electronic media, made advertising not only more fascinating and income generating but also socio-cultural influencing. Thus we can say that advertisements have become the part of life for every one through various mass media. In the present era of information explosion and media influence, advertising play a major role in changing the society. Thus, the impact leads to cultural and social changes to a great extent through mass media.

7

The Role of the Caricature in Presidential Election of USA

Dr. Bahareh Bakhshi

Introduction

Today, the media play an effective role in the development of awareness of people and their decision making. The more a subject is important for people, the more media are paid attention to.

Images can affect audiences on their emotions and drives their perception of news towards goal. Among various types of images, caricatures can be pointed out which are seen today in many newspapers, magazines and news sites alongside important news.

During the course of the twentieth century, photographic, film, and televisual images have played an increasingly important role in the construction and documentation of historic events. The advent of the mass media has led to a proliferation of images in non-imaginative communication. But images also play a central part in how imaginative discourses conceptualise history. W.J.T. Mitchell has coined the term "pictorial turn" for this increasing "imagine" in contemporary communication, taking up Richard Rorty's argument that the history of philosophy has progressed through a series of paradigm changes, or "turns"—"The picture of ancient or medieval philosophy as concerned with things, the philosophy of the seventeenth through the nineteenth century as concerned with ideas, and the enlightened contemporary philosophical scene with words has considerable plausibility". Rorty calls the last of these paradigm shifts the "linguistic turn"—a term that has found wide acceptance among literary critics. However, art historians like Mitchell and Gottfried Boehm have pointed out that by the end of the twentieth century, the "linguistic turn" has been replaced by another dominant paradigm: the "pictorial" (Mitchell) or "iconic" (Boehm) turn. Pictures, Mitchell argues, have a status "somewhere between...a 'paradigm' and an 'anomaly" in contemporary discourse, "emerging as a central topic of discussion in the human sciences in the way that language did: that is, as a kind of model or figure for other things (including figuration itself), and as an unsolved problem". Thus, images are not only the paradigm in which contemporary culture must define its unresolved issues, but they are also the medium in which these issues are represented[2].

One of the factors that helped Barack Obama win the forty-fourth presidential election was his strong media team. This article is dealing with the role of pictorial discourses in media, focusing on caricatures, in the forty-fourth presidential election of America.

What is a Caricature?

The term is derived from the Italian *caricare*— to charge or load. An early definition occurs in the English doctor *Thomas Browne*'s *Christian Morals*, published posthumously in 1716.

A caricature can refer to a *portrait* that *exaggerates* or distorts the essence of a person or thing to create an easily identifiable visual likeness.

In literature, a caricature is a description of a person using exaggeration of some characteristics and oversimplification of others.

Caricatures can be insulting or complimentary and can serve a political purpose or be drawn solely for entertainment. Caricatures of politicians are commonly used in *editorial caricatures.*

There have been efforts to produce caricatures automatically, or semi-automatically using computer graphics techniques. For example (E. Akleman, J. Palmer, R. Logan, 2000), provides warping tools specifically designed toward rapidly producing caricatures. There is very few software programmes designed specifically for automatically creating caricatures.

An interesting aspect of some computer graphic systems is that by necessity they require quite different skill sets to caricatures created on paper. Thus using a computer in the digital production of caricatures requires advanced knowledge of the programme's functionality. Rather than being a simpler method of caricatures creation, it can be a more complex method of creating images that feature finer coloring textures than can be created using more traditional methods.

A milestone in formally defining caricatures was Susan Brennan's master's thesis (Susan Brennan) in 1982. In her system, a caricature was formalised as the process of exaggerating differences from a mean face. For example, if *Prince Charles* has more prominent ears than the average person, in his caricatures the ears will be much larger than normal. Brennan's system implemented this idea in a partially automated fashion as follows: the operator was required to input a frontal drawing of the desired person having a standardised topology (the number and ordering of lines for every face). She obtained a corresponding drawing of an average male face. Then, the particular face was d simply by subtracting from the particular face the corresponding point on the mean face (the origin being placed in the middle of the face), scaling this difference by a factor larger than one, and adding the scaled difference back on to the mean face.

Though Brennan's formalisation was introduced in the 1980s, it remains relevant in recent work. Mo et al. (2004) refined the idea by noting that the population variance of the feature should be taken into account. For example, the distance between the eyes varies less than other features such as the size of the nose. Thus even a small variation in the eye spacing is unusual and should be exaggerated, whereas a correspondingly small change in the nose size relative to the mean would not be unusual enough to be worthy of exaggeration. Leopold et al (2006) found that individual face-recognising neurons in the infer temporal cortex respond more strongly to d faces than to the veridical representations of the same face, and suggest that the visual brain may code faces relative to a prototypical face, consistent with Brennan's formalisation.

Some, on the other hand, argue that a caricature varies depending on the artist and cannot be captured in a single definition (L. Liang, H. Chen, Y. Xu, and H. Shum, 2002). Their system uses machine learning techniques to automatically learn and mimic the style of a particular caricature artist, given training data in the form of a number of face photographs and the corresponding caricatures by that artist. The results produced by computer graphic systems are arguably not yet of the same quality as those produced by human artists. For example, most systems are restricted to exactly frontal poses, whereas many or even most manually produced caricatures (and face portraits in general) choose an off-center "three-quarters" view. Brennan's caricatures drawings were frontal-pose line drawings. More recent systems can produce caricatures in a variety of styles, including direct geometric distortion of photographs.

In a lecture titled *The History and Art of caricatures* (September 2007, Queen Mary 2 Lecture theatre), the British caricaturist Ted Harrison said that the caricaturist can choose to either mock or wound the subject with an effective caricature. Drawing s can simply be a form of entertainment and amusement, in which case gentle mockery is in order, or the art can be employed to make a serious social or political point. A caricaturist draws on (1) the natural characteristics of the subject (the big ears, long nose or whatever); (2) the acquired characteristics (stoop, scars, facial lines etc.); and (3) the vanities (choice of hair style, spectacles, clothes, expressions and mannerisms)[3].

Types of Caricatures

Caricatures are divided into five categories in terms of the type and design, which include:

1. *Simple caricatures*: In this type of caricatures, the caricaturist changes the matching between the figures of human body and objects.

2. *Syllable designs*: These caricatures are censorious and insinuating as well as changing the figures. This kind is mostly used in political issues.

3. *Comic designs*: Usually journalists, fill their humor page with these designs. The goal of this project is to make readers of newspapers or magazines laugh and the designer does not follow any social or educational purposes.

4. *Daily designs*: The main and fundamental role this type is criticism and interpretation of daily work and activities in newspapers and magazines.

5. *Fantasy designs*: These caricatures are more or less comic, but imagination plays an important role in them.

Research Main Goal

Research main goal includes finding out the role of pictorial discourses in the forty-fourth presidential election of America.

Research Methodology

This research is based on Content analysis of Internet sites of newspapers and magazines in the United States that had the highest audiences in Google site.

Information Gathering Techniques

In the first stage, during a period of one year, all the caricatures which in some way were involved in highlighting Barack Obama's targets have been collected. These caricatures are in connection with each of the research hypotheses in rejecting or approving them.

In the second stage, caricatures are analyzed by experts.

In the third stage, discourses of each part are described separately.

Research Statistical Population

The research data that includes 48 caricatures are extracted from the site http://www.google.com. Caricatures are selected which are most clicked. These caricatures should be designed in addition to news about the election of forty fourth presidents, Barack Obama.

Caricatures can be drawn in personal blog, online and specialty publications and news websites.

Statistical Sample

Statistical sample include 48 available items.

Sample Size

Sample size includes 15 items.

Research Variables

A: *Independent variable*: Obama's victory in presidential election

A1: *Dependent variables*:

1. Using film symbols
2. Victory in sports
3. Supporting by important individuals and organizations in the world
4. Supporting by Democrats
5. Supporting by nature
6. Supporting by well-known statues in America
7. Supporting by people
8. Being compared to competitors

B: *Independent variable*: Obama's defeat in presidential election

B1: *Dependent variables*:

1. Being disrespected by TV programs
2. Disrespecting former officials
3. Following the opinions of Bill Clinton
4. Inefficiency of Obama's programmes
5. Contradiction in his speeches
6. Supporting by unaware people
7. Denying his Muslim's roots

Factors Affecting the Victory of Obama in Presidential Election over Hillary Clinton and McCain

Row	*Scenario Type*	*Frequency*
1.	Using film symbols	2
2.	Victory in sports	4
3.	Supporting by important individuals and organisations in the world	4

4.	Supporting by Democrats	4
6.	Supporting by nature	1
7.	Supporting by well- known statues in America	2
8.	Supporting by people	11
9.	Being compared to competitors	6
	Total	**34**

Table # 1: Factors Affecting the Victory of Obama in Presidential Election over Hillary Clinton and McCain

5. Supporting by Nature.

1. Film Symbols

2. Victory in Sports

3. Supporting by Important Individuals and Organizations in the World

4. Supporting by Democrats

Row	Scenario Type	Frequency

6. Supporting by Well-Known Statues in America.

7. Supporting by People.

8. Being Compared to Competitors.

Factors which have degraded Obama in Presidential Election over Hillary Clinton and McCain.

1.	Being disrespected by TV programmes	2
2.	Disrespecting former officials	3
3.	Following the opinions of Bill Clinton	2
4.	Inefficiency of Obama's programmes	3
5.	Contradiction in his speeches	1
6.	Supporting by unaware people	1
7.	Denying his Muslim's roots	1
	Total	**13**

Table # 2: Factors which have degraded Obama in Presidential Election over Hillary Clinton and McCain.

1. Being disrespected by TV programmes.

Conclusion

McCain's intention: (a) Black (b) Stupid (c) Naive or (d) All of the above.

2. Disrespecting former officials

3. Following the opinions of Bill Clinton

4. Inefficiency of Obama's programmes

5. Contradiction in his speeches.

6. Supporting by unaware people.

7. Denying his Muslim's roots.

Media plays an effective role in the development of awareness of people and their decision makers. It applies to various types of pictorial discourses including caricatures as well as literature discourses to help representation of news, stories, politics, economics, cultural and social issues in a more clear way.

Images can affect audiences on their emotions and drive their perception of news towards goal. Among various types of images, caricatures can be pointed out which are seen today in many newspapers, magazines and news websites alongside important news.

Different types of caricatures are used to meet different goals and objectives.

The research findings indicated that pictorial discourses have a significant role in the forty-fourth presidential election of America and such factors as using film symbols, victory in sports, supporting by important individuals and organizations in the world, supporting by Democrats, supporting by nature, supporting by well- known statues in America, supporting by people and being compared to competitors have affected the victory of Obama in the forty-fourth presidential election of America. On the contrary such factors as being disrespected by TV programs, disrespecting former officials, following the opinions of Bill Clinton, inefficiency of programmes, contradiction in speech, supporting by unaware people and denying his Muslim's roots have degraded Barack Obama in the presidential election.

References

1. *In literature.*
2. E. Akleman, J. Palmer, R. Logan, "Making Extreme s with a New Interactive 2D Deformation Technique with Simplicial Complexes", Proceedings of Visual 2000. Mexico City, Mexico, pp. 165-170, September 2000. See the author's examples on *VIZ-tamu.edu*
3. Susan Brennan, The Generator, MIT Media Lab master's thesis, 1982. Also see Susan Brennan, Generator: The Dynamic Exaggeration of Faces by Computer, *Leonardo, Vol. 18, No. 3 (1985), pp. 170–178, doi:10.2307/1578048*
4. Mo, Z.; Lewis, J., Neumann, U. (2004), *"Improved Auto-matic by Feature Normalization and Exaggeration". ACM Siggraph. doi:http://doi.acm.org/10.1145/1186223.1186294.http://portal.acm.org/citation. cfm?id=1186294&jmp=references&coll=&dl=GUIDE&CFID=15151515&CFTOKEN=6184618.*
5. Leopold, D., Bondar, I., Giese, M. (August, 2006). "Norm-based face encoding by single neurons in the monkey inferotemporal cortex". *Nature* 442 (7102): 572. *doi:10. 1038/nature04951. PMID 16862123.*
6. L. Liang, H. Chen, Y. Xu, and H. Shum, Example-Based Generation with Exaggeration, *Pacific Graphics 2002.*
7. *http://www.uiowa.edu/~ijcs/mediation/horstkotte.htm*
8. *http://en.wikipedia.org/wiki/*

8

Mobilising Mass Media for a Vibrant Civil Society: A Study

Arijit Ghosh

Introduction

A Healthy civil society is characterised by the vibrancy and quality of the networks between individuals, group, institutions and organisations, and the social capital they create. Civil society refers to the multiplicity of voluntary, collective action and social organisation by citizen, typically motivated by shared interests, goals, identities, cultures, beliefs, values as such. We can term it as an opposing force to the state and to the market and as such had been referred to using economic terminology — as the third sector of society.

Civil society is formed by informal and spontaneous networks as well as formal organisations. Such as:

- Non Governmental organisations (NGOs)
- Registered associations and charities
- Clubs for sports or other leisure time activities.
- Self help groups
- Community groups (certain Neighbourhood villages as such)
- Campaign and protest actions
- Citizen lobbies and advocacy groups
- Social movements
- Religious groups

Civil society generally do not include political parties or trade Unions, rather it includes grassroot activities and organisations of citizens. The importance of a vibrant civil society to a democracy is widely recognised.

How civil society actors are using mass media for bringing a change in the society.

Bringing a change in the society means that it will benefit the Poor. The focus of attention needs to be on supporting and strengthening communication processes and channels used by the poor. And marginalised people, who, because of their disadvantaged situations are facing many barriers to receiving information – including illiteracy, not able to speak the majority or official languages and limited access to mass media. In this context, Panos London contends that four key areas need to be tackled using an integrated approach: Rights to Freedom and Speech and Access to Information; supporting Media; Developing and exploiting the revolutionary new opportunities offered by ICTs and enabling greater participation of poor and marginalised people in social, economic and political processes.

Civil society requires mass media to:

- Encourage public debate
- Uplift new themes and bring them to light
- Analyse causes and suggesting solutions to social problems
- Influence the public opinion, to create support and sympathy for the cause. For example we are seeing various organisations are using social media to enrich their support.
- Suggest alternatives values, consumer habits and so on.
- Give voice to the voiceless

Writing in 1993, William Grasson and Gadi Wolfsfold suggested that social movements rely on the mainstream media for three main services, (1) Mobilisation of Political support, (2) Legitimation in the mainstream discourse, and (3) to broaden the scope of conflicts.

Media coverage is very crucial for less well known social movements. Typical protests action which includes–sit-ins, pickets, strikes, rallies, mass demonstrations are being constantly reported in the media. Understanding the relationships between social movements and the media's coverage of their actions isvery significant, especially if this is to be utilised to bring a progressive social change. Most civil movements are not the centre of regular news beats. They struggle to get their message heard, as "the vast majority of demonstrations are ignored by the mainstream media".

According to Tarun Tejpal, editor-in-chief of the news magazine *Tehelka*, "the media today have became a purely commercial construct. Civil society, in contrast is not—there is no money to be made out of the activities that civil society is involved in. I think that that this has became the fundamental differences between the media and civil society organisation. Ideally, civil society should be amplifying what the media do, and media should be articulating the concerns of civil society. But, today this complementary is not very evident. Of course, there will always be issues on which journalism and civil society find themselves on the same side, but when this happens it is largely because the media do not see these issues as handicapping them commercially. So, on

Jessica lal, for example every body is one the same side and all the media houses clamber to project the story. But if it is about a SEZ acquired by Reliance, its another story."

How India is Bringing a Revolution in Social Change

2011 saw one of the largest rallies staged in Delhi where lakh of workers from nine central trade union – including the congress party INTUC- hit the streets to protest against rising food, unemployment. This was more bigger in intent than the modest numbers at Anna Hazare's fast for corruption and larger than Ramdev's rollicking yoga camp. These rallies provided the real taste of 'civil society'. The rally was covered by the *BBC*, Reuters and AFP but the mainstream media did not paid so much attention.

A clear contradiction is visible in mainstream media houses. Anna enjoyed the support of Media. Baba Ramdev did not got it fully. Both claimed to speak for 'civil society'. Both stressed the fact that their idea was best for the nation. They were above the legislature, the executive and the judiciary. Both felt that they were fighting corruption. Both saw themselves as 'Messiah' who will turn the filthy nation upside down. One would probably remember how the same media which is now trashing Ramdev came out in support when he clashed with smt Brinda Karat in 2006. The case was over the exploitation of 113 workers thrown out of the pharmacy controlled by Ramdev's trust and facing false cases. The media slammed Ms. Karat over this incident.

What we are witnessing in India, civil society is completely different. It is crowded with human rights activists, NGO, academics, high profile journalists and celebreties. The main burning issues like farmer suicides, landless labourers, trade unions are being kept aside by media houses for public debates.

India is seeing a new revolution in social Activism. From Gandhigiri, the following principles of non violences, to joining protests and marches, the citizens are raising voice for their rights. But this emergence has its flaws. Gopal Krishna, member, Citizen Forum for Civil Society, says, "the civil society intervention is more symbolic. When there is no one saying anything it makes sense to have at least this symbolism but we cannot depend on this symbolism for any substantive action."

Today, we are seeing that these social activists are using social networking media to vent their protests. Recent trends portray that Indian netizens are getting too vocal on social networks such as facebook and twitter. Pages like 'india against corruption' got huge fan followers.

How civil rights organisations are using social media :

- Breakthrough, an international human rights organisation, decided to utilise all media tools to drive home its message on domestic violence. Its blog www. Bellbajao.org continues to give people a platform to share their experiences and encounters with domestic violence.
- People for the ethical treatment of animals has also jumped on the social media bandwagon to reach out to more people, while the global @ PETA is drawing high 2,00,000 followers, the Indian peta india has jut over 2,00 followers on *Twitter*.
- Juvenis technologies private limited in Mumbai, has used 'India Against Corruption "on the android market place. The application allow users to make this movement solid by making a missed call to a number held by india against corruption. So far, it claims to have received close to 1.3 crore missed calls".

Participatory Media

Participatory media includes a multiplicity of publication, practices and projects. Their main aim is to involve and empower ordinary citizens. They are alternative to the mainstream media in terms of contents and practices. They give voice to the voiceless and present views which are not depicted by the mainstream media.

Various forms of participatory media:

- Citizen media
- Third sector media
- Community media
- Alternative media
- Radical media
- Grassroots media
- Do-it-yourself media
- Minority media
- Social media (in internet, also refered to as Web 2.0)

Community Radio as a Participatory Media

The community based organisations have been playing a significant role in the process of development in India. The historical philosophy of community radio is to use their medium as the voice of the voiceless, the mouthpiece of the oppressed people and generally as a tool for development. (AMARC 1981).

It is the most significant tool for participatory and democratic communication.

They are typically:

- voice of the civil societies, communities and various marginal/minority groups. For example 'Namma Dhwani', 'SEWA Radio', 'Helvel Vani' and many others reveal that Communities are coming together and making their vices heard. Some of the most recent community radio initiatives include Charkha's Pechu-wali Man Ker Swar in Ranchi, Self Employed Women's Association (SEWA'S), 'Radi no Radio' in Gujarat and Agragamees Vjjala in Jeypore, Orissa (Patil, 2010);
- open for participation by members of the community they serve;
- accountable to the community;
- Independent and non-profit;
- educational in nature;
- based on horizontal "many-to-many" communication and "bottom-up" communication (as opposed to "top-to-bottom" communication of the mainstream media),

Community radios – and community media in general – have several important functions, such as:

- bringing the community into public discussion;
- disseminating essential information for community members;
- educating, empowering and mobilising community;
- Serving special groups and communities, such as ethnic minorities, women, indigenous people, students, civic organisations and social movements;
- promoting development, human rights and freedom of speech; and
- providing media education citizen.

Conclusions

This paper demonstrates how civil groups are using media to bring about social change. In summary, we can say that civil group must use the media in a positive way to maximise its potential. The focus of attention needs to be on suppoting and strengthening communication processes and channels used by the poor. Media coverage is extremly useful for this civil groups to foster their agendas. Many groups went unnoticed because they were ignored by the mainstream media.

We have also witnessed in this paper how social activism is prospering in India. Social activists are using new media /social media to vent their protests. Finally, civil organisations must use community radio to reach the unreached. It is the ultimate medium for providing participatory and democratic communication.

References

1. AMARC (1981), "Community Radio Handbook," Canada.
2. Gamson, W. A. and Wolfsfeld, G.(1993), "Movements and media as interacting systems" in *Annals of the American Academy of Political and Social Science*, Vol. 528. pp.114-125.
3. Kulmakivi, Journalism for social change, Learning module 4: *Media and Civil Society.* http:// Kulmakivi.ning.com/
4. Patil. A. Dhanraj, (2010), 'A Voice for the Voiceless: The Role of Community Radio in the Development of the Rural Poor,' Maharashtra. Vol.17, No.1, April 2010.
5. Philipose, Pamela, 'We run with the hounds and hunt the hares', a series of conversation with Tarun Tejpal.
6. Subramaniam, karthik (2011), In India, civil and political movement warm to social media, *The Hindu*, Chennai, August 21, 2011. www.thehindu.com/news/national.

9

Media : The Fourth Pillar of Democracy

Dr. Vinod Kumar Pandey

Introduction

The mass media constitute the backbone of democracy. The media are supplying the political information that voters base their decisions on. They identify problems in our society and serve as a medium for deliberation. They are also the watchdogs that we rely on for uncovering errors and wrongdoings by those who have power. It is therefore reasonable to require that the media perform to certain standards with respect to these functions, and our democratic society rests on the assumption that they do.

The media has a crucial role in not only strengthening democratic processes in each of the countries in the region, but also in fostering greater cooperation and demand for change and ensure that the process is implemented in the best possible manner.

Democracy

Democracy is a form of government in which people are governed by their own elected representatives. It is a government of the people, for the people and by the people. In this system of government, it is the people who are supreme and sovereign. They control the government. They are free to elect a government of their own choice. Freedom of choice is the core of democracy.

Democracy existed in ancient Greek and Roman republics but with little success. It had very little scope in ancient India. Democracy entered its golden stage in he twentieth century. Many countries in the world today follow the democratic form of government. Democracy depends on the following conditions (i) co-existence of ideas and of parties; (ii) the right to free discussion; (iii) universal adult suffrage; and (iv) periodic elections.

Origins of Democracy

The word "democracy," as well as the concept it represents, can be traced back to the area surrounding the Mediterranean Sea. The beginnings of democracy can be credited to the Greeks of the sixth century BC. The word comes from two Greek words—*demos* meaning "the people," and *kratein* meaning "to rule." These two words are joined together to form democracy, literally meaning "rule by the people" (Pious). The Greek system of government was perhaps closer to a true democracy or rule by the people than any other in history. The Greeks viewed dictatorship as the worst possible form of government, so their government evolved as the exact opposite. Their civilisation was broken down into small city-states (never more than 10,000 citizens), and all the men voted on all issues of government. There were no representatives in the Greek system of government. Instead, they ruled themselves directly; each man was a life long member of the decision making body. This was almost a total democracy except for the fact that women and slaves (over 50 per cent of the population) were not considered citizens and were not allowed to vote. Despite this, no other civilisation has come as close to democracy as its creators, the Greeks, and many later civilisations have incorporated this Greek idea as part of the foundation for their government (Lee; Lefebvre).

Ideas of democracy similar to that of the Greeks were used by the Romans, though not to the same extent. The Roman Empire (509-27 BC) took some of their governmental ideals from the Greeks. Their government was a representative democracy, which had representatives from the nobility in the Senate and representatives from the commoners in the Assembly. Governmental power was divided between these two branches and they voted on various issues. Many Roman political thinkers were fond of democracy. The Roman Statesman, Cicero was one. Cicero suggested that all people have certain rights that should be preserved. He and other political philosophers of the time taught that governmental and political power should come from the people (Lefebvre; Lee). After the trend of democracy was started by the Greeks and carried on by the Romans, it has been seen in many later governmental systems throughout history.

Democracy in the Middle Ages

Though democracy was not directly instituted in the Middle Ages, many democratic ideas were prevalent throughout the period. Because Christianity, which taught that men were created equal in the eyes of God, was deeply ingrained into the society of the Middle Ages, the democratic idea of equality was understood by many of the people. The Middle Ages, however, utilised another form of government, which was developed during this period called feudalism. Feudalism stressed that all people have certain rights and developed a system of courts to defend these rights. From these courts came the modern day judicial branch of the American government along with many of the ideas such as kings councils, assemblies and eventually parliamentary systems (Sanford 20-27).

Democracy in England

In 1215 AD, the Magna Carta opened the door to a more democratic system in England. Nobles forced King John to sign this "Great Charter" that created the English "Parliament", or law-making body, and stated that the written laws held a higher power than the king, thereby limiting the power of the Royal family and giving some of that power to the people. Later, the Petition of Right (1628) stipulated that the King could no longer tax without parliament's permission and the Bill of Rights (1689) provided freedom of speech and banned cruel or unusual punishment. These strengthened Parliament further and gave the people more right to express themselves. Though these reforms did not make England a true democracy in any sense, they did incorporate democratic ideals, which would later be used to form the government of the United States (Lefebvre; Pious).

The concept of democracy continued to be prevalent in Europe with the philosophies of an English philosopher by the name of John Locke and a French philosopher named Jean Jacques Rousseau.

Democracy in America

Modern American democracy is in the form of a democratic republic or a representative democracy. A representative democracy came about in the United States because the colonists were tired of taxation without representation and wanted a more fair system where the people had more say in the rule of the country. They did not desire the Athenian form of democracy however; as they feared it would give the people too much power and would lend control of the government to the uneducated masses. What they came up with was a representative democracy wherein elected representatives rather than direct rule by the people rule the government. These representatives are elected with the idea that they will accurately represent their constituents, but in case some don't, the U.S. government is divided into three branches to keep corruption in check. These three branches are the Executive, Legislative, and Judicial branches. No one branch contains absolute power, rather, each branch is balanced off of the others creating a system of checks and balances to protect the principals of democracy. This system is in no way perfect, and this is why we must pursue a more perfect form of democracy and a more perfect union between our citizens, states and country (Pious; Sanford 20-27).

Indian is the largest democracy in the world. The Constitution of Indian was enforced on 26 January, 1950. It ushered in the age pf democracy. India became a democratic republic infused with the spirit of justice, liberty, equality and fraternity. The Preamble, the Directive Principles of State Policy and the Fundamental Rights reflect the Indian ideology as well as the caste, creed, religion, property, or sex have the right to cast their vote. After and election, the majority party or coalition forms the government and its leader become the Prime Minister.

Political parties are the vehicles of ideas. Parties act as the bridge between social thought and political decision in democracy. The Indian politics system is a multiparty system. However, gradually politics has become a game of opportunism and corruption. Most political parties are only interested in coming to power. Every party adopts different caste politics. Some try to influence the people thought caste politics. Some try to raise the religious sentiments of the people. The Indian ideology today is replaced by caste and religion.

We enjoy every right in theory, but not in practice. real democracy will come into being only when the masses are awakened and take part in the economic and political life of the country. There is inequality in every sphere-social, economic and political. Illiteracy is the main cause of inequality. The illiterate masses get easily lured by money during such an event. Also some of our legislators have criminal records against them. The people who make the laws themselves break them.

Even after more than sixty years of Independence, one forth of the population today goes to bed with an empty stomach, live below the poverty line without access to safe and clean drinking water, sanitation or proper health facilities. Governments have come and gone, politics have been framed and implemented, crores of rupees have been spent, yet many people are still struggling for existence.

Casteism today is more pronounced that it even was. Untouchability remains abolished only in theory with frequent newspapers reports of Dalits being denied entry to temples or other public places. Violence has been taken a serious turn in country, *Bandhs*, strikes and terrorist activities have become a common affair. Every sphere of national life is corrupted. Our democracy is capitalistic. Here, the rich exploit the poor who have no voice or share in the democratic structure. For a successful democracy, all these need to be checked.

But India, as a democratic country, has progressed in many aspects. It has archived self-sufficiency in food grains as a result of the green revolution. People vote for change whenever a government fails to come up to the expectations of the people. India has been a successful democratic country only because the people are law-abiding, self-disciplined and have the sense of social and moral responsibilities.

Role of Media in Indian Democracy

Newspapers play an important role in a democracy. They act as bridge between the government and the governed. Everybody, except a few read the newspaper everyday.

Different people read it for different purposes. Newspapers keep the people aware of the activities of the government. They mobilise public opinion. They play an important role in fighting the menace of corruption. In a democracy, there should be an efficient and fearless press. Press is he mirror of the society.

Everybody except a few read the newspaper everyday. One reads it with exciting curiosity every morning. Different people read the newspaper for different purposes. Young graduates scan the job-advertisement pages. Lottery addicts pour over the lottery results. The school boy looks about the detailed happenings in cricket and other sports. The head of the household reads about government matters and other events. Business entrepreneurs go thought the business news.

India is a developing country. Most of the people are poor and illiterate. For democracy to be successful, all the citizens should be illiterate. Politicians with selfish motive deceive the poor and illiterate with false promises. Newspapers help in spreading public opinion. They keep the people aware of the activities of the government.

In a democracy, there should be an efficient and fearless press. Press refers to newspapers, magazines, the news section of radio and television, and the journalists who work for them. Press is the mirror of the society. It acts as a watch0god of democracy. it is the duty of the press to watch the activities of the government. Its duty is to highlight the failure of the policies of the government and pinpoint its lapses.

Media give us the latest information on local, national and international events. They serve as a platform for discussion on public issues. Media focus on social and political evils prevailing in the society. Some of these evils are unsociability. dowry, drinking, gambling, drug addiction etc. Media can exhort the people to root out these evils.

Media make people aware of every field of society. Once in every week, every newspaper publishes vacancies in all fields. Job seekers get much benefited thought this. A weekly matrimonial supplement is also published with almost every newspaper and its related news and events. Newspapers also contain the schedules of Television and theaters. It helps people to plan their day accordingly. News related to sports becomes very important nowadays as it fetches large amount of revenue. So almost all the newspapers publish the sports-news with elaborate pictures and charts. People get informed about weather forecast, railway and airport time table.

In the present age, corruption is present in all walks of life. Media play an important role in fighting against the menace of corruption. The people can be made aware of the corrupt practices prevalent in various departments of Government and other agencies.

Media act as a link between the government and the people. They make the people aware of the policies, programmes and activities of the government. They also make the government aware of the problems, being faced by the people. Newspaper could make a great impact on its readers. So, they should concentrate on giving only the true picture of the society.

Television and radio have made a significant achievement in educating rural illiterate masses in making them aware of all the events in their language. Coverage of exploitative malpractices of village heads and moneylenders has helped in taking stringent actions against them by attracting government's attention.

The media also exposes loopholes in the democratic system, which ultimately helps government in filling the vacuums of loopholes and making a system more accountable, responsive and citizen-friendly. A democracy without media is like a vehicle without wheels.

In the age of information technology we are bombarded with information. We get the pulse of the world events with just a click of a mouse. The flow of information has increased manifolds. The perfect blend of technology and human resources (journalist) has not left a single stone unturned in unearthing rampant corruption in politics and society. We all are well aware of what Tehelka did. Thanks to technology that has brought a kind of revolution in journalism.

Impact of Media

The impact of media is really noteworthy. Excessive coverage or hype of sensitive news has led to communal riots at times. The illiterates are more prone to provocations than the literates. Constant repetition of the news, especially sensational news, breeds apathy and insensitivity. For instance, In

Mumbai terror attack case, the overloaded hype led excessive information exposure to terrorists. There is a plethora of such negative impacts. Media should take utmost care in airing or publishing such sensational news.

Commercialisation has created a stiff competition in media. In order to outdo each other print media has often gone one step further in publishing articles, cover stories, etc. on sex.

Media experts say this is one of the means of attracting readers who are glued to T.V. news channels, which have cropped up swiftly in a recent past and they believe this is a cheap form of journalism.

India's strength has always been its vibrant democracy. Ours is perhaps the only country where people from contrastingly different castes, creed, religion and race live together in peace and harmony. The other hallmarks of our country are a strong judicial system and a free press. The imposition of the emergency in 1975 struck at the very core of these ideals, which constitute our democracy. It was perhaps the darkest period in the history of independent India.

Free Press Vs. Fair Trial

The concept of '*Janta Adalat*' has lead to a serious conflict between free press and fair trial by the judiciary. Indian media leaves no stone unturned in its quest for gripping news. And what better news to grab viewership than an on going trial?

The Contempt of Courts Act, 1971 and Articles 129 and 215 of the Constitution of India are meant to protect the right of a citizen to have a fair trial. i.e. a trial uninfluenced by extraneous pressures. But the realm of aggressive journalism has severely compromised this right.

Instances of media uncovering 'evidences' and prejudicing the public opinion are not new. This leads to serious miscarriage of justice. In their relentless investigations and publicising of the same, they spare neither the seasoned criminal nor the innocent victim. Both their images are splashed in their channels. Even the witnesses and the kit and kin of the victims are not spared. Witness protection is seriously endangered and so is the likability of the victim ever returning to normal life.

Now for the Good Acts

The media may bias justice, it may broadcast senseless news for hours on end, but one thing that cannot be denied is that media forms the 4th wheel of the Indian democracy. With a secular state like ours with varied beliefs and traditions, a strong and independent media can mobilise us for the right cause.

The true spirit of journalism is showcased in instances such as the *Bofors* case and the *HDW* (Howaldswerske) marine case. Through media only the case of Narasimha Rao bribing the Jharkhand Mukti Morcha MPs, was revealed. Sting operations carried in the right spirit had resulted in the success of *Operation Duryodhana* in which MPs were caught taking bribe to raise questions in the Parliament. Similarly the *Tehelka* case had led the CBI to file a chargesheet against those who took the bribe.

As observed by the Delhi High Court in the Bofors case, the media plays a vital role in making the public aware of what is happening in their country. It can be rightly said that media is instrumental in making people aware of their rights and freedoms.

Moreover by telecasting such news media is in a way reducing the crime rate as more and more people disapprove of criminal behavior. As such it also facilitates public discussions on important issues.

Every Right or Freedom has its boundaries and cannot be adjudged as absolute in any manner. While exercising one's right it should be kept in mind that one shouldn't encroach on another's freedom. The media needs to be self-regulatory and humanitarian in its approach to the way it treats news. Only then the concept of *Free Press* can be realised.

Conclusion

No one is perfect in this world and so is the media. We don't intend to degrade the media; rather we would say there is still a lot of scope for improvement by which media can raise up to the aspirations of the people for which it is meant. we cannot think of a democracy without active and neutral media. From being just an informer it has become an integral part of our daily lives. With the passage of time it has become a more matured and a more responsible entity. The present media revolution has helped people in making an informed decisions and this has led to beginning of a new era in a democracy.

References

1. Andrew Vandenberg (Ed.) 2000, Citizenship and Democracy in a Global Era, Mac Millan Press, New York.
2. Dennis McQuail, 2000, Mass Communication Theory, Sage, London. Romila Thaper (Ed.) 2000, India Another millennium? Viking, New Delhi.
3. Edward S. Herman, Robert W. McChensney, 1998, the Global Media, New Missionaries of Corporate Capitalism, Madhyam, New Delhi.
4. Gordon Marshal (Ed.) 1994, The Consice Oxford Dictionary of Sociology, Oxford University Press, New York.

5. James Curran and Michel Gurevitch (Ed.) 2000, Mass Media and Society, (Second Edition), Arnold, London.
6. Lucian W.Pye, 1963, Communications and Political Developments, Radhakrishna Publishers, New Delhi.
7. Richard Gunther and Anthony Mugham, 2000, Democracy and the Media, Cambridge University Press, Cambridge.
8. Romila Thapar, (Ed.), 2000, India Another Millennium, Viking, New Delhi.
9. Sean MacBride, 1982, Many Politics, One World, UNESCO, Paris.
10. Naval Prabhakar, Narendra Basuk, Mass Media and Society, Commonwealth Publishers, New Delhi, 2007.
11. www.publishyourarticles.org-democracy in india
12. Library.thinkquest.org

10

Democracy and Media: An Overview

Debilal Mishra

Introduction

It is always true to say that the media is a vital element in democracy. Without media the existence of a democratic set up is almost impossible. Democracy, at its core, is concerned with the people and their fundamental rights, participation and representations. It refers to the 'rule by the people'. Since the people are rarely unanimous, democracy as a descriptive term is synonymous with majority rule. Undoubtedly, a democratic set up largely draws its sustenance from the media. The media in a democracy is a powerful as well as responsible asset. It is through the media that public discourse about the scope and nature of democracy is circulated. Peruvian communication theorist Rosa Maria Alfaro [2006] asserts that "today media constitute a crucial source of civic education and legitimisation of democratic power. Political elites legitimise themselves or join dissident discourses through their interactions with newspapers, magazines, radio and television. Notions of political authority, political values and general understanding of a nation's political institutions are consolidated through the daily programmes of the mass media and particularly via news. The national and international agenda emerge from daily mass media processes of production and consumption. Both the concept and feeling of nation and of the world are also articulated in the production and consumption of media".

THE ROLE OF MEDIA IN DEMOCRACY

The mass media are presumed not only to have certain objective effects on society, but also to serve a social purpose. This means that some of the effects that have been observed are both intended and positively valued. These include the effects of disseminating information, expressing different voices and views, helping public opinion to form on issues and facilitating debate [Denis McQuail, 2010]. The media carry out a number of important and essential tasks in a contemporary society and it is in the general interest that these are performed and performed well. Simply put the media and society share a reciprocal relationship. The media reflects the society, upholds the public interest and creates a process of societal development. According to McQuail, "we should have a media system that is operated according to the basic principles governing the rest of society, especially in relation to justice, fairness, democracy and reigning notions of desirable social and cultural values. It is clearly in the public interest that the media don't cause social problems or extreme offence. But media are usually established not to serve the public interest as such, but to follow some goal of their own choosing. The goal is sometimes defined in cultural, professional or political terms but more often it is the goal of making profit as a business. Sometimes it is both at the same time. This points to the key problem of determining just what the public interest might be and of who should decide it. There are always diverse and conflicting versions of what is good for a society as a whole, and there is even support for the view that it is better for the media not to pursue any normative goal at all. Rather, the many different media should be left free to do what they want, within the limits of the law. Where media are run on a commercial basis, as they mainly are, the media's view of what is the public interest tends to equate it with what interests the public. This shifts the responsibility for norms, ethics and values to the society". However, all aspects considered, media should play certain roles in certain contexts for the success of a democracy. Without these positive roles of media no democracy can ever be successful. Let's discuss these important roles in some detail.

PROVIDING INFORMATION AND KNOWLEDGE

Information is knowledge and knowledge is power. Today's society is information society and so has been today's democracy. The overload of information in every walk of life has made the time information-rich. And it is influencing democracy in a big way. It is desirable that the media system overall should exhibit a range of output that reflects the diversity of the society, especially in the key dimensions of region, politics, religion, ethnicity, culture and so on. Media channels should be open to new movements and ideas and give reasonable access to small minorities. The media should meet a wide range of public communication and information needs and the citizens should have access as senders and receivers to media that reflect their ideas and meet their interests and needs.

EDUCATION

In the present time the media assumes the role of an educator. It plays a key role in educating people about the different dimensions of democracy, may it be political power, representation, culture or socio-economic issues, through different approaches and projections. The media should also educate the public mind and contribute actively to the creation of positive citizenry for a better societal transformation.

PARTICIPATION AND COOPERATION

Participation and cooperation are the two vital components of a democracy. Without people's participation and cooperation no country can achieve its major objectives and goals of nation building. Media should allow people to participate in the affairs of the state by being participatory. The participatory approach of media is best prescribed in the process of socio-national development. And the media must arouse a sense of involvement among the people in a democracy and make them cooperative in a democratic way to reach a common consensus and start up point for action.

GENERATION OF OPINION

The media, as part of its important function, should highlight the informed opinion, or general view of the more educated and aware members of the society. By generating opinions the media supports the democratic process to a great extent. This contribution is made through publishing full, fair and reliable information on public matters, assisting in the expression of diverse points of view, sensitising the public thinking, giving access to many voices in society, facilitating the participation of citizens in the socio-political life and so on.

'WATCHDOG' STAND POINT

Media is the watchdog of the society, especially of the government. It safeguards the fundamental rights of the citizens and reacts to any violation. In a democracy there are so many differences and discrepancies. It is the media which brings everything to a common platform for the purpose of developing awareness and understanding. Media must keep a strict vigil on the emerging social problems and issues like corruption and other social evils. While the media are not normally required to do the work of the police or other authorities, on whom they should keep a critical eye, there is a widely held view in democracies that there are some matters on which they do have a duty to assist authority.

CULTURAL PROMOTION

The mass media, in a democracy, play a greater role in developing and nourishing culture and it can be effectively used to preserve and promote the precious cultural impressions. The media are expected to respect the dominant values and moral standards of their own society and to give expression to the traditional valued culture, and the arts and language of their own national society or region.

SUPPORTING THE DEMOCRATIC PROCESS

It is another important role of the media to support the democratic process by respecting the rights of the individuals, maintaining public order, meeting various socio-human obligations, maintaining healthy relationship with the government and facilitating inter structural harmony. The right media attitude is the basis of the democratic process. The approach of the media in a democracy should always be constructive and it should keep away from excessive commercialisation and intense sensationalism in the interest of a positive society.

THEORETICAL DIMENSIONS

There are several theories of media that explain the role of media in the society, especially in the democratic societies. These include the following theories.

FUNCTIONAL THEORIES

In 1948 and 1960 the renowned communicologist and media scholar Harold Lasswell and Charles wright explored the functional theory of mass communication. In their respective works on the communication and media- 'the structure and function of communication and society: the communication of ideas' and 'the functional analysis of mass communication'–both of them agreed to one point that the knowledge is universal and it is one truth that the mass communication functions as part of our society. It is a main source of surveillance, entertainment, correlation, transmission and mobilisation. The mass media serves many functions for our society. The five elements the theorists put together describe the audience's use for the media. Surveillance means that the media provides news and information. Correlation means that the media presents the information to us after they select, interpret, and criticise it. The cultural transmission function means that the media reflects our own beliefs, values, and norms. Media also entertains us in our free time and provides an escape from everyday life. Mobilisation refers to the media function of promoting society's interest especially in times of crisis.

Wilbur schramm also defined the functions of communication, in turn the functions of media, in terms of watcher, forum and teacher. The media plays the role of a watcher by keeping a watch on the environment. It is a forum for debates and discussions. And as a teacher it develops public opinion and persuades the public to be guided by the right thing.

COMMUNITARIAN THEORY AND THE MEDIA

A relatively new development is expressed in terms of 'communitarianism' which reemphasises the social ties connecting people, in contrast to modern libertarian individualism [MacIntyre, 1981; sandel,1982; Rorty,1989; Taylor, 1989]. It stresses duties owed to society as well as rights to be claimed. In respect of media, relations between media and audience take on a more mutual character, especially where they share a social identity and a place. One exponent of communitarian thinking stresses the ethical imperative of the media to engage in dialogue with the public it serves [Christians,1993]. 'In the communitarian model', according to Nerone [1995:70-1], 'the goal of reporting is not intelligence but civic transformation. The press has bigger fish to fry than merely improving technology and streamlining performance... in a communitarian world-view, the news media should seek to engender a like-minded philosophy among the public. A revitalised citizenship shaped by community norms becomes the press's aim. News would be an agent of community formation'. In some respects the call is to return to a more organic social form, in which the press plays an integrative, expressive and articulating role. Not self interest but partnership is seen as the way forward [McQuail].

SOCIAL RESPONSIBILITY THEORY

Freedom carries concomitant obligations; and the press which enjoys a privileged position under our government, is obliged to be responsible to society for carrying out certain essential functions of mass communication in the contemporary society. To the extent that the press recognises its responsibilities and makes them the basis for operational policies, the libertarian system will satisfy the needs of society. To the extent that the press doesn't assume its responsibilities, some other agency must see that the essential functions of mass communication are carried out [Peterson]. According to Peterson the responsibilities include servicing the political system by providing information, discussion and debate on public affairs, enlightening the public so as to make it capable of self-government, safeguarding the rights of the individual by serving as a watchdog against government and so on.

DEMOCRATIC-PARTICIPANT THEORY

This theory was propounded by McQuail. It emphasises and supports the media's multiplicity, local nature, small scale usage, de-institutionalization, reciprocal part of recipient and communicator, horizontal approach, involvement and interaction. This theory outlines certain important principles that consider communication and mass media as being very important and should be managed by the professionals. Democratic participant theory allows freedom to associated local data, freedom for answering back, freedom for using new communication means for the purpose of interaction and freedom of taking social-action in community, sub-culture's and interest-group's small scale settings.

MAJOR ISSUES WITH MEDIA IN DEMOCRACY

There are some issues that always keep on accompanying media in a democracy. Let's discuss the important ones.

FREEDOM

It is widely agreed that media should be free from control by government or other powerful interests, sufficient to allow them to report and express freely and independently and to meet the needs of their audiences. Freedom consists essentially in the absence of advance censorship or licensing, or of punishment after the event for publication or broadcast that is not otherwise unlawful. According to John stuart Mill, "the peculiar evil of silencing the expression of an opinion is, that is robbing the human race, posterity as well as the existing generation, those who dissent from the opinion even more than those who hold it. If the opinion is right, they are deprived of the opportunity of exchanging error for truth; if wrong, they lose what is almost as great a benefit, the clearer perception and livelier impression of truth, produced by its collision with error"[1859, on the liberty of the press].

The historical context of the struggle for press freedom was almost invariably one of antagonism between publication and some authority, first church and later government, in many aspects. The core idea goes back to John Milton's pamphlet, Areopagitica [1644] against licensing of the press in England. It is not surprising that press freedom came to be defined primarily as freedom from restriction. This was the meaning it had been given in legal terms in the United States, in the words of the first amendment to the US constitution[1791], to the effect that congress shall make no law...abridging the freedom of speech or of the press'. By contrast, reformed constitutions in many other countries have referred to a right guaranteed to citizens. For example, article 7 of the 1848 constitution of the Netherlands says: 'no one needs advance permission in order to make public through the printing press any thoughts or feelings, aside from everyone's responsibility in law'. Similarly, Articles 19-22 of the Indian Constitution give to the citizens the Right to Freedom as one of the Fundamental Rights. The right to freedom of expression enshrined therein gives the media not only a primary role but also a paramount responsibility of expressing public opinion. In India during the period of emergency the media received control and retribution from the government. However, it has been free throughout its course relatively.

By the early twentieth century it was clear to many reformers that press freedom in the economic sense and expressed in the purely negative terms of rejecting government interference was failing to give voice to the full meaning of freedom of expression, which includes some notion of a realistic opportunity of access to the channels of publication. Instead of being a vehicle for advancing freedom and democracy, the press was becoming more and more a means of making money and propaganda for the new and powerful capitalist classes, and especially 'the press barons' [McQuail].

Democracy can't function unless the people are well informed and free to participate in public issues by having the widest choice of alternative solutions of the problems that arise. The people can be given the fullest scope for thought and discussion on public issues, if only the media are allowed to represent different points of views without any control or bias; and with objectivity, truth and balance. The freedom of the press or media essentially refers to the freedom of the conscience of the journalist to see the reality and let others see it.

"The press, and particularly the newspaper press, stands by common consent first among the organs of the public opinion...The conscience and common sense of the nation as a whole keep down the evils which have crept into the working of the constitution, and may in time extinguish them...so long as the opinion of a nation is sound the main lines of its policy cannot go far wrong" [Bryce, American commonwealth].

DEVELOPMENT

From the early stages of the introduction of mass media, attempts have been made to expand their potential for development purposes. The terms development communication and development journalism were closely associated with the new world information order [NWIO] debate that centered in UNESCO in the 1970s and early 1980s. The argument that mass media could be mobilised to guide social change originated long before UNESCO, however. It derived in large part from the experience of the United States and a few other western countries early in the twentieth century. These countries created a variety of government programmes to promote development in rural areas. In the United States, a large bureaucracy called the Agricultural extension service was established to administer these programmes. The country 'ag agent' and 'home agent' are, still fixtures in rural court houses around the country, still working to improve agricultural production and rural life in general. Local radio shows and weekly newspaper columns prepared by the ag extension office are part of life in many rural areas of the united states. It was thought that this experience could be used to tackle some of the dreadful problems facing the newly independent nations of Asia and Africa in the 1950s and 1960s [Robert L Stevenson].

Media is an essential tool for national development and social change. Wilbur schramm in his book *MAGIC MULTIPLIER* has said that media can do a list of works in a democracy that include being social watchdogs and broaden horizons, focusing attention and raising aspirations, creating a climate for development, feeding interpersonal channels of communication, conferring status, enforcing social norms and helping form tastes. According to him, "this is the really exciting question: how much could we increase the present rate of development, how much could we smooth out the difficulties of the terrible ascent, how much more could we contribute to the growth of informed, participating citizens in the new nations, if we were to put the resources of modern communication skillfully and fully behind economic and social development".

Numerous development approaches have been made within democracies for the overall transformation of the developing conditions. Everywhere the vital roles of media have been acknowledged. No development programme has been feasible in any country so far without the valuable contribution of the mass media. In the Indian context there have been several experiments with the media for development–may it be SITE, Kheda or community development projects with rural radio. All these attempts were aimed at the change in attitude and behaviour of the target people in favour of the realisation of social worth and the major thrust was to promote the use of media as a support to the national development initiatives.

NEW MEDIA TECHNOLOGY

With the advent of the new technologies and new media environment the core of the democracy has also been renewed. Now the nation is going through the important phase of transition from action to experience and from experience to vision. Almost all the vital institutions of democracy have undergone transformation; both structural and functional. After the introduction of internet and the new media, the experiences of *e-governance, e-commerce, e-learning, e-communication* and *e-administration* have been wonderful. The new process is reflecting the people-centric vision, transparent approach, and easiness of dealing and the realisation of time value. The new electronic media have been widely hailed as a potential way of escape from the oppressive top down politics of mass democracies. The concepts of new politics based on new media are quite diverse and different perspectives are involved. Dahlberg [2001] describes three basic models. *First* there is the model of 'cyber-libertarianism' that wants an approach to politics based on the model of the consumer market. Surveys, plebiscites and televoting fit this outlook, replacing older processes. *Secondly*, there is a 'communitarian' view that expects the benefits to come from greater grass-roots participation and input and the strengthening of local political communities. *Thirdly*, there is a perceived benefit to 'deliberative democracy' made possible by improved technology for interaction and for exchange of ideas in the public sphere [Coleman, 2001].

However, the continuing making process of the *e-democracy* has triggered a real challenge in the form of digital divide or knowledge divide. With the new media social and information gaps widen rather than narrow and there emerges an information upperclass as well as a social underclass. Much is made of the digital divide as a successor to the information gap that was once predicted as a result of the coming of television [Norris, 2000; Castells, 2001; Hargittai, 2004].

The way the new communication technologies have developed and come to influence life, both challenges and opportunities are there. The only path to be followed is to address everything equally in the transformed democracy so that the new media don't become a divider in contrast to its equaliser perspectives.

CONCLUSION

We all know that the media is the fourth pillar of democracy; that means the democracy draws sustenance from the media. What is important for media is to realise its contribution required for making democracy successful. Challenges are bound to be there. But with the determination of media, the other side of a challenge is an opportunity. No democracy can be imagined without the role of media and it is only the media that is instrumental for making a positive democracy. Today most of the democracies are suffering from various problems like corruption and other socio-moral diseases. The only reason is the lack of efficient human resource. And this human resource can get created with the bright side of the media. Media must assume the role of a catalyst in the process of change towards positive directions. However in the process of well being it is to be realised that media is a resource, not a source. The fundamental role of the media lies in making something better for life, for society. The media and society share reciprocal effects. All the hypes played by media these days just symbolise an extreme frustration that the present society encounters. The process of mediatisation should bring forward the maximum projection of values and the media should better try to concentrate upon a development mind-style; rather than a sponsored life style.

References

Murphy, P, 'Media and democracy in the age of globalisation'

Stevenson, R. L. [1994], Global Communication in the Twenty First Century, USA: Longman.

McQuail, D. [2010], Mass Communication Theory, 10th edn., New Delhi: SAGE.

Laswell, H (1948), The structure and function of communication and society: The communication of ideas, New York: Institute for Religious and Social Studies, 203-243.

Wright, W. R. (1960), Functional Analysis and Mass Communication, *Public Opinion Quarterly* (24), 610-613.

Tomlinson, J. [1999], The globalisation of culture, Cambridge: Polity Press.

Thompson, J.B. [1995], The Media and Modernity, Cambridge: Polity Press.

Schramm, W. [1995] 'Information theory and mass communication', *Journalism Quarterly*.

11

Role of Media in 21st Century Indian Society: Issues and Concerns

Deepshikha Saxena, Jyoti Sankar Pradhan

Media refers collectively to all technologies which are intended to reach large audience via mass communication. This includes the broadcast media, the print media and also the new age media which refers to mobile phones, computers and internet. In today's world, media has made a very special place for itself in our lives. Media is playing a very significant role in making the world smaller. Through various mediums of media whether it is radio, television, newspaper or internet, we are able to connect with large number of people around us. Especially internet has truly become the need of every individual both for our work and to connect with our friends and well wishers. Besides connecting with our friends, media also informs us about the world happenings. In fact media is like a mirror of the society which reflect each and everything about the society to us. If we just look around then we would find that there is no aspect of our life which is not touched and affected by media. Be it our work, relationships, education or entertainment, media is seen everywhere. Our work places have become more efficient by relying on internet which is the fastest means of communication. Record keeping and day to day office work has become more convenient, faster, transparent and efficient through the use of new age media. This has also added value to environmental conservation by minimising the use of paper.

Through the use of social networking and other mediums a person is well connected with his friends and relatives. It is a means of exchanging ideas and also lately it has evolved as a means of social awakening and formation of public opinion. We have recently witnessed the social movement against corruption when the public came in front to support Anna Hazare's call to remove corruption from society and constitution of strong *Lokpal.*

In the present scenario media has a huge responsibility of conveying the truth and relevant information to the common man. But somewhere this seems to be taking a back seat for media people as they are focusing more on commercialization. But media is not just confine to informing us about the world happenings and serving a means to connect with people, in fact it also affects out thinking patterns as well. The way we think and perceive various issues about the world is also shaped up by media. Today everyone especially youth is growing so aware about his responsibilities towards society is because of media. Campaign such as *Teach India* and *Jaago Grahak Jaago* helps in spreading awareness about human rights and duties.

In the last fifty years the media influence has grown exponentially with the advance of technology, first there was the telegraph, then the radio, the newspaper, magazines, television and now the internet. We live in a society that depends on information and communication to keep moving in the right direction and do our daily activities like work, entertainment, health care, education, personal relationships, travelling. What we need to be aware is that most of our decisions, beliefs and values are based on what we know for a fact, our assumptions and our own experience. In our work we usually know what we have to do based on our experience and studies, however, on our daily lives we rely on the media to get the current news and facts about what is important and what we should be aware of. The media makes billions of dollars with the advertising they sell and that we are exposed to. We buy what we are told to be good, after seeing thousands of advertisings we make our buying decisions based on what we saw on TV, newspapers, or magazines to be a product we can trust and also based on what everyone else that we know is buying and their decision are also based on the media. The new communication and information technologies have profoundly affected our social structure. There is a growing interdependence between technology, information and society. At the policy level the use of communication technologies in education and training has been identified emphatically. The CABE Committee on Distance Education (1994)b recommended the urgent need for the use of electronic media in the educational process in view of its vital importance, particularly to support open distance education. It also recommended undertaking some experiments with new technological systems/ developments, with an eye on the future and in keeping with the technical expertise and advanced infrastructure available in the country.

Convergence of emerging communication and information technologies is taking place these days, thus maximising the strengths of individual technology. Telecommunication clubbed with computer technology has revolutionised the area of human communication. The capability to exchange information on a global basis is possible through a powerful communication tool; the satellite. Computer technology has provided tremendous capacity to store and exchange information. The human computer interface has made communication further efficient, in terms of cost, time and reliability. This is the reason why communication technologies are becoming popular in receiving and transmitting messages, data, voice and images.

The computer and telecommunication technologies are not leaving the education sector untouched. These are enabling the teachers to develop multimedia in which text, voice, pictures etc. can be integrated and delivered through computers as an interactive learning package. The technologies will enable us to develop what are often called virtual classrooms wherein C-IT will create learning environment suited to the needs of the learners.

Emerging technologies appear to offer the opportunity to gain access to knowledge and skills required in real life. This would lead us to a learning society where learning is a continuous process throughout life. This is a single new development that can revolutionise the future of education. Virtual reality and simulation will provide the ability for us to enjoy experience that we could not get otherwise. This is an experience without risks and promotes learning in a new way. So, communication technology will provide a new strategy for education, for training experience. We are not talking about the technologically developed countries only, virtual classrooms or institutions are now getting established in the developing countries.

There are the effects of mass media in teenagers, they buy what they see on TV, what their favorite celebrity advertise and what is acceptable by society based on the fashion that the media has imposed them.

There are some positive and negative influences in young people. Here is a positive influence example, if there is a sport that is getting a lot of popularity among your friends and society, you will more likely want to practice the sport and be cool with all your friends.

However, a negative influence in teenagers is the use of cigars by celebrity movie stars, the excessive images of violence and exposure to thousands of junk food ads. Young people are in a stage of life where they want to be accepted by their peers, they want to be loved and be successful. The media creates the ideal image of a beautiful man and woman and tells you what are the characteristics of a successful person, you can see it in movies and TV. It's a subliminal way to tell you that if you are not like them you are not cool yet so its time to buy the stuff they buy and look like they look.

Another negative influence in teenagers that has grown over the last years are anorexia and obesity. There are millions of adolescents fighting obesity, but at the same time they are exposed to thousands of advertisements of junk food while the ideal image of a successful person is told to be thin and wealthy.

But in this era of commercialisation media has to play a considerate role for the development of healthy society. Sometimes to serve their vested interests the media projects different incidents taking place in the society in negative way which is unethical. To gain overnight popularity the electronic media resorts to flashing catchy headlines and they keep on repeating the same hour after hour and they prevent themselves from providing the real information to the world.

Media can play an equally important role in education. Classrooms have become interactive and child centered by the use of advanced technology. This access to technology for the upcoming generation is also a threat to society as they are exposed to unwarranted information which plays an important role in influencing young minds. More information but less knowledge is available. So here comes the role of media in development of healthy minds and sound personality. Thus, media has to play a very responsible and restraint role in the present century.

References

1. Bhan, Suraj Prakash (2006); "Teacher Training": Lotus Press, Ansari Road, New Delhi.
2. Carnoy M., "Education and Open Society: A Critical Look at New Perspectives and Demands", Globalisation, educational trends and the open society; OSI Education Conference 2005, Stanford University, School of Education.
3. International Association of Universities' Survey Report (2003); 'Internationalisation of Higher Education Practices and Priorities'.
4. Kapoor K., Sahoo J., Lhungdim T. and Acharya P.K. 2007, 'Teacher Education in 21st Century', The Associated Publishers, Ambala.
5. National Knowledge Commission- Report (2009).
6. Prakash R. (2006); "Teachers for better schools", Alfa Publications, New Delhi.
7. Ramalingam, P. (2007), "Effective Teaching Skills", Puducherry Co-operative Book Society, Puducherry.
8. Rangarajan C., "Responding to Globalization: India's Answer", 4th Ramanbhai Patel Memorial Lecture on Excellence in Education, February 25, 2006, Ahmedabad.
9. Report of the committee on 'India Vision 2020' (2002), Planning Commission, Government of India, New Delhi.
10. Sagar, K.V. (23-09-2005), 'Globalization of Education', Counter currents.org.

11. Sharma, Prem Lata (2005), "Teaching and Learning in 21st Century", Sarup & Sons, New Delhi.
12. Shankar T. (2008), "Encyclopaedia of Techniques of Teaching", Crescent Publishing Corporation, New Delhi.
13. Singh, Sharma and Upadhya (2008), "Encyclopaedia of Educational Technology, Teaching Learning, Vol. I", APH Publishing Company, New Delhi.
14. Srivastava S.K. (2004), "Higher Education System in India: Challenges and Strategies for Reforms", World Bank Report.
15. Thorat S. (24-11-2006), "Higher Education in India: Emerging Issues", Nehru Memorial Lecture, University of Mumbai, Mumbai.
16. Venkataiah, N. (2006), "Curriculum Innovations for 2000 A.D.", Ashish Publishing House, New Delhi.
17. www.ugc.ac.in
18. www.unesco.org
19. www.knowledgecommission.gov.in

12

Hazardous Forms of Child Labour and Role of Media to Counter the Problem

Dr. Naseem Ahmad Khan and
Nadia Bilgrami

Introduction

A child is an invaluable asset of any society and has a definite role to play in the development of the nation. The future of a country depends on how its children are being nurtured to become the future citizens of the country. Some of the children, forced by their socio-economic conditions, take up work at a crucial formative age.

Government of India's most notable attempt to tackle the problem of child labour has been to declare this practice illegal and create laws and labour enforcement infrastructure to address the issue. Yet, the number of children joining the work force is growing more rapidly. More seriously, a major chunk of the growing child work force is engaged in activities which are highly damaging to their health and consequently to their productive life. Glass industry in Firozabad (UP) represents one such working environment where children are victims of pollution and economic exploitation.

From the perspective of various social problems prevailing in our country, the mass media have a decisive role to play in mobilizing the people for exploiting the children and forcing them into labour. The problem of child labour in India, its different types and abolishment pathways as a topic being focused for communication by the print media and how prevalent this topic has been addressed by the news media of India. The above analyses and investigation will display the status of interest the news media shows towards the societal issue of both national and international concern.

CHILD LABOUR : A GROWING PHENOMENA

Not all work done by children should be classified as child labour that is to be targeted for elimination. Children's or adolescents' participation in work that does not affect their health and personal development or interfere with their schooling is generally regarded as being something positive. This includes activities such as helping their parents around the home, assisting in a family business or earning pocket money outside school hours and during school holidays. These kinds of activities contribute to children's development and to the welfare of their families; they provide them with skills and experience, and help to prepare them to be productive members of society during their adult life. The term "child labour" is often defined as work that deprives children of their childhood, their potential and their dignity, and that is harmful to physical and mental development. It refers to work that is; mentally, physically, socially or morally dangerous and harmful to children; and interferes with their schooling:

By depriving them of the opportunity to attend school;

By obliging them to leave school prematurely; or

By requiring them to attempt to combine school attendance with excessively long and heavy work.

In its most extreme forms, child labour involves children being enslaved, separated from their families, exposed to serious hazards and illnesses and/ or left to fend for themselves on the streets of large cities – often at a very early age. Whether or not particular forms of "work" can be called "child labour" depends on the child's age, the type and hours of work performed, the conditions under which it is performed and the objectives pursued by individual countries. The answer varies from country to country, as well as among sectors within countries.

What is Hazardous Work?

Most child labour, 71 per cent, is found in agriculture and fishing. The main tasks in agriculture include working with machinery and agrochemicals, and picking and loading crops. Hazards may include unsafe machinery, hazardous substances (insecticides, herbicides), and heavy lifting and extreme temperatures. In deep-sea fishing, children might be diving to depths of up to 60 metres to attach nets to coral reefs, risking exposure to high atmospheric pressure and attacks by carnivorous and poisonous fish. In manufacturing, where 8.3 per cent of child labour is found, items such as glass bangles, matches, fireworks or bricks might be made. Hazards occur in the form of noxious fumes and radiant heat from the molten glass; stepping on or handling hot broken glass; exposure to hazardous chemical mixtures; stuffing cracker powder into fireworks, risking fire and explosion; exposure to silicate, lead and carbon monoxide; carrying excessive weights; and burns from ovens through the processing of clay in the making of bricks.

The Hazardous Work List

When countries ratify Convention No. 182 and Convention No. 138, they commit themselves to determining work to be prohibited to persons less than 18 years of age. Article 4 of Convention No. 182 says:

1. The types of work referred to under Article 3(d) [work which, by its nature or the circumstances in which it is carried out, is likely to harm the health, safety or morals of children] shall be determined by national laws or regulations or by the competent authority, after consultation with the organisations of employers and workers concerned, taking into consideration relevant international standards, in particular Paragraphs 3 and 4 of the Worst Forms of Child Labour Recommendation, 1999.

2. The competent authority, after consultation with the organisations of employers and workers concerned, shall identify where the types of work so determined exist.

3. The list of the types of work determined under paragraph 1 of this Article shall be periodically examined and revised as necessary, in consultation with the organisations of employers and workers concerned.

For short, we refer to this as the "hazardous work list". This list is extremely important because, once enacted into law, it forms the basis for a wide range of activities – advocacy, services, policies and enforcement – that can protect children and youth from exploitation and provide a clear rule on what children above designated ages can or cannot do.

Building a Protective Environment for Children

Government commitment and capacity

Providing all children with access to education is every government's responsibility, as well as a practical response to preventing child labour. Free, compulsory, relevant and quality education services are essential.

Legislation and Enforcement

Laws and regulations against child labour must be in place and rigorously enforced by governments. Time-bound national plans of action, as required by ILO Convention No. 182 on the worst forms of child labour, are crucial.

HUMAN RIGHTS

International Labour Organisation (ILO) Conventions 138 (1973) and *182* (1999) define child labourers as all children younger than 12 working in any economic activities, children 12–14 years old engaged in more than light work, and all children engaged in the *worst forms of child labour* – in which they are enslaved, forcibly recruited, prostituted, trafficked, forced into illegal activities or exposed to hazards.

Article 32(1) of the *Convention on the Rights of the Child* (1989) calls for the recognition of the right of children to be protected from economic exploitation and from performing any work that is likely to be hazardous or to interfere with their education, or to be harmful to their health or physical, mental, spiritual, moral or social development.

By March 2006, 143 countries had ratified Convention No. 138, setting minimum ages for general, light or hazardous work and 158 countries had ratified ILO Convention No. 182 on the worst forms of child labour.

ROLE OF MEDIA ON THE PROBLEM OF CHILD LABOUR

It will not be easy in a world of rapid technological change and globalisation of information, commercial competition has led to a perceptible fall in standards within traditional media. At the same time, many governments and state authorities manipulate information through regulation or forms of censorship, often to satisfy narrow political objectives rather than to meet the needs of people or to protect the rights of children. Whether driven by commercial objectives or subject to political controls, journalists and media professionals are under increasing pressure.

How can the media help to protect the dignity of the child in the Asia-Pacific region? There are perhaps three roles that the media, both mainstream and alternative, can play in ensuring that the self-worth and self-respect, the honour and integrity, of any person below the age of eighteen is safeguarded to the utmost in the most extensive region of the world, stretching from Syria and Iraq, at one end, to New Zealand and the Fiji, at the other end of the geographical spectrum. One, the media should be unrelenting in its mission to expose those circumstances and situations that undermine the dignity of the child in the Asia-Pacific region. Two, the media should never cease to remind policy-makers, other influential elements in society, and society as a whole, of the essential prerequisites of an environment that is conducive for the dignity of the child. Three, the media should convince today's child that if he is to live with dignity in tomorrow's world he will have to be imbued with values and principles that are different from some of the dominant motives and attitudes that have driven economic growth and development in various countries in Asia-Pacific in the last few decades. The media refers to the people and organisations behind mass communication. They have three primary purposes: to inform, to educate, to entertain.

CONCLUSIONS

The following conclusions were drawn from the present extensive study and are summarised as below:

✓ Recent Industrialisation and Globalisation is changing the occupational morbidity drastically the new pathologies like cancer stress, Aids, psychological disorders and heart disease are on raise.
The media have played a major role in defining what is "normal" and what is "deviant" in society, thus contributing to definitions of what is, and what is not, considered to be child abuse.
The problem of child labour in India, its different types and abolishment pathways as a topic being focused for communication by the print media and how prevalent this topic has been addressed by the news media of India.
Hazards occur in the form of noxious fumes and radiant heat from the molten glass; stepping on or handling hot broken glass; exposure to hazardous chemical mixtures; stuffing cracker powder into fireworks, risking fire and explosion; exposure to silicate, lead and carbon monoxide; carrying excessive weights; and burns from ovens through the processing of clay in the making of bricks.
The paper presents the various hazardous forms of child labour and the role of media to counter the problem.

References

1. Challenges in Young People's World of Communication Karlstad Sweden, June 14 to 18 June, 2010, Keynote Speech by Professor Dr. Chandra Muzaffar, Today's Child, Tomorrow's World: The Role of the Media in Protecting the Dignity of the Child in the Asia-Pacific Region.
2. Media World Vision, New Zealand.
3. Guidelines for Journalists and Media Professionals International Federation of Journalists with the support of the European Commission.
4. Guidelines for Journalists and Media Professionals International Federation of Journalists with the support of the European Commission
5. Human Development Report, 2000, UNDP, 2000.
6. Improving Environmental and Health Condition of Children Working in the Glass Industries at Firozabad.
7. International Programme on the Elimination of Child Labour Children in hazardous work: What we know, what we need to do (2011).
8. Inter-Parliamentary Union/ International Labour Office, 2002.
9. Karthi J., Abstract, The Role Of Mass Media On The Child Labour Problems of India.
10. The United Nations Children's Fund (UNICEF) 2006, The Child Protection Section Programme Division, UNICEF NY.

CONCLUSIONS

13

Technology in Education : The New Implementation

Dr. Abdul Hakim, Smt. Ruksana Begam, Smt. Rehana Begam

Technology is the main need of modern age. It is very helpful of development and prosperity of the country. Technology knowledge and equipments are used in different kind in all fields of development. Many means of technology were used pervious time, But now being development of new innovations, use of technology ran towards every where.

In 19th century, when India was ruled by the English then new educational pattern was adopted. Though the English rulers educated Indians for their needs, But educational technique changed. Traditional education system reformed the education which was only verbal changed. Written education started to be given. Technical tools were used. Examination were also conducted is written pattern. Science developed and new inventions created education changed in two part. Arts and second science. Science education mostly depended on practical. Different Laboratories were established in school and college. Student got science education in different branches such as physics, chemistry, Zoology, math's was the common subject of art and science. But with out math's science education in complete.

Now science development in all fields. There are several branches of science development. New Technical education opened. Engineering, Medical Sc., Astronomy and Geology etc. branches are of new technical education. Educational pattern totally changed. New challenges came in front of education, Competition performed some countries developed rapidly in this field. England, France, Germany became the nation of new invention. Then U.S.A. Japan, lately and other countries tried to run by side of scientific development. Technology covered all educational means. We may say that "No Technology No Education."

Several tools are now used to educate to now generation. Invention of computer changed all the system. It is used in different manners. Internet service is also related to with computer. About all information are stored in computer, and again can obtained according to our need. Print out may be obtained. With help of internet. Distant education become easy. Any body may talk and Ask with distant person. class room teaching is not sufficient to provide education. C.D. Projectors tape records etc. are very useful for providing advanced education. With the help of these equipments recent knowledge and changing events can be noticed. These system are also helpful to bring equality in countries. Backward countries are also running with developed countries. Developed countries also opened their doors for new technical education for the students of all world. Now nobody can say that he is fulfilled with new knowledge because new researche are coming in light very fast. "Today's knowledge will become old tomorrow". New fields of education created of today is better than his teacher had. Because he has gotten new education being conducted by Technological way. So teacher's knowledge is not sufficient to provide education. He should be maintained up to date by getting education, full of information technology. Otherwise, he will be obliged to set out from education, job being insulted. Mobile, the recent information system gets helpful to connect with required person.

Education with knowledge is very essential for development and personality as well as society then nation. Education become very fast so we will also be alert to complete. The man is going to be a machine. It is needed to open mind from all direction to be perfect.

Education is the basic need of human being. So education should be full with technological facts.

Technological Implementation in Education

In present time education is given on only by books and lectures. Several progressive instrument are now used to provide education. They are:

(1) *Computer and Internet*: There is vital use of computer in education. Subject matter and dates are feuded in computers and at the time requirement their scene, or prints out may be obtained. A minor computer is a book of vast knowledge. Computer are of two types: Desktop and; Laptop. Desktop is a big computer with monitor, processor, keyboard and mouse. It spread son a table in different bins. It is like a suitcase having monitor and keyboard. It can be carried like a book small suitcase. It is used Like a rough copy. Internet is

another system which is being joint with computer every information of any part of world can be found by its website.

(2) *Satellite System* : M.P. Govt. School education Depot has ordered to each school even primary schools to get connected with the set light system. Different subjects and their courses broad coasted by Bhopal It can be seen and heard by every school student concerning his subject and course. The Regular Time table of those Subject previously informed to each school heads. On particular time and subject student are gathered to listen those lectures student are also able to ask questions. They get response from other side.

(3) *Tape recorder C.D., V.C.D. and D.V.D.*: These Technological instrument are used very vastly cassets and CDs are the record instruments some CD records light also. Tape recorder is reflector of cassets sound, V.C.D. and D.V.D. are used for CD with sounder and TV.

(4) *Email* : Email address is useful to communicate to distant one with the help of passworda Email may be opened on computer and able to get necessary information of all directions. M.P. Higher education has provision of this facility each student, admitted in college should maintain email personal address directorate of higher education will communicable necessary information and give direction through email student will be aware time to time to open this email address. In this way latest information may be communicated to student by the head of education depot.

(5) *Telephone, Fax and Mobile* : Telephone is just ancient information system. It is and line connection. Internet facility may be achieved with connection with telephone. This is called Broad Band Connection. To improve education condition Telephone cum Broad Band Connection is very essential system. Fax is a printer machine of paper message. Quick information by Fax may be commutated. Now a days no body waits for postal letter. Fax machine quick provide printed matter of paper message sent from the other side. Mobile is available every where every time providing listening message. Without line connection and wire. Mobile towers are helpful to catch and throw message. With help of set light mobile is very tiny instrument. Now co lour mobile in with the facilities of sweet sons, photo camera are available. This tiny system is really a magic instrument proving different kind of facilities.

(6) *Projector and Slide* : Projector shows linger figures on screen of slide and film what matters contained on slide and film. It saves time of black board work. difficult material also be seen by projector which is feuded in slide and film. Teacher now freely. and fearlessly are able to teach with the help of slide, or film and projector. Screen may be the wall of room. No headache create this system against teaching.

(7) *Radio*: It is just old system of providing education in school education student some of subject and topics of different subject and different classes were broad coasted by radio. Timing of those education programmed were set up and informed to energy institution on particular time concerning class. Students gathered info through radio and listened to subject matters. This unloaded over-burden of teacher. They should not have to tension of preparation of hard topics and subjects.

(8) *Sum up*: The technical means are very helpful for improvement and development of education. Development of information technology gives proper information about course subject fee and time of admission. So Indian students now go to get higher and technical education in foreign institutions and foreign student come to India for this purpose. There is no distance between countries. Any person may go anywhere to get knowledge. The scope of knowledge now become very vast. We are now able to go to space and other planets due to our developed technical knowledge. Technical means are used in all field of education. The subjects modified and available in recent form.

14

Looking Beyond Information and Communication Technology Access: A Discursive Approach to Computer Mediated Communication

Uma Shankar Pandey

Introduction

The Internet originated in the 1960s from the Arpanet, a decentralised military computer-based communication network set up by the US government to survive a nuclear attack. The Internet-based technology that has had the greatest social impact is the World Wide Web created by Tim Berners-Lee at CERN in 1990.

The origin of the web was made possible through the Hyper Text Markup Language, published in 1990. It was originally developed to transfer images and text within the scientific community at CERN.

It was designed in the nineties to take care of the varied computers and their software with different processes for handling text and images. Instead of developing another international standard, the new code simply told the computer systems what to do with the files. The web browsers were developed to make the code user-friendly. This was the basis of the now ubiquitous 'Internet Explorer' (Lister, Dovey, Giddings, Grant & Kelly, 2009, p. 177).

In technical terms, Internet is a global system of computer networks linked by a globally unique address space based in the Internet Protocol, or its updated variants. It is also able to support communications using the Transmission Control Protocol or its extensions. Access to 'high level services layered on the communications' are also provided through the internet technology. (Lister, Dovey, Giddings, Grant and Kelly, 2009, p. 164).

The highly cooperative and interdependent nature of this technology which has now become an indispensable resource has its legacy in its origin.

It was developed in the public sector, as part of an attempt to promote co-operation and exchange. This was then made available to the private sector for social use.

The stipulations for the HTML code are vital for other software creators to be compatible with all web browsers.

This allows a user-friendly browsing in a common information highway making use of a standard browser (Fuchs, 2008, p.121).

Many scholars have seen this interplay between high technology and its social use as a "top-down process." According to a recent study this mediation of technology in human communication impacts 'emergent aspects of thinking and action' (Fuchs, 2008). The existing technological infrastructure stores objective human knowledge. Users make subjective use of this objective knowledge in their consumption of knowledge represented in the Internet. The same structure is repeated when human beings communicate or cooperate with other human beings via the Internet. In a "bottom-up-process," on the other hand human beings, communicate, or cooperate in such a way that the knowledge stored in technological infrastructure, is actualized, and extended. Here 'objective knowledge emerges from the cooperation of human actors' (Fuchs, 2008, p. 122).

Herein lies the difference in discourse on platforms which are more interactive than others. Use of interactive media leads to greater consolidation of ideas even converging to a degree of consonance.

Web 1.0

The first phase of the development of the World Wide Web (Web 1.0) was dominated by hyperlinked textual formations. This was established through the emergence of web sites. The key to the popularity of these sites was the links.

Creating links is the essential operation of networking in Web 1.0. It is reflexive in the sense that when a new link is created the system refers to itself by incorporating its content. Each Web page refers to a number of other Web pages that again refer to other Web pages, and so on. Self-referentiality is the defining feature of the hypertext; by creating links a hypertext is connected to a hypertext; the hypertext system of the www is referring to itself.

These sites were predominantly made up of dynamic pages. They are available across different platforms in the same physical format. In this sense, it is independent of the location or even the technological forms of access. The ease of access and production leads to an unprecedented volume of content. The ever-increasing structure of the Web content can neither be fully known nor even be controlled. This growth cannot be safely predicted. The complexity of the web structure too increases with its growth. The number of websites and the hyperlinks is a measure of this complexity. When a new site is introduced, it is implanted into the existing web extending it further.

For a site to be accessible through the internet platform, hyperlinks must be created that lead from and to the site. Hence the web sites are interdependent structures linked to search engines. In its initial *avatar* the content included informational pieces (texts, images, animations) (Fuchs, 2008, p. 124).

Computer-Mediated Communication

The advent of the internet technology led to intense research on its impact on human communication. An important strand of this research is the impact of Internet use on social ties. One of the earliest studies in this stream is Rheingold's conceptualisation of 'virtual community.' He described Internet as capable of 'bringing strangers together' to form intimate online networks (Rheingold, 1993).

This diverged with the observation of other scholars who regarded online social networks as 'the illusion of community' (Parks & Floyd, 1996).

The prevalent approach in the initial CMC studies has been the Reduced Social Cues (RSC). Lack of social cues that communicators have access to in Face-to-Face communication was regarded as a major hindrance in CMC.

The most obvious cues are that of direct and indirect physical appearance, indicators of behaviour, or personality traits and other more subtle prompts that emerge during social interactions. These can include signals in elucidation and other aspects of language. In addition, once we have framed our image of the communicators, we even employ a variety of strategies to create a desired impression about ourselves.

The exclusion of impression-forming signals leads to the development of relatively nebulous impressions in CMC. The reduced cues in CMC 'may lead people to forget that messages are communications, not just soliloquies to a computer'. Communicators are not aware of the nature and size of their audience or even that their communications will be read at all (Hancock & Dunham, 2001, pp. 325-326).

The lack of these nonverbal social and relational indicators in CMC produces a 'depersonalised form of communication' and decreased awareness of others, which in turn hinders interpersonal relations (Hancock & Dunham, 2001).

Other studies have pointed out other later latent effects of the RSC approach. They estimate development of such psychological states that undermine social influences on individuals. The result is 'uninhibited' and extreme behavior, as well as more 'polarized, extreme and risky' decisions (Sproull and Kiesler, 1991).

Another related phenomenon of the early computer-mediated communication is the notion of flaming. It is closely linked to the typical transient character of CMC, in which text messages appear and disappear from the screen without leaving behind any 'tangible artifacts.' Another estimation is that participants who communicate via computers imagine that they must use stronger language to get their messages across. According to an earlier study, 'electronic messages are often startlingly blunt and electronic discussions can escalate rapidly into name calling and epithets' (Sproull and Kiesler, 1991).

The hyperpersonal model was an adaptation of the RSC approach. The early form of CMC largely consisted of textual information. Participants deliberately chose cues which would frame a personality of their choice (witty, or matter-of-fact for example). Suppression of physical and behavioural cues is not possible in FtF interaction). The hyperpersonal model notes that this lack of cues may allow the user to reallocate cognitive resources to language selection, content and perception management.

Another important challenge to the RSC perspective is the Social Identification Deindividuation (SIDE) approach. The major consequence of this de-individuation, defined by visual anonymity and physical isolation, is an increased confidence on the few remaining social cues on which to form perceptions of a CMC partner.

Under these conditions, communicators are assumed to construct more 'stereotyped and exaggerated' representations of their partners, based on the indications emerging from the relevant contextual cues provided in text-based discourse. Perception-relevant information may also emerge from the partner's communication style.

When deindividuated CMC participants perceive themselves as part of a group, this group identity is intensified and becomes more significant than their individual self-identities. The primary consequences of this social perception are strong positive feelings toward the virtual community members and intensified attributions of similarity.

The fundamental difference in the SIDE model is between social and personal identities. Social identities refer to people's identification with certain groups, whereas personal identities refer to the unique attributes of the individual.

The SIDE model proposes that a deindividuation process in CMC actually augments social identity. Once people identify with a social group, possible intra-group differences become less significant as a result of visual anonymity. This reinforces normative behaviour and group response in an online group. On the other hand, when people do not identify with a social group but adhere to their personal identity, group salience will decrease as a result of anonymity and physical isolation (Spears & Lea, 1992, p. 47).

There are diverse views among scholars on whether computer mediated communication decreases or increases social ties or it has no effect on social ties (Wellman, Hasse, Witte, & Hampton, 2001).

The correlation between internet use and social ties is a factor of the qualitative use of online activities. An earlier study predicted those using the Internet for interpersonal contacts are likely to have more social connections than those who use it for solitary activities like net surfing. Also solitary web users are likely to have fewer social ties than nonusers. Heavy surfers on the net tend to have fewer social ties than light users do (Zhao, 2006, p. 858).

Web 2.0

Web 2.0 creates faster and easier network effects through an 'architecture of participation', going beyond the page metaphor of Web 1.0 to deliver loaded user experiences. Web 2.0 was a term coined in 2003 by the media consultant Tim O'Reilly. The notion of Web 2.0 is that combinations of user-friendly software, broadband access and collective use have disseminated the idea that there is something qualitatively different about the new web'. This new conception of the web is characterised by collective creativity, participation and openness. This is also backed by technological advances which make content creation across different formats easier and accessible with a paradigm shift in the volume and acceleration of information flow. This is represented by wiki based ways of creating and accessing knowledge, social networking sites, blogging, tagging and 'mash ups'. These subsystems of the new Internet can maintain and reproduce themselves only due to the fact that human actors make use of the technological structure as a 'medium of their symbolic exchange.' (Lister, Dovey, Giddings, Grant, & Kelly, 2009, p. 204). Web 2.0 emphasises interaction, sociability, and openness. Along with these characteristics are simple technologies and decentralised processing. It includes the concepts of weblogs, wikis, Really Simple Syndication (RSS) functionality, social tagging, mashups, and user defined content. Unlike traditional Hypertext Markup Language (HTML) web pages, blogs offer the ability even for the nonprogrammer to create content regularly. Traditional HTML style pages required knowledge of style, coding, and design in order to publish content.

Weblogs remove much of the constraints by providing a standard user interface that does not require customization. Weblogs allow readers to become content providers (Blood, 2004). The Web 1.0 platform was predominantly a system of cognition. 'Users Add Value' is the driving idea for Web 2.0 that argues in different ways that user behavior itself creates a commodity that has value (Lister, Dovey, Giddings, Grant & Kelly, 2009, p. 205).

Web 2.0 encourages user participation and derives its greatest value when large communities contribute to the content. User generated metadata, information, and designs enable a dense environment where the value is generated by the volume of users. This social software creates the foundation of cooperative intelligence (Weiss, 2005).

The idea of a blog is defined by small chunks of content referred to as posts and includes links, text and images (Baoill, 2004). The intransience of the content which has a unique Universal Resource Locator (URL) allows the content to be posted along with the comments to define a permanent record of information. This is critical since having such a collaborative record can be indexed by search engines increases the utility and spread the information to a larger audience.

Wiki is a web site that promotes the shared creation of content. Its pages can be edited by anyone at any point of time. Content can be created and easily organised within the wiki environment and then reorganised as required. Due to their simplicity and flexibility wikis provide different elements of documentation, reporting, online glossaries, dictionaries and discussion groups, in which the end user can provide value. The major difference between a wiki and blog is that the wiki user can alter the original content while the blog user can only add information in the form of comments. This creates an environment open to sharing information and knowledge to a large group of users.

Originally developed by Netscape, RSS, another defining feature of Web 2.0 was intended to publish news type information based upon a subscription framework (Lerner, 2006).

RSS is a content-syndication protocol that allows web sites to share information and aggregate information based on the users needs. In the simplest form, RSS shares metadata about the content without actually delivering the entire information source. The user needs an application – aggregator in order to receive the information. By having the RSS aggregator application, end users are not required to visit each site in order to obtain information. From an end user perspective, the RSS technology changes the communication method from a 'search and discover' to a 'notification' model. Users can locate content that they desire which enables a much faster communication stream.

Social tagging describes the collaborative activity of marking shared online content with keywords or tags as a way to organise content for future navigation, filtering, or search. Traditional information structural design utilized a central classification scheme to place in formation into a specific category. Tagging offers the benefit of bookmarking the information in a way that is easier for them to recall. The idea of social tagging allows different users to tag content in a way that makes sense to them. This creates an ecosystem where the opinions of the majority define the precision of the tags themselves. The act of creating a collection of popular tags is known as a folksonomy which is defined as a folk taxonomy of important and emerging content within the user community.

The final Web 2.0 technology describes the efforts around information integration, commonly referred to as 'mashups'. These applications can be combined to deliver additional value that the individual parts could not.

One of the basic themes of Web 2.0 is user contributed content. The value derived from the contributed content comes not from a subject matter expert, but rather from individuals whose small contributions add up.

With the rise of platforms such as *My Space, YouTube, Facebook, Wikipedia,* communication and cooperation have become more important features of the web (Fuchs, 2008).

Social Networking in India

Social Networking is an application that connects people by matching profile information with direct interactions. These connections may be in the form of dating interests, employment status, or political party affiliation (Counts & Geraci, 2005).

Social Networking provides two essential functions. The first is the ability to create and maintain a profile that serves as an online identity within the ecosystem. The second is the ability to create connections between other people within the network. Social networking technologies, such as *Facebook* offer a blend of interactive and static features in the users' profile. Others also contribute information to the site. Postings by other people on one's own profile create a perception of the person who made the postings. The observers' reactions to these postings may affect impressions of the target profile maker as well, even though the profile maker did not initiate the postings. This makes participative social networking technologies different from Web 1.0 applications that allow the initiator complete control over the content (Walther, Heide, Kim, Westerman & Tong, 2008, p. 29).

One way in which *Facebook* is unique for creating perceptions of individuals is the degree to which personal information is presented by means other than revelation by the person himself. In traditional communication environment, people make conscious decisions about when and how they will provide information about themselves. These decisions involve a multifaceted process in which people set rules about how and when they will disclose private information, 'negotiate those rules with other people', and make 'decisions on disclosure based on violations of those rules'. However, social networking sites to some extent 'obviate an individual's rules, negotiations, and disclosure decisions by placing discretion at the mercy' of the social networks (Walther, Heide, Kim, Westerman & Tong, 2008, p. 32).

In his important work on social psychology (Berger, 1979) identified three passive strategies, two active strategies, and three interactive strategies, that people utilise to acquire information about others. This can provide some information about the ways in which perceptions are created through third-party posts on sites such as the *Facebook*.

Passive strategies are defined as those situations in which information is collected about the target without affecting the target's or other actors' behaviour. The first passive strategy is the discreet observation of a person in a situation in which he interacts with others. The second is social comparison, exploring the behavior of the target when he interacts with people known to the observer. The third passive strategy is deviation testing which identifies the person's 'real' self in situations where he is not inhibited by social norms.

The active strategies involve proactive efforts to gain knowledge about others. However, they are indirect in the sense that they do not directly communicate with the target. The first strategy is asking others about their perception of the individual in question. The second is about creation of a set of circumstances followed by unobtrusive scrutiny of the individual in that setting, in order to view the effect of the 'manipulation.'

An interactive strategy involves direct communication and deals with trying to identify of falsifications and misrepresentations. The second is about questioning. Finally, the third interactive strategy is self-disclosure by the communicator who knowingly communicates to another about himself, to elicit disclosure from a target person (Tidwell & Walther, 2002, pp. 321-322).

Three sources of information can be distinguished on the social networking sites: self-generated cues, other-generated cues, and system-generated cues. Self-generated cues are cues that a person deliberately provides, such as posting visual and descriptive information. Other-generated cues are information/views on a user's profile that come from others, such as the wall postings on *Facebook* by friends of the communicator and also pictures of those friends. Finally, system-generated cues are cues that the system chooses to show on a user's profile, such as the number of friends etc. (Tong, Heide, Langwell & Walther, 2008).

Information gained about someone through others in that person's social network is common. People try to find out about one another via commonalities in the overlapping social networks. Objectivity and validity of other-generated cues and system generated cues are often considered more reliable than self-generated cues. Though these are not fully in control of the individual but since the salience of third party information is known, often the self-generated cues are generated with an effort to manipulate the other two.

Digital Divide

The idea of the digital divide initially was about denial of access to information and communication technology is now largely spoken in terms of access to online resources. The genesis of the concept is the belief of that new computer and telecommunications technologies will transform countries into 'knowledge economies' and 'network societies' (Castells, 1996; Reich, 1991). This was also expected to remove other social disparities. Over the years, development researchers, politicians and social welfare organisations, have promoted the use of ICT – largely for development objectives (Strover, 2003).

The raw data about the distribution of personal computers is one way of looking at the digital divide. Different studies have identified the divide across eight different elements across class, access, gender, physical location, as well as skills and the ability to contribute content or locate useful content (Lister, Dovey, Giddings, Grant & Kelly, 2009, p. 185).

More recent studies have defined digital divide in more qualitative terms not limiting to formal access to the information and communication technologies. The first consists of the 'theoretical' access to ICTs and content, which is about the availability of ICTs in home and work settings available to individuals in theory.

The other aspect is whether the access is effectual. In other words it is about the ease of 'access' to ICTs and content in home, surroundings and work settings.

Another important aspect of the qualitative dimension is the 'usefulness' of ICT content which may or may not lead to medium/long term consequences for the user. Use could be considered to be 'useful, fruitful, significant and relevant' to the individual.

The fourth dimension is the 'control' dimension where the user exercises a degree of control and choice over technology and content.

The fifth dimension is the activity dimension which could consist of 'production activity, political activity, social activity, consumption activity and savings activity' (Selwyn, 2004, p. 352).

Earlier studies have also considered the question of unequal access in terms of the ability to maximise the effectiveness of the technology in quest of various goals. For example, an individual can own a computer with an Internet connection but not know how to utilise it as a way of getting a technical job (Jung, Qiu & Kim, 2001).

In the first known study on qualitative aspects of internet use (Jung, Qiu & Kim, 2001) identified four categories of internet users: 'researchers', who use the Internet mainly for sending and receiving e-mail and also to explore varied issues/events; 'consumers', who use the Internet for online shopping; 'expressives', who express views and opinions online, and 'gamers', who go online to play games (Jung, Qiu & Kim, 2001, p. 512). This was, however, limited to the first generation of internet users of Web 1.0 as we have identified them.

Jung, Qiu & Kim (2001) extended this scheme further to arrive at what they described as the Internet Connectedness Index. Digital divide was described more in terms of identifying the various qualitative uses of the internet.

The first of element is the number of years a person has owned a personal computer with an internet connection at home.

Task scope is about whether the person connects to the Internet for work-related, academics or personal tasks. Site scope is a factor of the places where a person connects to the Internet, which includes home, work, school, a community center, library, or a cyber-cafe.

Goal scope was a factor of whether the internet was used for social understanding or as a medium of expression, work tasks, or to get advice on various issues.

Activity scope was another measure for Internet Connectedness Index, or Web activities which included categories other than e-mail. The categories included bulletin boards, chat rooms, online gaming, mailing lists, and newsgroups.

Time spent on interactive online activities indicates the frequency of participation in bulletin boards, chat rooms etc.

For measuring computer dependency an important study asked the respondents to imagine that their personal computer had vanished and noted their response (Jung, Qiu and Kim, 2001, pp. 515-517).

In a recent study on digital divide in post-socialist Europe (Vartanova, 2002) estimated the following reasons for unequal access. Lack of financial resources was the predominant reason for unequal access to ICTs. Lack of skills, lack of time, lack of awareness, lack of media activity, and lack of interest were the other factors observed. Other individuals also did not find any need to access the online resources among individuals (Vartanova, 2002, p. 450).

Internet Users in India

As can be seen in Table-1, there were 50,000 broadband users in India at the end of 2002, which was a mere 0.01 per cent of the population. By 2010, the number of broadband subscribers had grown to 1 per cent of the population. Internet growth has been pretty gradual over the years in India. However, in the last two years there has been a substantial growth of internet subscribers. There are 18.69 million Internet subscribers in India by the end of December 2010 compared to 17.90 million at the end of September 2010, registering a growth of 4.43 per cent. The percentage of subscribers is about 1.4 per cent of the total population.

There is a qualitative difference in internet subscribers in India. A substantial section of the internet users have access to what is known as narrowband or internet speeds of less than 256 kbps.

Number of Broadband subscribers increased from 10.31 million at the end of September 2010 to 10.99 million at the end of December 2010, registering a quarterly growth of 6.64 per cent and year on year growth of 40.48 per cent. The growth in the number of Broadband subscribers is more or less similar to the growth in overall telephone subscriber base (Telecom Regulatory Authority of India, 2011, p. 29).

Share of Broadband subscription in total Internet subscription increased from 57.6 per cent in September 2010 to 58.8 per cent in December 2010. Number of Narrowband subscribers increased from 7.59 million in September 2010 to 7.70 million in December 2010, registering a growth of 1.42 per cent as against a growth of 4.71 per cent in the previous quarter (Telecom Regulatory Authority of India, 2011, p. 30).

The number of cybercafes, most of whom provide narrow band access to consumers also went down to 8792 cybercafes at the end of December 2010 compared to 9288 at the end of September registering a decline of 5.34 per cent.

Apart from this, 332.43 million wireless subscribers have subscribed to Data services (Telecom Regulatory Authority of India, 2011).

Recognising the potential of Broadband service in enhancement in quality of life as well as employment generation by high-speed access to information the Government of India announced the Broadband Policy in October 2004. The main emphasis was on the creation of infrastructure through various technologies that can contribute to the growth of broadband services. These technologies include optical fibre and Asymmetric Digital Subscriber Lines (ADSL). Target has been set for 20 million broadband connections by 2012 and providing Broadband connectivity to all schools, public health institutions and all rural local governments at the 'panchayat' level by 2012.

Social Networking in India

The growth of the telephone infrastructure and broadband connectivity is a largely urban phenomenon. With the growth of high-speed internet connections, the time spent on web-based email declined by 10 per cent in 2010 compared to 2009. Within the region, markets showed varying levels of engagement trends (Comscore, 2011). *Facebook* grabbed the number one ranking in July 2010 in India with 20.9 million visitors, up 179 per cent versus year ago (Comscore, 2010).

According to international analysts, social networking continues to grow substantially worldwide, and India represents one of the fastest growing markets at the moment. More than 33 million Internet users age 15 and older in India visited social networking sites in July, representing 84 per cent of the total Internet audience. India now ranks as the seventh largest market worldwide for social networking, after the U.S., China, Germany, Russian Federation, Brazil and the U.K. (Comscore, 2011).

The total Indian social networking audience grew 43 per cent in the past year, more than tripling the rate of growth of the total Internet audience in India. *Twitter* had the highest rate of growth among the top five social networking sites, increasing 239 per cent to 3.3 million visitors (Comscore, 2010).

Discourse Analysis

A discourse analysis examines a media message as a discourse in its own right.

It primarily aims at the illumination of qualitative data paying attention to underlying semantic structures and makes explicit implications and presuppositions which are implicit in the discourse.

The discursive approach in our study involves the analysis of verbal expressions, such as sentences, texts, or messages, on different levels.

Discourse analysis generally involves specific sub-theories or even sub-disciplines of linguistics. Phonology for example, accounts for the structure of sounds and intonation. Morphology is about formulating the principles of word formation; syntax provides the rules according to which words of different categories are combined into grammatical sentences, and semantics, deals with the meaning of words, phrases, sentences, or whole discourses by formulating rules of interpretation (Van Dijk, 1983, p. 23).

In addition to these levels, different *units* of analysis can be distinguished in discourse: individual words, various structures of the clause, whole sentences, sequences of sentences (paragraphs), or whole discourses. The overall topic or theme of a discourse, for instance, can be studied only at the semantic level of the discourse as a whole, not at the level of individual words or sentences.

Stylistic variation can occur at several levels, such as lexical choice, word formation, or syntactic structures. There are different *modes* of the demonstration and use of discourse, such as spoken or written/printed discourse, monologues, and dialogues.

Discourses are not just isolated linguistic 'objects,' but are integral parts of communicative acts in some socio-cultural situations (Van Dijk, 1983, p. 24).

The following elements of discourse are analysed in our present study.

Functionality : A discourse is taken to be the expression of a sequence of sentences in some social context. The various properties of a discourse are assumed to be functional with respect to the social context.

The surface structures and meanings are produced and understood as indications about intentions, wishes and moods of the speaker and his effort to convey confidence, intimacy or even authority (Van Dijk, 1983, p. 25).

Meaningfulness : One condition for meaningfulness of a discourse is some kind of unity, which is described in terms of local or global *coherence.* Local coherence means that subsequent clauses and sentences are meaningfully related, since the information to which they refer are causally related. Global coherence is about larger parts of the discourse; described in terms of such notions as 'topic', or 'theme.' Such themes or topics are accounted for theoretically in terms of 'semantic macrostructures' (Van Dijk, 1983, p. 25).

Goal-directedness : People do not usually utter meaningful discourses on their own or randomly. Some 'speech acts' are meant to trigger other 'speech acts'.

A meaningful discourse is articulated, firstly, in order to perform a social act, that is, a speech act. In turn, such an act has in mind some goal that is sought to be realized the speech act (Van Dijk, 1983, p. 26).

Modality is a factor of whether the surface structure of the discourse is perceived terms of formal, informal, or matter-of-fact modes.

Colloquiality is a factor of the extent to which the local lingua is used in conjunction with the dominant means of discourse.

The discursive approach in our study will try to explain, how various structures of computer mediated discourse comes about and how it is understood in terms of underlying structures. The relation between content properties and specific 'effects' is split up in terms of a number of intervening variables (Van Dijk, 1983, p. 27).

References

Baoill, A. (2004), Conceptualizing the weblog: Understanding what it is in order to imagine what it can be, *Interfacings: Journal of Contemporary Media Studies, 5* (2), 1-8.

Berger, C. (1979), Beyond initial interaction: Uncertainty, understanding, and the development of interpersonal relationships. In H. Giles & R. S. Clair (Eds.), Language and social psychology (pp. 122-144), Oxford: Basil Blackwell.

Blood, R. (2004), How blogging software reshapes the online community, *Communications of the ACM , 47* (12), 53-55.

Castells, M. (1996), *The Information Age: Economy, Society and Culture, Vol. I – The Rise of the Network Society,* Oxford: Blackwell.

Comscore, (2011, January 27), *Email Behaviour Shifts in Asia Pacific*, Retrieved May 10, 2011, from Comscore Data Mine: http://www.comscoredatamine.com.

Comscore (2010, November 4), *Facebook and Orkut Growth in India*, Retrieved May 10, 2011, from Comscore Data Mine: http://www.comscoredatamine.com.

Counts, S. & Geraci, J. (2005), Incorporating co-presence at events into digital social networking, *CHI Extended Abstracts 2005*, 1308-1311.

Fuchs, C. (2008), Internet and Society: Social Theory in the Information Age, New York: Routledge.

Hancock, J. T. & Dunham, P. J. (2001), Impression Formation in Computer-Mediated Communication Revisited : An Analysis of the Breadth and Intensity of Impressions, *Communication Research, 28* (3), 325-347.

Jung, J., Qiu, J. & Kim, Y. (2001), Internet Connectedness and Inequality : Beyond the "Divide", *Communication Research, 28* (4), 507-535.

Lerner, R. (2006), At the Forge: Creating Mashups, *Linux Journal, 147* (10).

Lister, M., Dovey, J., Giddings, S., Grant, I. & Kelly, K. (2009), *New Media: A Critical Introduction* (2nd ed.), New York: Routledge.

Parks, M, & Floyd, K. (1996), Making friends in cyberspace, *Journal of Communication, 46* (1), 80-97.

Reich, R. (1991), The Work of Nations: A Blueprint for the Future, London: Simon and Schuster.

Rheingold, H. (1993), *The virtual community: Homesteading on the electronic frontier,* Reading, MA: Addison-Wesley.

Selwyn, N. (2004), Reconsidering Political and Popular Understandings of the Digital Divide. *New Media and Society, 6* (3), 341-362.

Spears, R. & Lea, M. (1992), Social influence and the influence of the 'social' in computer-mediated communication. In M. Lea (Ed.), *Contexts of computer-mediated communication,* London: Harvester-Wheatsheaf (pp. 30-65).

Sproull, L. & Kiesler, S. (1991), *Connections. New Ways of Working in the Networked Organisation,* Boston: MIT Press.

Strover, S. (2003), Remapping the Digital Divide, *The Information Society , 19,* 275-277.

Telecom Regulatory Authority of India (2011), *The Indian Telecom Services Performance Indicators October - December 2010.* Government of India, Department of Telecom, New Delhi: TRAI.

Tidwell, L. & Walther, J. (2002), Computer-Mediated Communication Effects on Disclosure, Impressions, and Interpersonal Evaluations: Getting to Know One Another a Bit at a Time, *Human Communication Research, 28* (3), 317-348.

Tong, S. T., Heide, B. V., Langwell, L. & Walther, J. B. (2008), Too Much of a Good Thing? The Relationship Between Number of Friends and Interpersonal Impressions on Facebook, *Journal of Computer-Mediated Communication, 13,* 531-549.

Van Dijk, T. A. (1983), Discourse Analysis: Its Development and Application to the Structure of News, *Journal of Communication,* 20-43.

Vartanova, E. (2002), Digital Divide and the Changing Political/Media Environment of Post-Socialist Europe, *International Communication Gazette , 64* (5), 449–465.

Walther, J. B., Heide, B. V., Kim, S.-Y., Westerman, D. and Tong, S. T. (2008), The Role of Friends' Appearance and Behavior on Evaluations of Individuals on Facebook: Are We Known by the Company We Keep? *Human Communication Research , 34,* 28-49.

Weiss, A. (2005), The power of collective intelligence. *networker 9* (3), 16-23.

Wellman, B., Hasse, A., Witte, J. & Hampton, K. (2001), Does the Internet increase decrease, or supplement social capital? Social networks, participation, and community commitment, *American Behavioural Scientist , 45* (3), 436-455.

Zhao, S. (2006), Do Internet Users Have More Social Ties? A Call for Differentiated Analyses of Internet Use, *Journal of Computer-Mediated Communication, 11,* 844-862.

15

Mass Media and the Challenges of Sustainable Democracy in Nigeria

Nicholas S. Iwokwagh

Introduction

The mass media play critical roles in the political processes of democracies, and indeed, other political systems. The nature and character of these roles, particularly in democracies is partly determined by the constitution, and partly by other structures upon which these democracies are built. These structures include institutions and organisations such as the government, made up of the executive, the legislature and the judiciary; the military, the police, the family the church, and the bureaucracy among others. Furthermore, these roles are influenced by the inter-dependent sub-systems which include, political, economic, cultural, and social sub-systems; and which work together to ensure the continuous growth and survival of these democratic societies.

In the Nigerian democracy, for example, Jibo (2003, p. 3) has noted that "the Nigerian media has been a major political actor long before the country was fashioned as a unified political system and has continued to play a central role in national politics since then." This paper, therefore, is an attempt at analysing the nature of this role, its impact on Nigeria's contemporary democracy and the challenges they have grappled with in their quest for sustainable democracy.

Sustainable democracy has been conceived as a dynamic, on-going, ever-changing democratic process that is positively responsive to the yearnings and aspirations of the people. The media, in turn, have been perceived as social institutions. As social institutions, the media have been defined as those highly structured or organised social systems with well defined authority relationships, which are responsible for gathering, processing, packaging and dissemination of information for public consumption.

A Look at the Social Functions of the Media

The media do not operate in a vacuum. They function within the confines of a society. A Society is an inter-dependent entity that is made up of different groups of people, culture and institutions. According to Otite and Ogionwo (2001, p. 41), a society refers to "a unit consisting of institutions and culture which are exclusive to a group of people." Clearly, this definition of society has three key elements: groups of people, the relationships between them, institutions and culture.

McQuail (2005, p. 96-97) offers another perspective of society, which we refer to here as *the systems perspective*. According to him, "society is viewed as an on-going system of linked working parts or sub-systems, each making an essential contribution to continuity and order." This definition highlights the fact that society is made up of inter-dependent parts called sub-systems. These sub-systems in turn, perform vital functions which ensure the continuous growth and survival of the entire system.

A close look at these definitions of society reveals that, a society:

(i) Is an organised entity with well delineated units called subsystems.
(ii) Has a mechanism of social control, which defines and regulates the relationship between its inter-dependent parts.
(iii) Defines roles and assigns specific functions to its inter-dependent parts to ensure order, and its continuous survival.
(iv) Has common goals for which it exists, and for which continuity is sought.

According to McQuail (2005, p. 97) "the media can be seen as one of these systems." Further, he says, "it is by responding to the demands of individuals and institutions in consistent ways that the media achieve unintended benefits for the society as a whole." What this means is that the media are institutions, which are vested with specific functions, both to individuals, other institutions and the sub-systems to ensure the survival of the society by responding to the demands of its three units structure. "These units are persons, institutions and sub-systems" (Otite & Ogionwo, 2001, p. 21).

The media, in discharging their duties to society network with other institutions to achieve homeostasis (social equilibrium). Among these institutions are the government, which is organised along the lines of the executive, the legislature, and the judiciary. Others include: the priesthood (church), the police, the military and the bureaucracy. The sub-systems on the other hand have been identified to include: political, economic, religious and social sub-systems.

Discourse on the social functions of the media dates back to 1948, when Harold Lasswell first prescribed the three cardinal functions of the media. These included: surveillance of the environment, correlation of the parts of society in responding to its environment, and transmission of the cultural heritage. Wright (1960) and Mendelsohn (1966) later added the fourth and fifth functions of entertainment and mobilisation respectively. Building on these functions, McQuail (2005) offers an expanded view of media functions in society:

Information

- Providing information about events and conditions in society and the world.
- Indicating relations of power.
- Facilitating innovation, adaptation and progress.

Correlation

- Explaining, interpreting and commenting on meaning of events and information.
- Providing support for established authority and norms.
- Socialising.
- Co-ordinating separate activities.
- Consensus building.
- Setting orders of priority and signaling relative status.

Continuity

- Expressing the dominant culture and recognizing subcultures and new cultural developments.
- Forging and maintaining commonality of values.

Entertainment

- Providing amusement, diversion and the means of relaxation.
- Reducing social tension.

Mobilisation

- Campaigning for societal objectives in the sphere of politics, war, economic development, work and some-times religion.

Of direct relevance to our discourse is the mobilising function of the media, particularly with reference to politics and the political process.

The Media and the Democratic System in Nigeria: A Critique

It is an incontrovertible fact that the media have served functional purposes in Nigeria's democracy particularly as a pool of mass information. As the proverbial "*watchdog*" – a metaphor which describes the real responsibility of the media to the Nigerian society, the media have worked hard at discovering the "truth" and mobilising the society towards worthy causes by presenting evidence and opinion as the basis for decision (Siebert, Peterson & Schramm, 1956). This function may have informed the position that the media play crucial roles in the political processes of democracies (Jibo, 1996).

One remarkable example with respect to this role is the "*Buharigate*" saga, which was made public by a popular news magazine *The News*. In its 10th July, 1999 edition, captioned "*Face of a Liar*", *The News* reported the certificate and age falsification scandal around the person of the erstwhile Speaker of House of Representatives, Alhaji Salisu Buhari. It presented details of Buhari's educational and business backgrounds and established prima facie, the allegations of forgery, perjury and fraud against Alhaji Buhari. This development consciously set national agenda for the Nigerian society by raising the spiral of public discourse, which culminated in his removal both as speaker, and as a member of the House of Representatives.

The media have also given impetus to the fight against corruption, and the drive towards transparency and accountability in Nigeria's democracy. In pursuing this role, they derived legitimacy from the Nigerian Constitution, which serves as the hallmark of Nigeria's democracy. Specifically, the 1999 Constitution provides in Section 22 that:

> The press, radio, television and other agencies of the mass media shall at all times, be free to uphold the fundamental objectives and directive principles of state policy, and highlight the responsibility and accountability of the government to the people.

In response to this provision, the media in Nigeria held the leadership of the country accountable for their actions. For example, the media indicted the then Deputy President of the Senate, Alhaji Ibrahim Mantu and the then Chairman of Senate Information Committee, Senator Zwingina for demanding a whooping sum of N54 million bribe from Mallam Nasir El-Rufai before he could be cleared for a ministerial post.

A more dramatic episode involved the erstwhile Minister of Education, Professor Fabian Osuji, who offered N55 million to the former Senate President Chief Adolphus Wabara, and some members of the Education Committee in both houses of the National Assembly to facilitate the passage of the budget proposal of his ministry in the 2005 appropriation bill. Commenting on the issue, *Newswatch* of April 4, 2005, reported in its lead story that: "The anti-corruption war of Obasanjo's administration recorded two major casualties last week (March 29), Adolphus Wabara and Fabian Osuji for their ignoble roles in the N55 million bribery scandal that rocked the National Assembly." The magazine gave details of the proceedings of the case and a graphic profile of the perpetrators of this fraud. It particularly reported the thesis of the pre-scandal meeting between the two parties. According to magazine (p. 17), "the Senate President emphasised the need for Ministry of Education to come forward with necessary PR or risk cut in his budget. The minister was given 5 days up till December 3, 2004 to produce N55 million gratification or forget the budget."

In its own account of the scandal, *The Source* magazine gave details of the scam, noting that "the entire amount of N55 million delivered to the house of Senator Chris Adighije was in the presence of Senator A. Ibrahim, Hon. Dr. Matazu and Senator Mbata" (*The Source*, 2005, p.17). Sequel to this development was the removal of Chief Adolphus Wabara as Senate President, and professor Fabian Osuji as Minister of Education. In a related development, the media indicted the then Police Chief, Tafa Balogun for embezzling and stashing away in foreign accounts the scandalous sum of N13 billion which was unfit for his status as the Police Chief. As a result, he lost his job, was arrested and prosecuted. All these go to say that the Nigerian media through investigative journalism, have exhibited a high level of social responsibility, patriotism and commitment to the policy and principle of transparency and accountability.

The Nigerian media have also created an enabling environment for dialogue and have ensured that different shades of opinion are brought to fore. In other words, they have served as the market place of ideas for political thought. An outstanding instance of this role was the "*Anti-third term*" campaign they orchestrated against the administration of former president, Chief Olusegun Obasanjo. Expectedly, the public consensus, built through agenda setting compelled him to conduct general elections and to hand over power to another democratic government-the Late Yar A'dua/Goodluck Jonathan administration.

The media have also made remarkable contributions towards national and rural development in Nigeria. Development (national and rural) has been seen as a many sided process which aims at the material well being of the greatest number of the people in society. This includes better nutrition, low mortality rate, capital accumulation, skilled labour formation and technological progress. These conditions are better brought about by policy makers, who make up the government, while the policies are implemented by the people. The Nigerian media, in this regard, have partnered with policy makers and implementers though in a limited manner, to feed the people with the necessary information - what roles they are to play, how they should play such roles and when they should play such roles. In other words, they (media) inform the policy makers about the people's problems on the one hand, and mobilise the people for development and enlighten them on their responsibilities on the other hand. For instance, the media heralded the inter-sectoral reforms of the President Obasanjo's administration, giving in-depth interpretations of the reforms, and noting their implications on the country and its peoples. The media, in doing this, also stated the roles of the people, and the expectations of government from them with respect to these reforms to ensure successful implementation.

Further through their contents (news, features, editorials, opinions, columns) and programmes (documentaries, talk shows, discussion etc.) the media have suggested corpus of strategies that policy makers and implementers could engage to improve development efforts in Nigeria. Some of these strategies have been enumerated by Sonmonu (1990) :

(i) Development of human resources
(ii) Satisfaction of the basic needs of the African (Nigerian) peoples, and the continuous improvement of same
(iii) Maintenance of healthy environment
(iv) Creation and generation of employment
(v) Food security and food self-sufficiency
(vi) Population management
(vii) Integrated industrialization
(viii) Development of sports and culture
(ix) The integration of African Economies
(x) Full participation of the people in all aspects of governance

In spite of this seemingly wonderful score card, the Nigerian media, however, are far from meeting the general expectations of their roles in Nigeria's democracy. This means, in other words, that their operations have been compromised by a plethora of challenges. Some of which are discussed in subsequent parts of this discourse.

Ownership Influence

Ownership influence has been a major challenge to the media in their bid to consolidate democracy in Nigeria. Udoakah (1992, p. 100) for instance, has argued that "the mass media do not exist for a 'common good' but as promotional fora for their proprietors and dossiers of shortcomings for their owners' political and economic or social rivals." Further, he posits that:

> What determines news…are the goals of the different mass media organisations. Which is to say that the mass media select and publish

> only those things they hope would win their audience to a point of view beneficial to their proprietors.

In addition, he provides that the quest for political power is what often informs the birth of newspapers or magazines, both by individuals and government(s) According to him (1992, p. 101)

> One of the fundamental reasons for the birth of newspapers or magazines is the desire by some persons to wield political power. Because the mass media have come to be seen as 'powerful' means of communication, aspirants to political offices and those in power or who want to influence politics, have ventured into newspaper and magazine publishing.

At the level of individuals he argued that (p. 101)

> ... during the transitional periods of the Second and Third Republics, many newspapers and magazines sprung up to serve political parties or individual politicians. Among such publications during the transitional period of the Second Republic were the Pro-NPN *National Concord* and *The Call* newspapers. The Pro-NPP *Satelite* newspaper and the Pro-PRP *African Progress* newspaper. The publisher of the *Concord,* Chief MKO Abiola had a presidential ambition but later backed out, while the publisher of the *Call* Late Chief Victor Akan became Senator. Chief Jim Nwobodo, publisher of the *Satelite* became the Governor of the former Anambra State, while Dr. Una Akpan, the publisher of *African Progress* failed to realise his governorship ambition.

At the level of the government, he maintained (p. 100) that

> Equally of political reason is government ownership of newspapers... state governments have embarked on establishment of newspapers as political weapons. These papers are expected to serve as advocates for their people, report with intensity and editorialise on issues affecting the wellbeing of their people. They are to play a public relations role for their governments. In other words, government financed newspapers are for the spread of political propaganda, publicity of government activities, and countering of opposition.

Clearly, the above suggests that the mass media do not exist for common good of society; rather, they give impetus to the accomplishment of the political, social and economic goals of their proprietors. Further, they serve as megaphones for the propagation of their owners' political ideology on the one hand, and as instruments of political vendetta on the other hand.

What has been said about the print also applies to the broadcast media, both at the individual and the government levels. According to the report of the Political Bureau (1987, p. 213), "there is little doubt that government controlled media have often been used to essentially serve the interest of those in government and their colleagues outside it rather than the larger interest of the society." According to Jibo (2003, p. 8), "this selfish use of the state owned media has been a major issue in Benue politics." Specifically, he provides (p. 8) that

> Radio Benue has been used by incumbent regimes to harass, intimidate, and malign opponents at the slightest provocation. Governor George Akume in a Radio Benue programme, *platform*, described Senator Joseph Waku, a key opposition member, as an illiterate who had failed to represent his people well in the senate. After such attacks, the affected opposition politicians were invariably denied the right of reply on the state owned radio. In the Second Republic, the National Party of Nigeria (NPN – then ruling party) used Radio Benue in a similar manner.

These situations serve only as a microcosm of such occurrences across different states of the country in the 2003 general elections. Government owned broadcast media were particularly indicted during these elections for denying opposition parties access to their facilities for their electioneering campaign programmes, even when such political parties were willing to pay money so that their activities will be publicised. Jibo (2003, p. 7) notes that this was the case in Ekiti, Oyo, Benue, Abia, Enugu, Ondo and others. According to him (p. 7), "the unwillingness of certain state radio and television stations to allow the opposition parties access to their facilities to air their viewpoints has been a sore point in many states such as Ekiti, Oyo, Benue, Abia, Enugu, Ondo and others." The situation was not radically different in the 2007 elections.

Regrettably however, exercising this form of control over media institutions and their contents in a democracy, particularly, during elections, totally negates the very essence of the democratic process. The reason is that political information is a necessary component of the democratic process, and the media serve as channels for the provision of such political information. Therefore, restricting opposition parties' access to media facilities especially during elections, amounts in real terms to disenfranchisement of the electorate. The question then is: *to what extent will this practice promote democracy?*

Ethnicity

Ethnicity has been the Achilles' heel of media operations in Nigeria's democracy. A look into the historical trajectory of Nigeria reveals that ethnicity has been the bane of Nigeria's media since colonial days. Uche (1998) for instance, observed that the use of the media (press) to defend the interest of political parties, has birthed and intensified ethnic and sectional politics in Nigeria. To anchor this claim, he provides that in 1959, Azikiwe and the National Council of Nigerian Citizens (NCNC) Party controlled 10 newspapers, while their rival, Awolowo and the Action Party controlled 14 newspapers. The rivalry, as he argues, was mainly, between the Eastern and Western regional press because the newspapers in the Northern Region then had not come into limelight.

However, after independence in 1960, the Northern Region established the *New Nigerian Newspaper*. According to Charles Sharp, its pioneer Managing Director, the *New Nigerian* "was a political creation that represented the views and aspirations of the North and all aspects of Northern Nigeria which had to be also communicated to readers in other parts of the federation" (Sharp, 1986, p.10). In other words, Nigeria inherited a highly sectarian, and a deeply tribalised media at independence (Iwokwagh, 2004, p. 100). Evidence abounds to show that the ethnic or tribal inclination of the media indeed gave impetus to the termination of Nigeria's First Republic in 1966.

Anifowose (1982) for instance, shows how the Western Regional election of 1965 provided the media (press) opportunities to whip up negative inter-ethnic and inter-regional sentiments of Yoruba verses Igbo and the East versus the West respectively. According to him, what happened in the exchange between UNTV/WNBS and ENTV/ENBS, *The Eastern Nigerian Outlook* and *The Sketch* amounted to media war in which no rules of the profession were respected. As a result, insults were freely exchanged, hard earned reputations were not spared and the ground was silently prepared for the coup of 1966.

Also, Jibo (2003, p. 52) observes that "when a national issue enters the public domain for debate, the Nigerian media often… takes a North versus South position on it." Further, he laments the situation where ethnicity has been used, especially in recent times, to excuse the excesses of government. According to him (p. 65) "in the past, legislation was used by government to close the prying eyes of journalists; today, ethnicity and money are thrown at many of them, and they are encouraged to soften their criticism of government."

Recently, the Nigerian media demonstrated the schism that exists in their operations along regional, sectional and ethnic lines in the celebrated cases of Alhaji Salisu Buhari, erstwhile Speaker, House of Representatives, Governor Bola Tinubu, former governor Lagos State, and Evans Enwerem, erstwhile Senate President. These three personalities were charged with the allegation of perjury and forgery. However, it is interesting that the media were selective in their reports, in the treatment of the issues. Put differently, the editorial treatment of this issue clearly showed media bias. The media were seen to have sympathised, and even protected a party in the scandal, while they opened the floodgate of malevolence to the other two parties. Put in practical terms, the media were instrumental to the removal of Alhaji Salisu Buhari and Senator Evans Enwerem as Speaker, House of Representatives, and Senate President respectively, while Governor Tinubu's case was treated with kid gloves. The point is, *The News* magazine prosecuted Buhari's case till he resigned as Speaker, House of Representatives, and lost his position in the House; while *Tell* magazine ensured that Evans Enwerem also lost his position as Senate President. However, none of these magazines, which incidentally, are Lagos/Ibadan based, beamed their searchlight of probity on Governor Tinubu's case.

Lawan (2000, p. 18) gives an explanation to this scenario:

> It has been the policy of the Ngbatis (Yoruba) to ensure the total and complete destruction of leaders from non-native areas. Such that in the end, they would not be able to produce nationally acceptable leaders...Because Buhari and Enwerem don't belong, they helped in denting them, when Governor Chicago (Tinubu) was exposed, they kept completely sealed lips...using their ethnic orientation to good advantage...

The underlying argument here is that the media have become entangled in the pursuit of ethnic interests and agendas at the expense of national interest. This practice, however, is inimical to the deepening of the democratic process in Nigeria, as it has the capacity to "make group grievances more intense, and divisions' deeper" (Udoakah, 1998, p. 35).

Policy Defects

According to Jibo (2003, p. 4), "the media helps the elites and the broad masses to articulate their views and positions on political issues and public policy." It follows from this observation that one of the fundamental roles of the media in a democratic society is contribution towards policy formation and execution. However, to accomplish this task effectively, the media are expected to partner with policy makers and implementers, and to feed the people with the necessary information: what roles they should play, when and how they should so do, much more, they are to serve as channels through which the people can contribute to the formation and implementation of such policies.

Udoakah (1998, p. 18) articulates this point:

> To get citizens to participate in development, those to benefit should be given the opportunity to contribute to the decision on the projects. In other words, they should be allowed to determine their needs and

be allowed to play some roles at the execution stage. This can be done through liaison with the people's groups such as community development.

Observation however shows that the reverse is the case in Nigeria. It has been noted for instance, that government agencies and media organisations still subscribe to the notion of the all powerful media in their bid to mobilise the people to participate in the implementation of newly fashioned development policies of the government without the people's prior participation in the early stages of policy formulation. Put another way, the media have erroneously been placed at the centre of policy formation and implementation instead of the people for whom these policies are articulated.

Commenting on this issue, Egbon (2006, p. 163) notes painfully that:

> One thing that is becoming clear in the Nigerian situation is the perception of those wielding powers that the mass media is almighty in its ubiquity and persuasiveness, and so can always be used to sell government ideas to the helpless populace the target audience of government campaign or brainwashing. But this is the same way the early media theorists deluded themselves by believing that an all – pervasive media phenomenon was also likely to be all–persuasive.

In other words, there is a structure of vertical communication, where the flow runs from top to bottom, where the few talk to many about the needs and problems of the many from the standpoint of the few through the media (UNESCO, 1980). The question then is, and remains: to what extent does this promote democracy?

Iredia (2004, p.15) has provided another perspective into how the Nigerian media have sabotaged otherwise laudable government policies in Nigeria. According to him:

> ...the media in Nigeria operate with a mindset that a successful journalist is one who is anti-government and hyper critical of all public policies. This helps to a great extent to sustain societal prejudices and also enhances the cynical posture of civil society. As a result, the social responsibility role of the media is hardly performed. With poor public enlightenment, every public policy is politicized and the people are mislead into sabotaging policies which are otherwise in their interest

In other words, the Nigerian media through their critical attitude to government policies particularly in the on-going democratic dispensation have reneged on their social responsibility, thereby jettisoning promising policies that would have served the national interest.

Legal Constraints

According to Nimmo and Combs (1992, p. xv), "the press and the broadcast media have become the principal means of 'mediating' - that is, standing between people and the world and reporting to them what they could not see or experience themselves." However, for the media to perform this societal obligation at peak efficiently there is need for an enabling environment. Within the context of this discourse, such an enabling environment will be consummated within the framework of the law. As we know, the constitution is the watershed of all democracies. It stands as the supreme authority, or hub around which the business of the state revolves.

In Nigeria, however, there is a consensus that the present constitution (1999, Constitution) is fraught with a myriad of defects particularly in the area of media freedom and freedom of expression. A cursory look at Section 39 of the 1999 Constitution, which purportedly guarantees freedom of expression and the press, clearly reveals the contradictions inherent in this constitutional provision. Section 39 (1) for instance, provides that "every person shall be entitled to freedom of expression, including freedom to hold opinions and to receive and impart ideas and information without interference." A critical evaluation of this provision, however, reveals inherent contradictions. For example, it is clear from this provision that an essential component of this fundamental right "*right to seek information*" otherwise termed "*freedom of information is missing.*" What it has provided for is the "freedom to hold opinions, receive and impart ideas and information without interference." The implication of this provision for individuals is the *denial of access to information* which could empower them to freely express themselves on the one hand and to help them take rational decisions on the other hand.

At the level of the media, this provision *restricts free access to information*, which otherwise could have fostered national interest. In practical terms, this provision has posted to the media the ferocious challenge of access to sensitive information which is often tagged "*classified*", or "*top secret.*" Usually, national security is traded as an excuse for doing so. The argument, however, is that the absence of this all important "freedom of information" provision, has been inimical to journalism practice in Nigeria. For instance, it makes it an offence, punishable by law, if a journalist so publishes any information that has been tagged "*classified"* even if the dissemination of such information was intended for national interest. Again, this provision has cost some journalists and citizens their lives, jobs, and opportunities for improved living. A few examples of the restrictive nature of this constitutional provision will buttress this point.

An example that readily, comes to mind is that of the harassment and bombing of the village residence of the Chief Executive Officer of the African

Independent Television (AIT), Chief Raymond Dokpesi, by State Security agents, for his TV Station's (AIT) live coverage of the National Assembly's Proceedings on Constitutional amendment (tenure elongation), and its live, on-the-site report of the Bellview crash of 2005.

Also worthy of mention is the invasion of the office of *Thisday* on 5th April, 2000 by State Security agents, for publishing information that exposed the involvement of some government officials in questionable business transactions (*Vanguard*, April 6th, 2000). Earlier in the same year, government security officers seized copies of the *Abuja Mirror* without explaining their action beyond saying that some classified information was divulged (*Vanguard*, April 6th, 2000).

In another instance, Mr. Akintunde Akinleye, a *Daily Independent* photojournalist was arrested by officers of the state police on August 30, 2003 while covering a public event that featured the former Vice-President Atiku Abubakar.

From the perspective of individuals, a good example that comes handy is that in which the rights of expression of the citizens (of Bayelsa State in petition and demonstration) were suppressed using extra-judicial and arbitrary measures. As a result, many lost their lives. The incident occured in 1999, when armed naval and army troops engaged peasant demonstrators in Odi, Bayelsa State in a pitched battle for several weeks, largely resulting from the citizens exercise of their rights to protest perceived unjust government policies. Dozens of unarmed civilians were killed, as soldiers razed down the entire town (*Tell*, January 17, 2000).

All these go to say that lack of freedom of information has often led to incidents of harassment of journalists, and the citizenry as well as use of arbitrary and extra-legal actions by State Security agents on them (journalists/citizens). This trend does not encourage the development of a democratic culture and cannot sustain democratic governance in Nigeria.

Poverty

Poverty has had a profound negative effect on the role of the media in sustaining Nigeria's contemporary democracy. According to Udoakah (2003, p. 15):

> To keep its responsibility to help an average citizen to take part in democracy alive, the press must inform the public accurately. It owes the public an obligation to monitor the environment and its agents in their conduct of public affairs and report to it. As an institution, the press is a crucial part of the political environment, providing

platform for a variety of political viewpoints, judging and criticizing the viewpoint in circulation.

This, however, will be possible only where the teeming populace have sweeping access to media channels. Unfortunately, it has been found that only few average citizens have access to the media. Jibo (2003, p. 21) decries this state of affairs, noting that "whereas in the past many people could buy a number of newspapers from the newsstand, at the moment, due to diminished disposable incomes, many people now hardly afford to pick a daily or a magazine."

Egbon (2006, p. 161) lends credence to this argument, when he remarked that:

> The Nigerian (hungry man) battling for survival may not be too enthused about owning these instruments of information dissemination (media). So we are locked in this vicious circle of poverty and power that incapacitate and inhibit exposure to the information to bring the change we envisage through the mass media of communication.

The point is that, poverty limits access both to the media of information and to contributions on policy matters. This robs the people of active participation in the process of governance, and breeds ignorance, rumour and suspicion. These states, least contribute positively to the sustenance of a democracy. In fact, they only brew distrust, acrimony, and conflict, as witnessed severally in Nigeria's contemporary democracy.

Illiteracy

Literacy is the key that opens the way to development. However, available statistics show that in Nigeria, only "40 per cent of the total population is literate; while illiteracy accounts for 60 per cent" (Tsavmbu, 2003, p. 157). This condition does not offer a favourable climate for deepening of the democratic process in the country. The reason for this is that access to information is necessary for the development and promotion of a national entity. In fact, free access to, and exchange of information is necessary for persuading citizens to accept the rules of social and political life; join in pursuing agreed goals, and above all, living together in peace (UNESCO, 1980).

Onabanjo (2002, p. 11) remarks that "about 98 per cent ruralites are non-literates and the print media will not benefit them." The radio, however, is revered for its reach and capacity to break language, literacy, and geographical barriers. However, even with these characteristics one notices few disturbing issues. For instance, what percent of the programmes that are produced in indigenous languages adequately address issues of concern to this teeming rural populace? Again, how much involved are these teeming rural populace in the production of the programmes for which it is believed will be beneficial to them? There is also a fundamental problem of poverty, such that, even where these *ruralites* have transistor radios, it becomes increasingly difficult for them to purchase dry cells on regular basis. This situation is aggravated by the fact that these *ruralites* hardly have access to electricity.

The import of this condition is lack of direct access to the mass media, and by extension, vital information which is an essential ingredient of a democracy through which the teeming rural populace can be mobilised to get involved in the processes of governance in their country. This trend often leaves these *ruralites* with the alternative of word of mouth transmission. However, one disturbing issue about this mode of information dissemination is the distortions that attend its practice. In other words, these messages are subjected to *sharpening, leveling* and *assimilation*, which are some ways of information distortion. The result is that these *ruralites* end up with misinformation, and sometimes misconceptions of government policies and what their roles should be in the implementation of these policies. This situation certainly does not augur well for a fledgling democracy like ours.

Corruption

Corruption has been identified by media scholars and professionals as one of the portent challenges with which the media have had to grapple since the First Republic. It has been observed that corruption has compromised the capacity of the media to effectively champion social engineering in Nigeria. Jibo (2003, p. 23) for instance, has established that "corruption has weakened the resolve of the media to fight corruption and it continued to do so in the run up to the 2003 elections." Earlier, Ray Ekpu, Chief Executive Officer, *Newswatch* Communications noted that "we have found out to our dismay, that instead of practising competitive professional and ethical journalism, these fellows have resorted to the dubious practice of pack journalism that is governed by cheque-book arrangement" (*Newswatch*, September 16, 2002).

The implication of corruption for the media and sustainable democracy in Nigeria has been articulated by media scholars. Jibo (2003, p. 23) for instance, has noted that "electoral officials and politicians cut deals to subvert the electoral process without fear of being exposed by a journalist determined to unearth it to make a name…." in other words, the thesis of Jibo's argument is that "the electorate in Nigeria should look elsewhere for protection for their votes, other than from the media." This means that corruption has compromised the capacity of the media to safeguard democratic values, structures and process in Nigeria's contemporary democracy. It's easy to perceive that such an attitude cannot engender sustainable democracy.

Towards Re-positioning the Mass Media on the Path of Sustainable Democracy in Nigeria

Our concern in this segment of the paper is to suggest possible ways through which the media in Nigeria will re-position in order to brace up to the challenges discussed above, and to consolidate sustainable democracy in Nigeria. We shall, therefore, examine the issues of national interest, cultural relativism, communication policy, and Freedom of Information Law among possible alternatives.

National Interest

Sustainable democracy in Nigeria can only be actualised when media organisations will truly embrace and consciously practice the principle of national interest. This principle suggests that, the interests of a country and its citizens should supersede the primordial interests of individuals and ethnic groups. McQuail (2005, p. 171) seemed to express this principle when he observed that media ownership should be viewed "as a form of public trust or stewardship rather than as an unlimited private franchise." The implication of this is that the media should demonstrate to society their obligation of social responsibility, which would make for its growth and continuous survival. Further, the principle bequeaths on the people the *right of expectation from the media*. For instance, it empowers the people to expect from the media truthful, accurate, fair, and objective information. This information will help them to function better as members of the society. In other words, this principle de-emphasises the over bearing influence of proprietors on media contents on the one hand, and the corrupt tendencies of the media on the other hand.

The point, therefore, is that, national interest, rather than primordial sentiments should be the sole determinant of media contents. The media should always be conscious of the fact that they hold the power they wield in trust for the good of society, and should work assiduously towards the realisation of positive social goals. A lot of positive impact could be made if media proprietors would re-define and re-align their goals and objectives with national goals and expectations. This way, the pursuit of their goals will naturally lead to the pursuit and achievement of national goals. This trend will bring about development and progress, and will make for mutual understanding; and strengthen the ties between the different interest groups in society. This in turn, will strengthen democratic structures as well as deepen the democratic process. The result, of course, will be a sustainable democracy.

Cultural Relativism

This principle entails that the media should be used to build bridges of mutual understanding and co-operation between the constituent parts of Nigeria. Put differently, this principle advocates that the media should institute; doggedly pursue, and consciously entrench the spirit and attitude of brotherhood among the ethnic groups that make up Nigeria. This way, the vision of "*though tribe and tongue may differ, in brotherhood we stand*" will be consolidated, and the esteemed mission of "*one nation bound in freedom, peace, and unity*" will be attained. Thus, it is easy to see that the media will be instrumental to the attainment of sustainable democracy in Nigeria, if they adhere religiously to this principle in the execution of their activities.

Communication Policy

There is an urgent need for a well defined, and a carefully articulated communication policy that will offer the framework and determine the direction and focus of communication activities in Nigeria's democracy. For instance, it is necessary for such a policy to state in clear terms, how interpersonal channels can be formally used to compliment media channels in mobilising people to get involved in the process of decision making in governance, and in an attempt to eliminate the inherent structural problems that make room for rumour, misinformation, and misconceptions thereby endangering the democratic process. In other words, it is crucial to evolve a comprehensive, practicable and realistic communication policy that will involve both the people and policy makers in key decision making processes of the government. This way, the people will not feel marginalised and sidelined in the process of governance, a feeling which often breeds discontent and festers conflict. Again, this arrangement will eliminate the practice where development programmes of the government tend to be media-centred rather than people-centred. Put differently, this arrangement will put the people at the centre of decision making and give them a sense of belonging; this in turn will attract their goodwill, which the government needs both to gain legitimacy, and to survive. It is our pious assumption that sustainable democracy will ensue when the government enjoys the goodwill of the governed.

Freedom of Information Law

As noted earlier, the freedom of expression provided for in Section 39 (1) of the 1999 Constitution is defective, and extremely restrictive on access to information. It is therefore suggested that the Freedom of Information bill which was just passed into Law by the National Assembly and assented to by the President in January, 2011 be religiously enforced. When this is the case, it will liberalise access to information, remove bottlenecks and break barriers associated with access to information. This means, the enacted Freedom of Information Law should guarantee both journalists and the public alike the legal right of access to information in possession of government officials and agencies; public institutions, and private bodies executing public functions, therefore removing unnecessary secrecy.

Further, the Freedom of Information Law should empower public officers to disclose public records of information to journalists without prior authorisation thereof, provided it is for public interest. According to the Executive Director Media Rights Agenda (MRA) Mr. Edetem Ojo, the Freedom of Information Law will strengthen the country's current war against corruption amongst other things (*Guardian*, January 4, 2006). In the thinking of the former Chairman, Nigeria Union of Journalists (NUJ) Akwa Ibom State Chapter, Mr. Sunday Antai, the law will not provide journalists with guns to kill government functionaries. Rather, the law would raise the level of the people's participation in governance, build confidence and promote transparency (Media Rights Monitor, 2003). It is difficult for democracy to fail under these conditions.

Although a case has been made for Freedom of Information, it is necessary to observe that no country in the world enjoys absolute press freedom. Often, there are restrictions in the interest of national security. Therefore, in clamouring for the engagement of Freedom of Information Law in Nigeria, we are not advocating for absolute freedom. What we are saying, however, is the need for the country to borrow a leaf from the constitutional provisions of most democratic countries of the world, which believe in, and acknowledge freedom of the press and freedom of information. For example, the Constitution of the United States of America provides that: "Congress shall make no law abridging the freedom of press" (Opadokun, 1991). In Africa, South Africa, Malawi, Mozambique and Tanzania have clearly acknowledged and provided for Freedom of Information. Section 32 of the 1996 Constitution of South Africa, for example, provides for the right of access to (a) any information held by the state, and (b) any information that is held by another person and that is required for the exercise or protection of any rights. (http://mediarightsagenda.org/agonfia).

Also, Article 37 of the Constitution of Malawi provides that:

> Subject to any Act of Parliament every person shall have the right of access to all information held by the state or any of its organs at any level of government. In so far as such information is required for the exercise of his rights.

In a nutshell, our call for the enforcement of the Freedom of Information Law stems from the realisation that such a law will consolidate Nigeria's democracy by enforcing inherent democratic principles. According to Wilson (2005), the Freedom of Information Law:

- Is a human right
- Guarantees the right of access to information
- Guarantees the right to know
- Ensures the right to express oneself within the law
- Promotes the right to receive information
- Guarantees the right to publish
- Protects whistle blowers
- Protects democracy and its institutions
- Guarantees the rights to education
- Helps in the fight against corruption
- Ensures transparency and accountability
- Ensures the emergence of honest and dedicated leadership
- Ensures effective participation in governance.

However, that Freedom of Information Law does not suggest absolute media freedom does not in any way infer that the media should keep mute in the event of bad governance and oppression of citizens. Professional ethics demand that they should be socially responsible to the citizenry. It is against the backdrop of this assertion that we commend the *Nation* newspaper for making public the content of former President Obasanjo's letter to the incumbent Goodluck Jonathan on issues that had implications for national security, and condemn in totality the unjustified attack on the newspaper by sealing its premises, arresting and detaining its editorial staff and using police to harass and intimidate the editorial board members of the newspaper. As it stands, our own brand of Freedom of Information is an aberration, for our democracy to equate western models, for example America's there is need to enforce the provisions of the Act in all its ramifications.

Conclusion

This paper has examined the role of the media in Nigeria's democracy vis-à-vis the challenges they have grappled with in the bid to foster sustainable democracy especially in recent times. It has shown that, although the media have had a central role in Nigerian politics since the colonial era, these roles have been controversial and contradictory. For instance, it has been demonstrated that the media have worked assiduously towards discovering truth, solving social problems, creating an enabling environment for dialogue and contributing towards national development in Nigeria. However, further evidence has established that such factors as ownership influence, ethnicity, policy defects, legal constraints, poverty, illiteracy, and corruption have negatively influenced the performance of the media at consolidating democracy in Nigeria.

Against the backdrop of these contradictions, suggestions have been made on how the media would consolidate democracy in Nigeria. National interest, cultural relativism, communication policy, and strict enforcement of the freedom of information law have been proffered as strategies which the media should engage to bring about the much needed change.

References

Anifowose, R. (1982), *Politics and violence in Nigeria: The Tiv and Yoruba experience*. Enugu: Nok Publishers.

Egbon,M. (2006), Communication, the media and the democratic process in Nigeria. In M. Maduagwu & A. Mohammed (Eds) *The challenges and prospects of democratisation in Nigeria* Kuru: Fulbright Association of Nigeria, (pp. 161-168).

Federal Government of Nigeria (1987), *Report of political bureau*, Abuja: MAMSER http://mediarightsagenda.org/agonfia.

Idang, G. (1973), *Nigeria: International politics and foreign policy*, Ibadan: University of Ibadan Press.

Iwokwagh, N. (2006), Education for sustainable democracy in Nigeria: A case for effective media involvement, *Nigeria Journal of Social Research*, 1(1), 87-99.

Jibo, M. & Simbive, A. (2003), *Contemporary issues in Nigerian politics*, Ibadan: JODAD Publications.

Jibo, M. (2003), *The Nigerian media and the 2003 elections*, Ibadan: JODAD Publications.

Lawan, B., Media terrorism, *The Post Express*, October 12, 2000. p. 28.

McQuail, D. (2005), McQuail's mass communication theory, (5th ed), London: SAGE Publications.

Media Rights Monitor (2003, June), Re-present Freedom of Information Bill to National Assembly, 8(6).

Mendelshon, H. (1966), Mass entertainment, New Haven, CT: College and University Press.

Nimmo, D. & Combs, J. (1992), Political pundits, New York: McGraw Hill Publishers.

Onabajo, O. (2002), Elements of rural broadcasting, Lagos: Gabi Concepts Ltd.

Opadokun, A. (1991), *Freedom of expression and the right to inform*, A Paper Presented at Seminar on Law and Social Justice. June 9th under the auspices of NBA Benin.

Otite, O. & Ogionwo, W. (2001), *An introduction to sociological studies*, Ibadan: Heinemann Edcational Books (Nigeria) PLC.

Sharp, C., Twentieth anniversary of New Nigerian, *The New Nigerian*, January 1, 1986, p.10

Siebert, F. Peterson, T. & Schramm, W. (1956), *Four* theories of the press, Urbana: University of Illinois Press.

Tell (2000, January 17).

Tsavmbu, B. (2003), The Critical Issues of the Future. In D. Denga (Ed.) *Local government administration in Nigeria: Past present and futuristic projections,* Calabar: Rapid Educational Publishers Limited. (pp. 152 - 163).

The Source (2005, April 4).

Uche, L. (1989), Mass media, people and politics in Nigeria, New Delhi: Concept Publishing Company.

Udoakah, N. (1993), The anatomy of mass communicated messages, *Journal of Humanities*, (3), 88 - 93.

Udoakah, N. (1998), *Development Communication*, Ibadan: Stirling Horden Publishers.

Udoakah, N. (2003), *The Nigerian press and political communication the place of political cartoons*, Uyo: Mediamark Associates.

UNESCO, (1980), *Many voices, one world*, Ibadan: University of Ibadan Press Ltd.

Vanguard (2006, April 6).

Wilson, D. (2005), Freedom of Information: The People's Right, *Media Rights Monitor* 8(6).

Wright, C. (1960), Functional analysis and mass communication, *Public Opinion Quarterly*, 24, 606 - 620.

16

The Real Democratisation of Society through Media Democracy

Dr. Minal

Introduction

Media democracy is a set of ideas advocating reforming the mass media, strengthening public service broadcasting, and developing and participating in alternative media and citizen journalism. The stated purpose for doing so is to create a mass media system that informs and empowers all members of society, and enhances democratic values. Media democracy entails that media should be used to promote democracy as well as the conviction that media should be democratic itself, media ownership concentration is not democratic and cannot serve to promote democracy and therefore must be examined critically. The concept, and a social movement promoting it, have grown as a response to the increased corporate domination of mass media and the perceived shrinking of the marketplace of ideas.

The term also refers to a modern social movement evident in countries all over the world which attempts to make mainstream media more accountable to the publics they serve and to create more democratic alternatives.

KEY PRINCIPLES

Media democracy advocates that corporate ownership and commercial pressures influence media content, sharply limiting the range of news, opinions, and entertainment citizens receive. Consequently, they call for a more equal distribution of economic, social, cultural, and information capital, which would lead to a more informed citizenry, as well as a more enlightened, representative political discourse.

Despite the difficulties in defining the term, the concept broadly encompasses the following notions:

that the press Media democracy remains an under-defined concept because of deliberate structural pressures that prevent individuals from questioning the connection between the press and democracy;

that the ability to comprehend and scrutinise the connection between press and democracy is important because media has the power to tell a society's stories and thereby influence thinking, beliefs and behaviour.

That the concept of "democratising the media" has no real meaning within the terms of political discourse in Western society. In fact, the phrase has a paradoxical, or even vaguely subversive ring to it. Citizen participation would be considered an infringement on freedom of the press, a blow struck against the independence of the media that would distort the mission they have undertaken to inform the public without fear, or favour... this is because the general public must be reduced to its traditional apathy and obedience, and frightened away from the arena of political debate and action.

MEDIA OWNERSHIP CONCENTRATION

A key idea of media democracy is that the concentration of media ownership in recent decades in the hands of a few corporations and conglomerates has led to a narrowing of the range of voices and opinions being expressed in the mass media; to an increase in the commercialisation of news and information; to a hollowing out of the news media's ability to conduct investigative reporting and act as the public watchdog; and to an increase of emphasis on the bottom line, which prioritises infotainment and celebrity news over informative discourse.

Cultural studies have investigated changes in the in-creasing tendency of modern mass media in the field of politics to blur and confuse the boundaries between journalism, entertainment, public relations and advertising. A diverse range of information providers is necessary so that viewers, readers and listeners receive a broad spectrum of information from varying sources that is not tightly controlled, biased and filtered. Access to different sources of information prevents deliberate attempts at misinformation and allows the public to make their own judgments and form their own opinions. This is critical as individuals must be in a position to decide and act autonomously for there to be a functioning democracy.

While it is vital to be able to scrutinize the choices made by media providers in terms of what information is included and excluded, individuals possess distinctive knowledge, habits and interests that affect what media they will view and how they will be affected by the media they are exposed to. The content is only one factor among many others that will shape an individual's powers of judgment.

This concentration has been encouraged by government deregulation and neo-liberal trade policies. For example, the U.S. Telecommunications Act of 1996 discarded most media ownership rules that were previously in place, leading to massive consolidation in the telecommunications industry. Over 4,000 radio stations were bought out, and minority ownership of TV stations dropped to its lowest point since the federal government began tracking such data in 1990.

The past decade has also seen a number of media corporate mergers and takeovers in Canada. For example, in 1990. These changes, among others, caused the Senate Standing Committee on Transport and Communications to launch a study of Canadian news media in March 2003. Specifically, the Committee discussed their concerns regarding the following trends: the potential of media ownership concentration to limit news diversity and reduce news quality; the Canadian Radio-television and Telecommunications Commission (CRTC) and Competition Bureau's ineffectiveness at stopping media ownership concentration; the lack of federal funding for the CBC and the broadcaster's uncertain mandate and role; diminishing employment standards for journalists (including less job security, less journalistic freedom, and new contractual threats to intellectual property); a lack of Canadian training and research institutes; and difficulties with the federal government's support for print media and the absence of funding for the internet-based news media.

Media democracy advocates in favour of legislative policies that encourage a stronger commitment to serving the public interest and a commercial framework that facilitates independence.

As a response to the shortcomings of the mainstream media, proponents of media democracy often advocate supporting and engaging in independent and alternative media, in both print and electronic forms as well as video documentary. Through citizen journalism and citizen media, individuals can produce and disseminate information and opinions that are marginalised by the mainstream media.The media must be free from persons with vested interests like politicians and the advertisers.

Democracy Now! is an example of a resource for information that is independent of both government funding and corporate advertising. *Democracy Now*! provides alternative perspectives and voices not present from media sources of concentrated media ownership and promotes access to diverse sources of news and information in order to enable true democracy.

Feminism and Media Democracy

Despite attempts to democratise the media, feminist media theory argues that the media cannot be considered truly inclusive or democratic insofar as they rely on the masculine concepts of impartiality and objectivity. Creating a more inclusive and democratic media would require reconceptualising how we define the news and its principles. According to some feminist media theorists, news is like fictional genres that impose order and interpretation on its materials by means of narrative. Consequently, the news narrative put forward presents only one angle of a much wider picture.

Feminist media literature frames the news and its central tenants of objectivity and impartiality as a masculine construction that subverts the personal voice, through which femininity is conveyed. To include the voices of women, speaking as women, would challenge the principles of objectivity and impartiality, upon which the media and news is founded. Some feminists media theorists argue that too much "feminisation" in the media is perceived as undermining the objectivity of the news by interjecting too much emotion or subjective content.

It is argued that the distinction between public and private information that underpins how we define valuable or appropriate news content is also a gendered concept. The feminist argument follows that the systematic subversion of private or subjective information excludes women's voices from the popular discourse. Further to this point, feminist media theorists argue there is an assumed sense of equality or equalness implicit in the definition of the public that ignores important differences between genders in terms of their perspectives. So while media democracy in practice as alternative or citizen journalism may allow for greater diversity, these theorists argue that women's voices are framed within a masculine structure of objectivity and rationalist thinking.

Despite this criticism there is an acceptance among some theorists that the blurring of public and private information with the introduction of some new alternative forms of media production (as well as the increase in opportunities for interaction and user-generated content) may signal a positive shift towards a more democratic and inclusive media democracy. Some forms of media democracy in practice (as citizen or alternative journalism) are challenging journalism's central tenants (objectivity and impartiality) by rejecting the idea that it is possible to tell a narrative without bias and, more to the point, that it's socially or morally preferable. Rhiamyers (talk) 23:59, 24 October, 2011, UTC).

CONCLUSION

In Indian democracy media has a responsibility which is deeply associated with the socio-economic conditions. The present scenario is not quite encouraging and certain areas need to be addressed. Media organisations, whether in print, audio visual, radio or web have to be more accountable to the general public. It should be monitored that professional integrity and ethical standards are not sacrificed for sensational practices. The freedom of press in the country is a blessing for the people. However, this blessing can go terribly wrong when manipulations set in. The self regulatory mechanism across media organisations need to be strong enough to stop anomalies whenever they occur. Agencies like Press Council of India need to be vigilant to stem the rot. Big media conglomerates are a serious threat. To counter this problem pluralistic media organisations which are financially viable need to be encouraged. Community participation is a goal that the media should strive for in a country like India.

References

1. Exoo, Calvin F. (2010), The Pen and the Sword: Press, War, and Terror in the 21st Century, California: Sage Publications, p. 1. ISBN 978-1-4129-5360-3
2. Exoo, Calvin F. (2010), The Pen and the Sword: Press, War, and Terror in the 21st Century, California: Sage Publications, p. 4. ISBN 978-1-4129-5360-3.
3. Hazen, Don and Julie Winokur, ed. (1997), New York: The New Press. ISBN 1565843800.
4. Exoo, Calvin F. (2010), The Pen and the Sword: Press, War, and Terror in the 21st Century, California: Sage Publications, p. 1-2. ISBN 978-1-4129-5360-3.
5. Meyer, Thomas; Hinchman, Lew (2002), Media Democracy: How the Media Colonize Politics, Cambridge: Polity Press, p. x. ISBN 0745628443.
6. Williams, Frederick and John V. Pavlik, ed. (1994), The People's Right to Know: Media, Democracy, and the Information Highway, New Jersey: Lawrence Erlbaum Associates. p. 153. ISBN 0805814914.
7. Exoo, Calvin F. (2010), The Pen and the Sword: Press, War, and Terror in the 21st Century, California: Sage Publications. pp. 195-196. ISBN 978-1-4129-5360-3.
8. Meyer, Thomas; Hinchman, Lew (2002), Media Democracy: How the Media Colonize Politics. Cambridge: Polity Press. p. 1. ISBN 0745628443.
9. Exoo, Calvin F. (2010), The Pen and the Sword: Press, War, and Terror in the 21st Century, California: Sage Publications. pp. 1-3. ISBN 978-1-4129-5360-3.

10. Meyer, Thomas; Hinchman, Lew (2002), Media Democracy: How the Media Colonize Politics. Cambridge: Polity Press, p. ix. ISBN 0745628443.
11. Meyer, Thomas; Hinchman, Lew (2002), Media Democracy: How the Media Colonize Politics. Cambridge: Polity Press. p. ix. ISBN 0745628443.
12. Steve J. Sherman, *Democracy Now*!, retrieved from http:// www.democracynow.org/about.
13. Thornham, Sue (2007), Women, Feminism and Media, Edinburgh: Edinburgh University Press. p. 97. ISBN 978 0 7486 2071 5.
14. Thornham, Sue (2007), Women, Feminism and Media, Edinburgh: Edinburgh University Press. p. 97. ISBN 978 0 7486 2071 5.
15. Thornham, Sue (2007), Women, Feminism and Media, Edinburgh: Edinburgh University Press. p. 90. ISBN 978 0 7486 2071 5.
16. Thornham, Sue (2007), Women, Feminism and Media, Edinburgh: Edinburgh University Press. pp. 90-91. ISBN 978 0 7486 2071 5.
17. Thornham, Sue (2007), Women, Feminism and Media, Edinburgh: Edinburgh University Press. pp. 91-95. ISBN 978 0 7486 2071 5.
18. Thornham, Sue (2007), Women, Feminism and Media, Edinburgh: Edinburgh University Press. p. 97. ISBN 978 0 7486 2071 5.
19. Thornham, Sue (2007), Women, Feminism and Media, Edinburgh: Edinburgh University Press. p. 110. ISBN 978 0 7486 2071 5.
20. Thornham, Sue (2007), Women, Feminism and Media, Edinburgh: Edinburgh University Press. pp. 91-92. ISBN 978 0 7486 2071 5.
21. Thornham, Sue (2007), Women, Feminism and Media, Edinburgh: Edinburgh University Press. p. 92. ISBN 978 0 7486 2071 5.
22. Thornham, Sue (2007), Women, Feminism and Media, Edinburgh: Edinburgh University Press. p. 95. ISBN 978 0 7486 2071 5.
23. Thornham, Sue (2007), Women, Feminism and Media, Edinburgh: Edinburgh University Press. p. 95. ISBN 978 0 7486 2071 5.
24. Thornham, Sue (2007), Women, Feminism and Media, Edinburgh: Edinburgh University Press. p. 109. ISBN 978 0 7486 2071 5.
25. Atton, Chris (2008), Pajnik, Moj.

17

Approach of two National Dailies on Anna Hazare's Movement Against Corruption: A Comparative Study of TOI and The Hindu

Shahzad Alam

Anna Hazare: A Versatile Character

Born on June 15, 1937 as Kisan Baburao Hazare in Bhingar, a small village near the city of Ahmednagar, in Maharashtra, Anna Hazare is a renowned Indian social activist and right to information crusader. Despite having studied up to the seventh standard Anna Hazare has become the role model for most of the Indians because of his contribution towards making India corruption free.

Anna Hazare proved himself as an optimist from early days of his childhood. His study was discontinued because of the economic problem in the family and he started selling flowers at Dadar station to support his family. He never lost his confidence and always thought for the better tomorrow. He soon started his own shop and brought two of his brothers to Bombay.

Anna Hazare joined Indian Army in 1963 and took voluntary retirement from the Army. He later shifted to his native village Ralegan Siddhi and started to work for farmers. He came to be inspired by reading "Call to the youth for nation building" of Swami Vivekananda and decided to sacrifice his life for others. As a result for his work towards development of the vellage, Anna Hazare made remarkable economic, social and community regeneration in Ralegan Siddhi.

Anna Hazare also made incomparable efforts in making people aware about the hazardous effects of alcohol. He organised the youth of the village into an organisation named the Tarun Mandal (Youth Association) to take up the issue of alcoholism. Anna as well as youth of the village resolved to close down liquor dens and ban alcohol in the village. Despite the regulations passed, many villagers continued to drink alcohol. After sometime Anna Hazare appealed the government of Maharashtra to bring in a law about prohibition of liquor. In July 2009, the state government issued a government resolution amending the Bombay Prohibition Act, 1949.

In his recent move of development Anna Hazare started the Grain Bank in 1980 to provide food security to needy farmers during times of drought, or crop failure. Anna Hazare also established a watershed embankment in the village to stop water and allow it to percolate and increase the ground water level and improve irrigation in the area.

For his movement towards anti-corruption, Anna Hazare launched the Bhrashtachar Virodhi Jan Aandolan (BVJA-People's Movement against Corruption), a popular movement to fight against corruption in Ralegaon Siddhi in 1991. He then protested against the collusion between 40 forest officials and timber merchants. Similarly Anna Hazare protested against malpractices in the purchase of powerlooms by the Vasantrao Naik Bhathya Vimukt Jamati Vikas Manch and the Mahatma Phule Magasvargiya Vikas Mandal in 1997.

He also led a movement in Maharashtra state which forced the state government to pass a stronger Maharashtra Right to Information Act in early 2000s. This Act was later considered as the base document for the Right to Information Act 2005 (RTI), enacted by the Union Government.

As far as Anna Hazare's recent movements against corruption is concerned, he initiated a Satyagraha movement for passing a stronger anti-corruption *Lokpal* (ombudsman) bill in the Indian Parliament as conceived in the *Jan Lokpal Bill* (People's Ombudsman Bill). He began his fast unto death on 5 April 2011 at Jantar Mantar in Delhi to press for the demand to form a joint committee of the representatives of the government and the civil society to draft a stronger anti-corruption bill. The hunger strike was ended on the morning of April 9, 2011 after 98 hours. Since the government was not found to be serious to pass Jan Lokpal Bill, Anna Hazare gave said a deadline of 15th August, 2011 to pass *Jan Lokpal Bill.* Further, he announced his next hunger strike to be started from August 16, 2011.

Corruption: A Conceptual Framework

Section 161 of the India Penal Code defines 'corruption' in legal terms, as under.

"Whoever being or expecting to be public servant accepts, or obtains, or agrees to accept, or attempts to obtain from any person for himself or for any other person any gratification whatever other than legal remuneration as a motive or reward for doing or forbearing to do any official act, or for showing, or to show, in the exercise of his official function, favours or disfavor to any person, or for rendering or attempting to render any service or disservice to any person, with the Central or any State Government or Parliament or Legislature of any State or with any public servant as such, shall be punished with imprisonment of either description for a term which may extend to three years, or with fine, or with both."

Another Species of Corruption not generally recognized as corruption is extravagant expenditure of public money. The Prevention of Corruption, 1947 calls it criminal misconduct and defines it as follows:

(a) If he habitually accepts or obtains or agrees to accept or attempts to obtain from any person for himself or for any other person, any gratification (other than legal remuneration) as a motive or reward such as is mentioned in Section 161 of the Indian Penal Code,

(b) If he habitually accepts or obtains or agrees to accept or attempts to obtain for himself or for any other person, any valuable thing without consideration or for consideration which he knows to be inadequate, from any other person, whom he knows to have been or to be, or to be likely to be concerned in any proceeding or business transacted or about to be transacted by him, or having any connection with the official functions of himself or of any public servant to whom he is sub-ordinate, or related to the person so concerned;

(c) If he dishonestly or fraudulently misappropriates or otherwise converts for his own use any property entrusted to him or under his control as a public servant or allows any other persons so to do;

(d) If he, by corrupt or illegal means or by otherwise abusing his position as public servant, obtains for himself or for any other person any valuable thing or pecuniary advantages;

(e) If he or any person on his behalf is in possession or has at any time, during the period of his office, been in possession, for which the public servant cannot satisfactorily account of pecuniary resources or property disproportionate to his known source of income.

(f) If public servant who commits criminal misconduct shall be punishable with imprisonment for a term which shall not be less than one year but which may extend to seven years and is liable to time.

Provided that the court may, for any special reasons recorded in writing, impose a sentence of imprisonment of less than one year.

Jan Lokpal Bill: An Introduction

The *Jan Lokpal Bill*, or Citizen's Ombudsman bill is a draft anti-corruption bill drawn up by Justice Santosh Hegde (former Supreme Court Judge), Prashant Bhushan (Supreme Court Lawyer) and Arvind Kejriwal (RTI activist) seeking the appointment of a *Jan Lokpal*.

According to the proposed Bill, anyone, except for a public servant, can file a complaint of corruption against the prime minister, other ministers and members of parliament with the ombudsman. The *Lokpal* has to complete the inquiry within six months. The *Jan Lokpal* will be responsible to investigate corruption cases, complete the investigation within a year and envisage trial in the case getting over in the next one year.

The first *Lokpal Bill* was presented by Shanti Bhushan during the 4th Lok Sabha in 1968 and passed there in 1969 but could not get through in Rajya Sabha. It was again presented in 1971, 1977, 1985, 1989, 1996, 1998, 2001, 2005 and 2008 but never passed.

The main objective of the *Jan Lokpal bill* is to provide speedy, non-expensive form of justice to people.

According to the proposed system of the bill, *Lokpal* will have powers to probe or prosecute any judge, even CJI, without any permission. The politicians will also not have any role in selections of chairperson and members of Lokpal. The *Lokpal* will be a three-member body with a chairperson who is or was a chief justice or Supreme Court judge, and two members who are or have been high courts judges or chief justices.

Methodology

The research methodology adopted to carry out the paper is comparative study through content analysis.

Content Analysis: According to Kerlinger (1973), "Content analysis in a method of studying and analyzing communication in a systematic, objective and quantitative manner for the purpose of measuring variables."

Method: Content analysis and comparative study of Anna Hazare's movement news material was carried out in two national newspapers, *The Times of India* and *The Hindu* during the days of movement in different phases.

The study comprises the analysis of newspapers in three different phases as the movement took place in three different parts.

First analysis comprises the newspapers from April 6-10, 2011 as the first hunger strike took place from April 5-9, 2011.

First Phase Coverage (From April 6-9, 2011) in The Times of India

Article	*Editorials*	*Letter to Editor*	*One Column News*	*Two Column News*	*Three Column News*	*Four Column News*	*Five Column News*	*Six Column News*	*Full Page News*
02	02	03	03	05	09	02	01	00	01

Second Phase Coverage (From August 17-29, 2011) in The Times of India

Article	Editorials	Letter to Editor	One Column News	Two Column News	Three Column News	Four Column News	Five Column News	Six Column News	Full Page News
08	08	03	14	16	39	17	11	04	08

First Phase Coverage (From April 6-9, 2011) in The Hindu

Article	Editorials	Letter to Editor	One Column News	Two Column News	Three Column News	Four Column News	Five Column News	Six Column News	Full Page News
01	02	02	04	04	07	02	01	01	00

Second Phase Coverage (From August 17-29, 2011) in The Hindu

Article	Editorials	Letter to Editor	One Column News	Two Column News	Three Column News	Four Column News	Five Column News	Six Column News	Full Page News
07	05	04	11	15	25	12	09	03	03

In the same manner the second analysis comprises the newspapers from August 17-29, 2011 as the second hunger strike took place from August 16-28, 2011.

These newspapers were selected for the study because of their wide circulation, readership and a good reputation among readers of diverse groups.

Coverage of Anna Hazare's Movement

The two newspapers (*The Times of India* and *The Hindu*) in same language (English under the aegis of two different publications left no stone unturned in giving the maximum coverage to the movement as well as reactions and responses of the masses in connection with *Jan Lokpal Bill.*

As far as *The Times of India* in concerned, it tried to give all the glimpses of the movement in all the forms like editorial, article, letter to editor and news. *The Hindu* also gave maximum attention in covering the movement of Anna Hazare.

Conclusion

Anna Hazare successfully caught the attention of English media in different newspapers. Both the newspapers showed their interest in catching every moment of the movement. However, *The Times of India* shown to be more interested in giving the news about the movement in all the forms of news as compared to *The Hindu. The Times of India* published eleven articles as compared to the eight of *The Hindu* during both the phases of the stir. Similarly in the form of editorial, letter to editor and full page story *The Times of India* published ten, six and nine stories as compared to seven, six and three of *The Hindu* respectively. As far News items with different number of column (viz one column, two columns, three columns, four columns, five columns and six columns) are concerned, *The Hindu* seemed far behind as it published only 94 stories as compared to 121 of the Times of India.

References

The Times of India, Newspaper, a publication of *Bennett, Coleman and Co. Ltd.*

The Hindu, Newspaper, a publication of *Kasturi and sons.*

Singh Jaspal: Indian Penal Code, *Allahabad Law Agency,* 1994.

Vittal N. Corruption in India, *Academic foundation, New Delhi,* 2003.

Tiwari, Prateeksha M. Anna Hazare: the new revolutionary, *Diamond Pocket Books,* 2011.

http://www.*annahazare.org/*biography.html

Berelson, Bernald, *Content Analysis in Communication Research,* 1971.

Krippendorff Klaus, *Content Analysis: An introduction to its methodology,* 2004.

18

Bhagvad Gita Vis-À-Vis Business Schools

Dr. Ahsanuddin Haider

Business week published sometimes back an article Karma capitalisation the influence of Bhagwad Gita in modern business school. Hindu daily reported Bhagwat Gita has entered in the classrooms of Business management in India. Business schools like Indian Institute of Management-Ahmedabad (IIM-A), IIM-Kozhikode (IIM-K), Narsee Monjee Institute of Management Studies (NMIMS), Indian School of Business (ISB) are some of the B-schools who are overhauling their syllabus to match contemporary business and corporate life. Leading business schools in the USA such as Kellogg have included the Bhagavad Gita as an elective subject in their curriculum. Terms such as 'Karma Capitalism', 'Exit Plan' and the likes are being explained on the basis of the teachings of Lord Krishna and the message of the Bhagavad Gita. An American university The Seton Hall University has made study of Bhagvad-Gita compulsory for all its students by including it in its "core course".

Management has become a way of life, be it at home office, factory, Government or in any other organisation where a group of human being assemble for a common purpose. Management principles come into play through their various facets like management of time, resources, personnel, materials, machinery, financial planning, etc.

Management is a systematic way of doing all activities in any field of human effort. It is about keeping oneself engaged in interactive relationship with other human beings in the course of performing one's duty. According to Management Guru Peter Drucker, its task is to make people capable of joint performance to make their weakness irrelevant. It strikes harmony in working equilibrium in thoughts and actions, goals and achievements, plan and performance, products and narket. It resolves situation of scarcities be they in the physical, technical or human fields through maximum utilization with the minimum available processes to achieve the goal.

The success and failures of any organization can be attributed to leadership. The leader/manager of organisation needs to set example to their followers as whatever the leader does, the followers will follow and whatever standards or example the leader sets people in general will follow.

The managerial functions can be viewed as follows:

- Conceptualising a vision and planning the strategy to realise such vision.
- Cultivating the art of leadership.
- Establishing the institutional excellence and building an innovative organisation.
- Developing Team building and teamwork.
- Delegation, motivation and communication and
- Reviewing performance periodically and taking corrective steps whenever needed.

Thus management is a process of aligning people and getting them committed to work for a common objective to maximize social benefit in search of excellence. The million-dollar question in the mind of every manager is how to be effective in their job. The answer of this basic question can be get from Gita which proclaims that you must try to manage yourself. In simple words without self introspection a manager cannot reach a level of excellence and effectiveness.

One of the greatest contributions of India to the world is holy book Bhagwad Gita. The Bhagavad Gita is one of the world's most important books—indeed, one of the greatest books of human culture, Eastern and Western alike. No doubt the Bhagwad Gita is a message addressed to each and every human being to help him or her to solve the irritating problem of overcoming the present and progressive towards a bright future. This book portrays the experience of everyone in this world from hopelessness to a state of perfection understanding, clarity, renewed strength and triumph. The philosophy of Bhagavad-Gita should not be viewed from spiritual perspectives only but also as a guide in developing and inculcating managerial effectiveness. The philosophical approach of the Bhagavad Gita is today considered relevant and essential to introspection and to handle war like situations in this globalised business world to survive, even in the western world. The Bhagvad Gita deals with a basic ways we should act because of who and what we are. In particular, the Bhagvad-Gita is about a moral quandary in which the characters in the Mahabharata war faces fundamental questions about the right way to survive.

Bhagwad Gita expounded thousands of years ago by the super management guru Bhagwan Sri Krishna enlightens all of us on all managerial techniques leading to a harmonious and blissful state of affairs as against conflicts, tensions, lowest efficiency and least productivity absence of motivation and lack of work culture etc common to most of the enterprises today.

The modern management concepts like vision, leadership, motivation, excellence in work achieving goals, meaning of work attitude towards work nature of individual, decision makling, planning etc., are all discussed in the Bhagwad Gita with a sharp insight and finest analysis to drive through our confused grey matter making it highly eligible to become a part of modern management syllabus but there is major difference between modern management concept propounded by great scholars of their time and super management guru of all times Bhagwan Sri Krishna. It may be observed that while western design on management deals with the problems at superficial, material, external and peripheral levels the contained in the Bhagwad Gita the issues from the grass roots level of human thinking because once the basic thinking of human is improved it will automatically enhance the quality of his actions and their results.

Whatever the excellent and best ones do, the commoners follow and this is the leadership quality so says Sri Krishna in the Bhagvad-Gita. The visionary leader must also be a missionary extremely practical intensively dynamic and capable of translating dreams into reality. This dynamism and strength of a true leader flows from an inspired and spontaneous motivation to help others. It has been presumed for long that satisfying lower need of a worker like adequate food, clothing and shelter, recognition, appreciation, status, personality development etc are the factors in the Maslow's hierarchy of need theory.

It is the common experience that the spirit of grievances from the clerk to the managing director is identical and only their scales and composition vary. It should have been that once the lower-order needs are more than satisfied, the managing director should have no problem in optimizing his contribution to the organisation. But more often than not it does not happen like that the eagle soars high but keeps its eyes firmly fixed on the dead animal below. On the contrary a lowly paid school teacher, a self employed artisan, ordinary artist demonstrate higher level of self-realisation despite poor satisfaction of their lower-order needs. This situation is explained by the theory of self transcendence or self-realisation propounded in the Bhagvad-Gita. Self-transcendence is overcoming insuperable obstacles in one's path. It involves renouncing egoism, putting others before oneself, teamwork, dignity, sharing, co-operation, harmony, trust, sacrificing lower needs for higher goals, seeing other in you and yourself in others etc. The portrait of a self-realising person is that he is a man who aims at his own position and underrates everything else. On the other hand the self-transgender is the visionaries and innovators. Their resolute efforts enable them to achieve the apparently impossible. They overcome all barriers to reach their goal.

Pedagogy of management education keeps changing in changing scenario. Now a day's worlds over Business schools are realising the lessons of Bhagwad Gita. Management gurus considering Bhagvad-Gita itself as management school of thoughts. The purpose of introducing Gita in management school is not to discarding modern management models of efficiency, dynamism and striving for excellence but to incorporate holistic approach of leadership in modern models for the welfare of society because there is indeed a moral dimension to business life.

Conclusion

The philosophy of Bhagavad-Gita should not be viewed from spiritual perspectives only but also as a guide in developing and inculcating managerial effectiveness. Now a day's it is considered relevant and essential to introspection and to handle cut throat competition in this globalised business world to survive and to improve the efficiency through inculcating the leadership quality. Modern leaders and managers can benefit from the philosophy of Bhagavad-Gita, which serves as a guide in developing managerial effectiveness. The philosophy of Bhagavad-Gita has remained and will remain as a guide for developing managerial effectiveness. Good leaders are selfless, take initiative, and focus on their duty rather than obsessing over outcomes or financial gain. This is absolutely applicable to corporate leadership today'. The purpose of introducing Bhagvad-Gita in Business school is not to discarding modern management models of efficiency, dynamism and striving for excellence but to incorporate holistic approach of leadership in modern models for the welfare of society because there is indeed a moral and social dimension to business life.

References

M.P. Bhattathiri: Bhagavad Gita, A Motivational Management Book
Swami Ranganthananda :The Universal Message of Gita", *Advaita Ashrama, Kolkatta,* **Vol. 1**, pp. 430 – 437.

B. Mahadevan: Bhagavad Gita, Ideas for Modern Management
Mahadevan, B. (2012). "Leadership lessons from Bhagavad Gita", Impact, July 2012, pp. 13 – 16.

Mohammad Vazeeruddi: Bhagwad Gita, First Manual on Management
Balakrishnan Muniapan: Managerial Effectiveness from the Perspectives of the Bhagavad-Gita.

Desh Raj Sirswal: Ethics of Bhagvad Gita

Shankar B. Chandekar: Principles of Management and The Bhagavad Gita, Dharmaram Journal **Anubhuti Vishnoi** (2009): **IIM-Indore's corporate solutions lessons from the Bhagavad Gita, The Indian Express**

Debashis Chatterjee(2012): Bhagwad Gita holds lessons for managers of all faiths, The Economic Times

http://www.esamskriti.com

http://www.kamyabology.com/bhagwadgita

http://wwwadvaita-space.org

http://www.shraddhananda.com

19

Corruption in Communication

Venudhar Routiya

The first pillar rests firmly on the belief that our drive against corruption must start at home within our organisation but should not stop at our own doors. We cannot hold our clients to a higher standard than we hold ourselves. Although we don't believe corruption to be widespread in the Bank, we would be naive to believe that there is none in an organisation that disburses about twenty billion dollars annually. And, even one case of corruption is one too many.

Let me provide a few examples of initiatives the Bank is undertaking to more effectively prevent corruption in projects financed through its own loans and credits.

- In May 1998, an Oversight Committee on Fraud and Corruption was established. The Committee is responsible for reviewing all allegations of fraud and corruption received by any member of the Bank Group and then determining when and how an investigation should be conducted.

To help ensure that allegations of fraud and corruption are reported, we have also set up a telephone hotline with multi-lingual capabilities, which operates 24 hours a day, seven days a week. It is available for use by Bank group staff and the public.

We have retooled our procurement training, with heigh-tened emphasis on procurement ethics. We have initiated new approaches to building borrower capacity, and are reaching out to other multilateral development banks to share best practices and harmonize our approaches. We are also tightening up our oversight of the Borrower's procurement processes. As part of this move, we are now periodically commissioning procurement audits undertaken by independent firms of international repute. Some 20 such audits have been commissioned in the past 12 months and are now underway. Fifty firms have been debarred from doing business with the World Bank; some for short periods, most of them permanently. The list of the firms and consultants is publicly available on the World Bank's web site. These and other such examples serve to illustrate that our efforts to address both *prevention* and *enforcement*, and demonstrate that these efforts rely not only on *capacity building*, but also on *enhancing transparency*.

Helping Countries Reduce Corruption

The Bank has for some time focused on measures to address administrative corruption by reforming public administration and public finance management. But with the increasing recognition that the roots of corruption extend far beyond weaknesses in the capacity of government, the repertoire has been gradually expanding to target broader structural relationships. These include the internal organisation of the political system, relationship among core state institutions, the interactions between the state and firms, and the relationship between the state and civil society. Jim Anderson will provide a detailed explanation of this approach in his presentation; but just permit me to mention what the Bank views as the five key pillars of any serious strategy for reducing corruption:

- ***Institutional Restraints*** : Examples include: independent and effective judiciary, legislative oversight, independent prosecution, enforcement.
- ***Political Acountability*** : Examples include: political competition, credible political parties, transparency in party financing, disclosure of parliamentary votes, asset declaration, conflict of interest rules.
- ***Competitive Private Sector*** : Examples include: economic policy reform, competitive restructuring of monopolies, regulatory simplification for entry, transparency in corporate governance, collective business associations.
- ***Civil Society Participation*** : Examples include: freedom of information, public hearings of draft laws, role for media/NGOs.
- ***Public sector management*** : Examples include: merito-cratic civil service with monetised, adequate pay, budget management (coverage, treasury, procurement, audit), tax and customs, sectoral service delivery (health, education, energy), decentralisation with accountability.

In recounting the five key pillars of our strategy for reducing corruption, I hope I have been able to emphasise the diversity and breadth of efforts that are required in order to effectively address corruption. In short, this is a task that is not for the faint of heart. It is a very challenging task and its success is dependant, first and foremost, on the political will to bring in the changes.

The *Anticorruption in Transition* report was launched at the World Bank/ IMF Annual Meetings in Prague, in August 2000. The report unbundles the phenomenon of corruption in transitional economies to identify and analyse different types and patterns of corruption in an effort to address the considerable variation in the nature of the problem across the region. By unbundling corruption, the report provides a differentiated approach to the prioritisation and sequencing of reforms in the economy, political system and the role of civil society that can serve as a basis for tailoring anti-corruption strategies more effectively to the specific contours of the problem in different countries.

The report *Diagnostic Surveys of Corruption in Romania* is based on our staff's analysis of surveys carried out last year of households, public officials and enterprises. The surveys gathered information about both perceptions and experiences with corruption. The analysis provides a rich and informative examination of the pattern, profile, causes and consequences of corruption in Romania.

The World Bank's Programme of Support for Anti-Corruption Efforts of the Government of Romania

The Bank stands ready to assist governments that request its help in combating corruption. Since the Bank adopted its comprehensive anti-corruption policy framework in 1997, it has been working to develop new, more targeted forms of assistance to curb corruption. The Bank's assistance can be conveniently grouped into two broad categories: (i) learning programs and (ii) lending and technical assistance programs.

Learning Programs: This includes workshops, training courses, and other activities conducted by the World Bank Institute (WBI). Also included is diagnostic work, such as surveys of households, enterprises and government officials. The reports being presented today are an example of this sort of assistance.

Lending and Technical Assistance Programs: These refer to loans and technical assistance the Bank provides to client governments to improve governance and strengthen public sector institutions. These programs help to build effective institutions to reduce incentives and opportunities for corruption. The Country Assistance Strategy, which the Government and the Bank are developing for Romania, includes a series of programmatic Institutional and Governance Reform Adjustment Loans as well as a Technical Assistance Loan to address several of the public sector pillars of any serious anti-corruption strategy. It also includes a follow-on to the already existing Private Sector Adjustment Loan and its supporting Private Institution Building Loan, which are supporting Romania's efforts to build a more vibrant and competitive private sector – another of the pillars of a serious anti-corruption strategy, which I mentioned earlier. Gary Reid will provide more details on the public sector-focused side of this program of assistance immediately after Mr. Anderson's presentation.

1. It is my privilege to be amongst senior officers from police, prosecution and judiciary. It is a laudable effort on the part of Central Bureau of Investigation and National Institute of Criminology and Forensic Sciences, New Delhi to organise a 2-day National Seminar on the issue of 'Fighting Crimes Related to Corruption'.
2. The menace of corruption is an important issue that is bothering the policy makers, administrator and the general public for a long time. There is an emerging global consensus that fighting corruption and building 'good governance' are essential for the socio-economic development of any nation. The prevalence of corruption undermines social cohesion, wider participation of citizens in economic and political processes, distorts allocation of resources and delivery of public services particularly damaging the interest of the poor and marginalised sections of the society. It also hinders the economic growth by skewing public and foreign investments, distorting the markets and weakening the rule of law. The corruption essentially undermines the credibility and effectiveness of the State and its instruments. The prevalence of widespread corruption and ineffective anti-corruption interventions in this country has led to public cynicism. We have chosen the system of democracy in our pursuit of growth and prosperity of our people and the corruption is a major hindrance in our pursuit.
3. In the words of Alexander Solzhenitsyn: "The line separating good and evil passes not between states nor between classes... but through the middle of every human heart". If governance is by men who are derelict, the governed will suffer. We have to keep in mind Plato's injunction:
4. "The punishment suffered by the wise who refuse to take part in government, is to suffer under the government of bad men". The focus should be on *e-governance* and systemic change. An honest system of governance will displace dishonest persons. As Gladstone so aptly said, "The purpose of a government is to make it easy for people to do good and difficult to do evil".

"Rivers do not drink their waters themselves, nor do trees eat their fruit, nor do the clouds eat the grains raised by them. The wealth of the noble is used solely for the benefit of others."

5. The constitutional vision of strong and prosperous India where freedom, equality of opportunity, rule of law is guaranteed to its citizens can never become a reality if we do not address the issue of corruption in our polity, economy and society in general. The fight against corruption is not only a moral imperative but an economic necessity for a nation aspiring to emerge as a global player. Corruption discourages investment (foreign/ domestic), harnessing of best technologies, resources etc. that requires transparency, fair play and is an impediment for integration with global economy. The issue of fighting corruption and building good governance are of paramount importance for achieving rapid economic development.
6. The six perceived governance quality measures, each an aggregate of a number of sub-measures, are: voice and accountability; absence of political instability and violence; government effectiveness; reasonableness of the regulatory burden; the rule of law; and the absence of graft. Of these, the last two are the most directly significant in the context of ethical governance. 'Rule of law' measures whether crime is properly punished or not; enforceability of contracts; extent of black market; enforceable rights of property; extent of tax evasion; judiciary's independence; ability of business and people to challenge government action in courts etc.
7. Robert Cooter's study shows that a society with high levels of corruption, has low levels of social interaction and weaknesses of the rule of law.
8. Two studies by Isham, Kaufmann, and Pritchett demonstrate that societies with high levels of corruption have low levels of mass participation in politics and weak protection of civil liberties. The study by Easterly and Levine establishes that a society with large incidence of corruption is characterised by deep ethnic divisions and conflicts.

9 In fact, as the Santhanam Committee on Prevention of Corruption wryly remarked, 'Article 311 of the Constitution as interpreted by our courts has made it very difficult to deal effectively with corrupt civil servants'. Even after Article 311 was amended, the panoply of safeguards and procedures still available is interpreted in such a manner

as to make the proceedings protracted, and therefore, effete in the ultimate analysis. There is no gainsaying that the provisions of Article 311 have come in the way of bringing the corrupt civil servants to book.

Article 311 would Require a Revisit

(i) *Strict enforcement of law* : The rule of law is an important element for good governance. The enforcement of contracts, plugging of leakages, ensuring bureaucratic accountability, punishment for the corrupt and dishonest, blocking the growth of black markets, minimising the tax evasion, accessibility to the aggrieved to challenge the decision of the states and its instruments in a court of law etc. are the test of prevalence of rule of law. The people facing criminal charges continue to hold key positions, inordinate delay in the issue of sanction for prosecution and huge pendency of cases before the court are indicative of lax and ineffective enforcement.

There is a need for effective intervention by anti-corruption agencies to make a dent on the gigantic problem facing the system. A swift and certain action against the corrupt, dishonest, delinquent elements in the system can only make the corruption a high risk and low return business.

Corruption and Hypocrisy Corruption and hypocrisy ought not to be inevitable products of democracy, as they undoubtedly are today.

- *Mahatma Gandhi*

10. Independence of the judiciary is inextricably linked with judicial ethics. An independent judiciary enjoying public confidence is a basic necessity of the rule of law. Any conduct on the part of a judge, which demonstrates a lack of integrity and dignity, will undermine the trust reposed in the judiciary by the citizens. The conduct of a judge should, therefore, always be above reproach.

"A judiciary independent of a king or executive alone is a good thing; but independence of the will of the nation is a solecism, at least in a republican government".

- *Thomas Jefferson*

11. The Law Commission in its 195th Report, examined the draft Judges (Inquiry) Bill, 2005. It stated: Judicial independence is not absolute. Judicial independence and accountability are two sides of the same coin. The present proposals in the Bill of 2005 together with our recommendations for enabling the Judicial Council to impose 'minor measures' including stoppage of assignment of judicial work are

constitutional. They ought not to be viewed as an encroachment on Judicial Independence by the Executive or by the Legislature.

The internal vigilance and departmental action : There is a perception that public services have largely been exempted from the imposition of the penalties due to complicated procedures that have arisen out of the constitutional guarantee against the arbitrary and motivated actions. The people who abuse public office for private gain at the cost of the public and national interest are being shielded from facing swift and stringent punishments. There is a feeling that the protection given to the public servants under Art. 311 of the Constitution of India is being used to create obstacles for expeditious punitive action. A huge body of jurisprudential precedents have further complicated the issue resulting in the distortion of real intent of the provision itself. There is a need for rationalisation and simplification of procedures to prevent the corrupt and dishonest elements in the system from cornering the benefit of the constitutional safeguards.

12. Out of 153 cases for sanction, 21 cases were pending for more than three years, 26 cases between 2-3 years, 25 between 1-2 years. The departmental enquiries are soft-pedalled either out of patronage, or misplaced compassion.

    Good governance: The fight against corruption calls for multi-pronged strategy as the problem is essentially systemic. It is important that those vested with power are made accountable and their functioning is made more transparent. Social Audit through empowered, autonomous and credible citizen groups is another way by which the check on corruption at cutting edge level is to be attempted. The system need to be fine tuned to make it easy for a honest, upright, committed public servant to take bold decisions quickly and to make it difficult for the self serving public servants to indulge in loot of the public money and aggrandize his personal wealth. If there is an effective solution to the menace of corruption it is good governance and it alone can help restore the credibility of the State and to win back the confidence of people in our public institutions. A major part of a good governance system is an efficient, effective and fair criminal justice system.

13. Abraham Lincoln, said:- "I see in the near future a crisis approaching that unnerves me and causes me to tremble for the safety of my country...an era of corruption in high places will follow, and the

moneypower of the country will endeavour to prolong its reign by working upon the prejudices of the people until the wealth is aggregated in a few hands and the Republic is destroyed.

14. The views evolved in UN Economic and Social Commission for Asia and the Pacific are almost identical. It holds that "Good Governance has eight major characteristics. It is participatory, consensus oriented, accountable, transparent, responsive, effective and efficient, equitable and inclusive and follows the rule of law. It assures that corruption is minimized, the view of minorities are taken into account and that the voices of the most vulnerable in society are heard in decision-making. It is also responsive to the present and future needs of society." While we all know that cancer of corruption has seeped into the blood stream of our polity, the million dollar question that stares us in the face is what can be done other than what we have been doing in the name of combating this evil all along. If a part of human body suffers from gangrene, doctors might advise surgery. When gangrene spreads to all nooks and corners, probably surgical amputation cannot be the mode of management. The punitive methods in the form of criminal law on corruption and disciplinary action for breach of conduct rules of the public servants on one hand and preventive measures in the form of pro-active vigilance on the other may need to be strengthened and the loopholes plugged. But, to my mind, this may not suffice. As history shows, unscrupulous elements have always been one step ahead of the law. We need to do something over and above law enforcement.

15. I was heading the 2nd Administrative Reforms Commission constituted by Government of India and the 4th Report submitted by the Commission dealt exclusively with the issue of ethics in governance including issues related to anti-corruption strategies. We had looked at the whole gamut of issues related to ethics, in public life, legal frameworks, institutional framework, social infrastructure, systemic reforms and international cooperation. We had made host of recommendation for electoral reforms including certain amendment to the Representation of Peoples Act – 1951 which have also been recommended by UN Convention against Corruption, establishment of watchdog agencies like *Lokpal* and *Lokayukta*, appointments to constitutional and statutory bodies, anti-defection measures, code of conduct for people occupying public offices, code of conduct for all professionals etc.

16. We had specifically looked at the way anti-corruption law has evolved in India in the post-independence period. The issue of collusive bribery was also looked into in great detail. The Sec. 24 of the Prevention of Corruption Act, 1988 provides protection to the victims of corruption in a bribery case. However, in a collusive corruption, there is no victim, both bribe giver and the bribe taker are the beneficiaries at the cost of public exchequer. Our inability to deal with such crimes undermines the efficacy of the anti-corruption regime.

    Therefore, an offence could be classified as collusive bribery if the outcome or the intended outcome of the transaction leads to a loss to the State, public or public interest. We need to consider legislative changes in contract laws, protection of witnesses, corruption by foreign and international public organisations, confiscation of assets on the lines of UN Convention against Corruption. All this will help in curbing collusive corruption. These are some of the issues which need greater debate and scrutiny.

17. You are aware that India is a signatory to the UN Convention against Corruption. To ratify the same, there is requirement for certain changes in existing rules and procedures which can be brought about only be suitable legislations. In this regard I shall like to make a special mention of Articles 6 & 36 of the Convention. These articles require that Preventive and Specialized Investigation anti-corruption bodies/ authorities need to be established and that they should have necessary independence so that they are able to carry out their functions without any undue influence. In order to fully comply with these articles, the State Anti-Corruption Organisations and CBI have to be made functionally autonomous/independent by removal of provisions such as pre-enquiry permissions [under section 6A of DSPE Act and Vigilance Manuals of State Governments], prosecution sanctions [section 19 of Prevention of Corruption Act, 1988], power to file appeals, engagement of counsels, budgetary resources and appropriate training, etc. We also look forward to a stage when even private sector will be brought within the ambit of anti-corruption agencies as envisaged in the UN Convention against corruption.

18. A host of initiatives have been taken by Government of India for administrative reforms, *e-governance*, restructuring of democratic institutions, reengineering of processes to minimize the opportunities for corruption and to strengthen the democratic institutions. The enactment of the Right to Information Act, 2005 to bring greater

transparency in governmental functioning, enactment of the CVC Act, 2003 for the independent functioning of the Central Vigilance Commission, setting of Serious Fraud Investigation Office for the investigation of serious corporate frauds, appointment of Ombudsmen for various sectors etc. are some of the examples. However, there is an urgent need for the strengthening of anti-corruption regime in the country. A comprehensive study of sect oral spread of corruption, innovative modus operandi adopted by the corrupt public servant in collusion with outsiders and devising suitable strategy to deal with the same is necessary for effectively combating corruption.

19. Another issue of great concern is the huge pendency of cases in various courts including the Appellate Courts. Indian judiciary is known for its independence, quality jurisprudence and its commitment for upholding the fundamental rights of the people. However, delays in trials lead to a general perception that the corrupt continue to hold official power despite criminal cases pending against them.

20. The delivery of expeditious and qualitative justice is important for strengthening the rule of building a fair, just and equitable society. The judicial system need to be strengthened to cope with the pressure of the pendency of cases and capacity building in terms of manpower, training, material resources, technology, specialisation etc. should be our priority for meeting the emerging challenges. There are a large number of vacancies at all levels of judiciary. The State governments and the High Courts need to work in co-ordination for the immediate filling up of vacancies. It is extremely important to attract young and talented persons to the judicial profession so as to bring in a new work ethics in its functioning. The use of information technology in the record keeping, listing and allocation of cases etc. is extremely important for bringing in speed and transparency in the functioning of the courts. The computerisation of the Supreme Court of India and a large number of High Courts of States has been completed. However, a lot needs to be done for the computerisation of trial courts and subordinate courts as the highest pendency of cases are in these courts. The other options of Alternative Dispute Resolution Methods such as, *Lok Adalats*, Mediation, Negotiated Settlements, and Arbitration etc. need to be pursued vigorously for reducing the pendency. The Criminal Procedure Code-1973 has been amended for making provisions for Plea Bargaining which need to be made popular among the judiciary, law practitioners and contending parties.

The Govt. of India has enacted the Grama Nyalaya Act, 2008 providing for setting up of *Panchayat* Level courts for expeditious dispute resolution at the grass-root level which can help in bringing down pendency in the trial courts and to achieve greater social harmony in our villages. The government is one of the biggest contributor to litigations and hence, our Government is proposing a National Policy on Litigation so as to limit the scope of the litigation to essential issues involving questions of law and of great public interest. Our Govt. is resolved to strengthening the physical and human resources of the judicial system as we believe that "Investment in Judiciary is investment in business/ economic development of the country". We are pursuing the matter of greater financial allocation for the Judiciary with Planning Commission and have also been urging/promoting the various State Govts. for creating the necessary physical infrastructure.

21. Paolo Mauro's study indicates that high levels of corruption are associated with lower levels of investment as a share of the GDP in a cross-section of the countries studied. Mauro demonstrates that countries with high levels of corruption invest very little in human capital and in particular, investment in education is only minimal. This is because education provides fewer opportunities for corruption when compared to other types of more capital intensive public spending such as infrastructure and defence. Knack and Keefer's study shows that high levels of corruption mean reduced investment, a lack of credible guarantees of property and contract rights, and poor institutionalisation of the government. A study by Shang-Jin Wei linking corruption to international investment proves that corruption acts like a tax on foreign direct investment. While a one point increase in the tax rate reduces FDI by 5 per cent, an increase in the corruption level from that of Singapore to Mexico is the equivalent of 32 percentage point increase in the tax rate. In another study, a one standard deviation (2.4) improvement in the corruption index is associated with over a 4-percentage point increase in the investment rate and half a percentage increase in the annual growth rate of per capita GDP.

22. I was told that you have discussed various issues such as, legal constraints regarding sanction for prosecution, stay on trial proceedings and appreciation of electronic evidence etc. in the various sessions held during the seminar. You must have also deliberated on

various issues related to the reasons for delay in investigation, trial of cases, poor rate of conviction and strategies to overcome the same. There are 9310 cases of Central Bureau of Investigation pending before various courts and more than 2000 cases are pending for more ten-years. A large number of these cases are against dis-honest and corrupt public servants and their associates who have allegedly played havoc with the system in their pursuit of self-aggradisation. The delay in the trial of these cases essentially means delay in effective action against the corrupt elements and relief to the ordinary citizens of this country who are victims of corruption. Therefore, the law officers appearing in these cases need to make all out efforts for overcoming the legal hurdles created by the defence advocates. A co-ordinated effort is needed on the part of the police officers, law officers and the judicial officers to secure early disposal of the cases. Govt. of India proposes to set up 71-new CBI courts for dealing with the cases investigated by the Central Bureau of Investigation and I am sure these additional courts will help in expediting the trial of anti-corruption cases. The impact of anti-corruption efforts of the Govt. will be felt, if the cases are registered and trial is completed in a time frame of 2 to 3 years. A coordinated effort on the part of all the stakeholders in the system will lead to effective anti-corruption interventions and help building good governance. Moreover, it is important that even as petty cases are solved, the big fishes should not escape punishment. There should be zero tolerance for corruption.

23. Apart from this, I would suggest the following Reforms to Curb Corruption:

    (a) The scope of Prevention of Corruption Act should be widened to include:

    - Gross perversion of the Constitution and democratic institutions amounting to willful violation of the oath of office;
    - Abuse of authority by unduly favoring or harming someone
    - Obstruction of justice;
    - Squandering public money; and
    - Collusive bribery.

    (b) The Corrupt Public servants (Forfeiture of Property) Bill as suggested by the Law Commission should be enacted without further delay.

(c) Steps should be taken for immediate implementation of the Benami Transactions (Prohibition) Act, 1988.

(d) There should be statutory protection for whistle-blowers and victim protection.

(e) A multi-member *Lok Pal* at the national level and *Lok Ayuktas* at the State level should be set up under the Constitution.

(f) False Claims Act should be enacted.

(g) Article 311 of the Constitution may be repealed along with the Article 310 and legislation should be passed under Article 309 to provide for the terms and conditions of service of public servants including necessary protection against arbitrary action.

(h) Prior sanction should not be necessary for prosecuting a public servant who has been trapped red-handed, or found in possession of assets disproportionate to known sources of income.

24. The focus should be on *e-governance* and systematic change. An honest system of governance will displace dishonest persons. As Gladstone so aptly said, "The purpose of a government is to make it easy for people to do good and difficult to do evil". We always find alibi for our lapses by quoting trespass from other democratic institutions, by resorting to a blame game. The executive/ civil services blame interference by the political executive or legislatures and *vice versa*; legislators blame the judiciary and *vice versa*–the main problem lies in each one leaving the space for the others to occupy. If any one of the democratic institution leaves space, the mafia or extra-constitutional authority occupies that space. Realisation of its own authority and discharging its sphere of responsibility, developing accountability and responsiveness are the real solutions to the conflicting situations of eroding democratic polity.

I would like to quote here an ancient *subhashit* (good message):

"Rivers do not drink their waters themselves, nor do trees eat their fruit, nor do the clouds eat the grains raised by them. The wealth of the noble is used solely for the benefit of the others"

25. I will await the recommendations of this National Seminar, I promise to extend all help and cooperation from my Ministry for the implementation of the recommendations. Our Government is committed to strengthening the Criminal Justice System. I once again congratulate Director, Central Bureau of Investigation and Director,

NICFS for organising this conference, which has provided a platform for exchange of ideas between investigators, prosecutors and judiciary.

References

1. Director, Central Bureau of Investigation.
2. Director, NICFS.
3. The Corrupt Public servants (Forfeiture of Property) Bill.
4. Central Bureau of Investigation.
5. Prevention of Corruption Act, 1984.
6. Grama Nyalaya Act, 2008.
7. Constitution of India, J.N. Pandey.
8. Right to Information Act, 2005.
9. CVC Act, 2003.
10. UN Convention against Corruption.

20

Barriers of Communication and Management Communication

Devdas Saket Scholar, Prof. Skay Lamb Toofan, Dr. Abdul Hakim

Introduction

Communication is the passing of information and understanding from one person to another. It is a sharing of meaning and is the process by which managers teach other to manage their work. Since managers work through other, all of their management acts pass through the bottle neck of communication. One person can initiate the process but he cannot complete it, i.e. a communication is complete only when the person received it. The purpose of communication is to supply the information necessary to those to whom it is conveyed for better job performance and active co-operative, i.e., to develop the skill and the will to work. If the message, decision etc., are efficiently and effectively communicated, the magement function also can be executed effectively and effeciently. No organisation exists without communication network.

Communication is a two way traffic. Not only the management communicates the messages and decisions to the sub-ordinates but sub-ordinates too can communicate their problems, demands, report of job performance etc., to the mangement. So it is a process of interacting and understanding each other in the organisation. It is an essential part of the management function to know what is going on in the organisation and what type of behaviour. The work force can meet the organisational objectives and then take necessary decisions corresponding to such behaviour. Likewise workers also expect a right type of behaviour from the management and they also expect that they and their work should be recognised and their problems should be tackled amicably. All these are possible only through an efficient system of communication.

Communication from management to workers is a downward communication and from workers to management may be called upward communication. communication may be oral or written. Communication is made through communication symbols, i.e., language, pictures and action (including body language).

Normally, recived translate the meaning of the message from communication symbols.

Definition

Communication is the nervous system of an organisation. It keeps the members of organisation informed about the internal and external happenings relevant to the task and interest. The success of an organisation depends very much upon the co-ordinated efforts of people working at different levels to achieve the common goal, only effiective communication can integrate thoughts and efforts of the people. Without communication the very existence of the organisation is in danger. It is a managerical skill based upon human behaviour.

Communciation is a process of passing information and understadning from one person to another. Communication is a system through which two or more person come to exchange ideas and understanding among themselves. In otherwords, communication means the imparting, conveying, or exchange of deas, knowledge etc., whether by speech, writing, or signs.

The term commincation is derived from the Latin word. *Communis* that means 'common' and thus if a person affects communication he has established a common ground of understanding. Literally, communication means to inform, to tell, to show, or to spread information. Thus, communication may be interpreted as an interchange of thought ot information to bring about understanding and confindence for food industrial relations. It brings about unity of purpose, interest and efforts in an organisation.

- Wibur Schramn has said that "the essence of communication is getting the receiver and the sender 'tuned together for a particular message".
- Louis A. Allen has said "Communication is the sum of all the things one person does when he wants to create understanding in the mind of another. It is a bridge of meaning. It involves a systematic and continous process of telling, listening and understanding."
- According to Koontz and O'Donnell, "Communication is a way in which one organisation members shares meaning and understadning with another."

- According to C.G. Brown "Communication is the transfer of infromation from one person to another, whether or not it elicits confidence. But the infromation transferred must be understandable to the receiver."
- D.E. Mc Farland has said, "Communication may be broadly defined as the process of meaningful interaction among human beings. More specifically, it is the process by which meaning are perceived and understadnings are reached among human beings."

To conclude from the abvoe definitions communication does not merely mean sending or receiving message. It is much more than that. It includes proper understadning of the message, it acceptance and action on it. In the broadest sence, communication refers to the whole process of man's life in relation to the group and includes an exchange of infromation, a system of communicating and a process by which meaning are exchanged anmong human beings.

Principal Barriers of Comunication

Physical Barrier or Personal barriers	Socio-Psychological	Organisational barriers	Semantic Barriers	Mechanical barriers	Miscellaneous barriers

Intoduction

When a message is sent by the sender to the receiver, it may be possible that it may not be effectively understood by the receiver in the same sense as the sender intended it to. There are several reasons for its ineffectiveness. The message may not reach the receiver at all or some problems may arise in its encoding and decoding or communication channel may be wrong or defective and there may be noise in the channel or there may be several personal reasons.

The barriers to communication in an organiusations are as follows:

- Physical barriers.
- Socio-Phychological or Personal barriers.
- Organisational barriers.
- Semantic barriers.
- Mechanical barriers.
- Miscellaneous barriers.

Physical Barriers

This is envirnonmental factor which obstructs or reduces the sending and receiving of communication. It includes physical, distracting noises and other interferences. Communication of message becomes difficult as the physical distance increase.

Personal, Or Socio-psychological Barriers

Personal barriers arise from motives, attitudes, judgement, emotions and social values of people which may create psychological distance. Siomilar to physical distance psychological distance prevents the communication, or cause misinterpretation.

Persons differ in their motives, attitudes, or sentiments. A person may be unaware of his motives, attitudes, or sentiments, or there may be problems in encoding and decoding other's sentiments, attitudes and motives and therefore interpersonal perceptions, or interpersonal emotions may cause breakdown because each perceives the things in the light of his own experiences, prejudices and thinking. The interests of people differ and so their attitude. A problem may be important for one person but may carry no weight for another.

It has been seen that sometimes it so happens that the ideas, questions, attitudes, feelings etc., of other party present an obstacle to his own personal goal. In the absence of adequate selfconfidence, or for fear of relation one restrains the expression of his true wants and needs. When we think of a person to be fool, any message from him is locked upon only in that sprit.

Division of people into classes, castes and communities also affects communication of ides and view points. In an organisation dominated by people of certain cases or communities, these belonging to minority group may have less opportunities of being heard. Viewpoints may differ and so organisation and communication suffers. Productivity, for example, may be looked from profit of view by mangers and from wages point of view by workers and trade unions. An executive may be harsh enough not to hear and accept other viewpoint whether right or wrong. Thus, acceptability and creditability of messages are subject to several mental and social barriers.

Organisational Barriers

Hierarchical structure promotes downward communication. Since there are several layerism on this structure, the chances of information being filtered are there. An information received from top may not reach the bottom in the same shape, or reverse may happen. The manager in between these two ends act as communication filters and communication prisms. They may colour the information. Generally, the possibility of filtering the information is there when he decides to pass on only a part of the infromation received from the below or above and in this way he may deprive people at the bottom of the wishes of the executives at the top and similarity may keep the top executive in dark from the happenings at the lowest level.

Sometimes, the manager diverts the information, meant for one person, or group to another. For example a message meant for personnel manager, is spent direct to personnel officer on account of which personnel manager is put to an awkward situation. Thus, manager may reflect or deflect a message.

Further, the manager may also colour the infromation. Sometimes, intentionally with a view to twist the situation in his favour, or sometimes it is out of situation. It is also possible than an offer may quote his sub-ordinate wrongly, or may tell something against him before his boss just to spoil the carrier of the sub-oridnate, or his chance of promotion or his image in the eyes of the boss.

Next, status is also a barrier of communication in a formal organisation. An executive in the middle of management hierarchy, may worry so much about what his senior, bosses are thinking and pay minimum attention to the thoughts of his juniors or sub-ordinates. The sub-ordinates are reluctant to communicate anything which their boss does not like or may have 'Negative effect' on their relationship. Dislike, distrust, dissatisfaction with jon and work environment are other reasons for deluctance to tell anything to their bosses. H. Kelly discovered a few interesting effects of status upon communication as follows:

- Low Status members communicate more task irrelevant information than high status members.
- High status person appear to be restrained from communicating criticism, negative attitudes, or confusion about their own job to those of lower status.
- Communication with high status persons tend to servce as a substiture for upward locomotion on the part of low status persons who have little, or no possibility of real upward locomotion organisation interaction and communication are thus influenced by the status and the role expectations. The status barriers may be overcome by creating an environment of trust and confidence in the organisation.
- Poor Supervision aslo serves as a communication barrier. When a supervisor suspects his sub-ordinates or acts as a self-appointed censor, or listens his sub-ordinates with closed minds, the communication is blocked.

Semantic Barriers

Semantic refers to the relationship of signs to their reference. It arises from the limitations of the symbolic system. Symbols may have a number of meaning and we have to select, or choose any of them according to the extent of the text of the communication. For this purpose a distinction is essential between inferences and facts.

Inferences : are an essential part of most communication. We cannot avoid them. Since inferences can give a wrong signal and we should, therefore, be aware of them and appraise them carefully. In case of any doubt more feedback should be sought.

Symbols : May reach a person's brain through any of the senses such as feeling or hearing. Symbols may be calssified as: Language; Pictures; Actions; Body Language.

Language : Words are the principal communication instrument of all employees in verbal as well as in non-verbal communication. Most of the time of managers and other executives is spent in verbal communication. A study of research managers showed that first level supervisors spent 74 per cent of their time in communication. Second level superior spent 81 per cent and the third level supervisor 87 per cent.

Difficulty with language: A major difficulty with language is that nearly every common word has several meaning and unless the context is known to the receiver, he is free to accept any one of them as he chooses.

In a face communication (i.e. verbal) a clarification may be sought if doubts exist about a particular word but it is very difficult in non-verbal communication. Consequently, effective communication are idea-centred, rather than word centred, because communications known that words do not mean people mean. Without context, language is just like a smog that irritates our senses and interferes with out perception.

Pictures : A second type of symbol is pictures. Pictures are visual aids worth thousand words. An organisation uses extensive use of pictures like blueprints, charts, maps, films, three dimentsional models and similar devices. A viewer may come to know the whole story when he sees them.

Sometimes, a picture may create confusion in the mind of an observer and this can done away if pictures are supplemented with well choosen words and actions to tell the whole story.

Action, or Non-verbal Communication : An action is an effective means of communication to the extent it is interpreted by others. To do or not to do both have meaning, for example, if a sub-ordinate wishes 'good morning' to his boss, a smile, or the absence of it, wishining or not wishing in return, both have meaning. In this sense, we do communicate all the time at work whether we intend to do or not.

Further, Action Speaks Lower than Words. If a person says one thing and does another, he will find in the long run that people listen to what he does. This is credibility gap. The more the gap the less seriously, the people will take him and he will lose confidence among his sub-ordinates.

Body Language : Body language is an important part of land supplement to non-verbal communication. People communicate meanings to other with their bodies in interpersonal interaction. Body language means communicating the message with the movement of the whole body, or a part of it. Mostly face and the hands are useful symbols generally used in body language. Examples are eye contact; eye movement, smiles and frawns, touching, furrowed brow, closeness, hip movements, breathing rate and odour.

Machanical Barriers

Mechanical barriers include :

- Inadequate arrangement for transmission of new facts and figurs;
- Poor office layout;
- Defective proceddures and practices; and
- The use of wrong media lead to poor communication.

The above are some of the barriers in effective communication of message. They all vitiate the message in several ways. It may result in message (a) distortion, (b) filtering, and (c) ommission.

- *Distortion* means changing the context of the message or the meaning of the message; whereas *Filtering* means reducing the message only a few basic details; and *Omission* represents deletion of all or part of the message.

We must be careful about these barriers in communicating the message.

Methods to Remove the Barriers of Communication

In order to remove the barriers of communication following steps may be adopted.

- An open door communication policy must be prepared and followed by the managers in the organisation.
- They should also create an atmoshphere of trust and confidence in the organisation so as to fill up the capacity gap.
- No Manager can acquire a passport of credibility unless the facts communicated by him are well understood and accepted by the people concerned.

The communication policy should aim at :

- **Promoting Two Way Communication**: There should be no communication gap. That means communication should folw both ways downward. A sound feedback system should be provided for, so the misunderstanding and distortion of messages cab be avoided.
- **The Communication Network be strengthened**: In order to improve the communication network, procedure of communication should be simplified layers in downward communication should be reduced to the minimum possible, decentralisation and delegation of authority should be reduced to make the informal communication less important through frequent mettings, conferences and timely dissemnination of information to the sub-ordinates.
- **Message should be Listener Oriented:** The message must be of interest to the listener. It should be clear, complete, concise, concrete and correct, so that it may be receive and interpreted in the same sense by the receiver.
- **Proper Communication Media be Selected** : The Media of communication should be such selected that the message reached its destination in time, to the right person and in the sense in which it was framed. Hove Land's pursuation model of communication may help the policy-makers in this regard.
- **Organisational Barriers be Removed**: Barriers to communication should be avoided as far as possible. Filtering or twisting of information, bossism and status consciousness should not come in the way of communication. Other barriers such as physical, or socio-psychological, or semantic should be reduced to the extent possible.
- **Promoting Participative Approach** : The management should promote the participative approach in management. Sub-oridnates should be invited to participate in the decision-making process. It will seek co-operation and reduce many communication barriers.

Therefore, a well defined, open door policy of communication covering all the point should be followed in the organisation to promote the cohensiveness oridnate.

MANAGEMENT COMMUNICATION

Introduction

Communication within the management group is called management communication. Management at different levels play different roles that also affect communication partners. As the management is to explain organisational policies, preactices and programmes further to their sub-ordinates, they are supposed to know these policies etc. beforehand from the top management.

Inspite of many barriers among people and group in the organisation one of the bais proposition of organisational behaviour is that open communication is better than the restricted communication. So, Communication among various groups should be tried to improve wherever possible.

Definition

Communication within the management group (from board of directors to supervisor) is called management communication or intra-management communication. This aspect of communication is important because if managers at different levels remain uncommunicated, they are not supposed to explain the policies and practices of the organisation to their sub-ordinate employees.

Importance of Management Communication

Management Communicationshould be emphasised and encouraged due to the following reasons:

- **It is pre-requisite to employee communication :** Management Communication is prerequisite to communication with the operating workers. The main responsbility of the managers and supervisors at all levels is to communicate the message to the employees sub-ordinate to them. Top management expect supervisors to interpret and explain the plans, policies etc. to the workers but they fall to explain the plan to the supervisors so the supervisors remian unsuccessful in explaining it to the workers, inspite of the fact that they have sufficient papers explaining the plan remians either unimplemented or badly implemented.
- **It is necessary for sound decvision :** Decision-making is one of the functions of the management. Though they are quite isolated as regards to performance, but they are served as a competent decision centres only to the extent that they develop suitable information channel. Many of these channels must be within the mangement group. If the management communication channels are not appropriate sound decisions are not expected.
- **If has greater scope of managerial influence :** Another reason for emphasising management communication is that they cover greater area of influence, than that of workers. Inadequate information to managers affect a broad area of performance (i.e. productivity,

profitability and morale) because they influence many persons and activities within the organisation.

- **Various links in communication chain are within management group:** If we study communication chain in detail we will be able to know that there are five links in the communication chain from top to bottom and from bottom to top. Four links out of five are in management group and only one link, i.e. between supervisor and operative employee is outside the management group. Each link has an equal opportunity to distort, fade, or make delay the communication. Thus, the greater proportion of these problem are intra management. When the communication chain is long, so effective management communication is necessary for the effective employee communication upward and downward. Communication chain may be depicted in the following figure.
- **Communication for self :** For self-management itself communication is necessary because they are also employee of the organisation and need proper communication like any other person in the organisation.

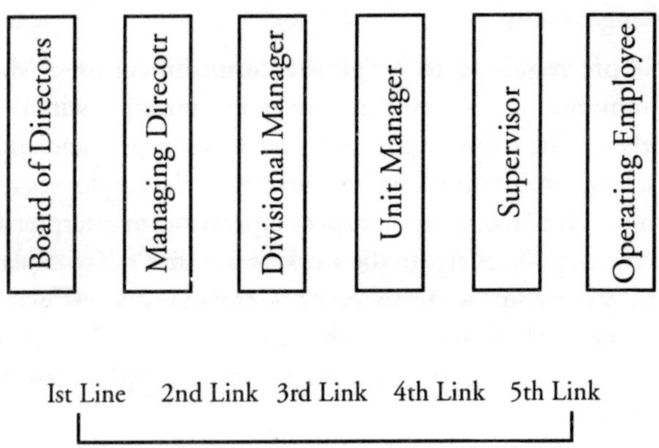

4 Links in Management Group
Most Links in Communication Chain are within the management

Methods within management for improving communication system

- **Committee, Conference, Board etc. :** In order to improve the flow of management information, managers who are generally the members of various boards, committees, conferences and meetings should represent their department in such committees etc. and discuss different common problems relating to the organisation or their department.

- **Written Communication like Bulletin, News leter etc. :** Many organisation have deloped special written communication for their management people through newsletter, bulletins and special booklets to keep their managers well informed of the policies, practices, services and products of the organisation, Some employees have a practice to provide copies of their magazines before general release so that they may come to know their contents well in advance.
- **Conferences Outside the Place of Job or Business:** In order to have better management communication some organisation's conferences at locations away from their work just to avoid work interference on a particular subject. Sometimes some distinguished person is called upon to initiate the debate. It is a good method for inter-organisation communication.

Thus management communication must be improved to have a better understanding of the polices and practices of the organisation and to convey such polices etc. to the operating employees in an effective manner.

21

The Positive Aspect of Media in Indian Democracy

Sandhya Singh

Introduction

"The popular media of the modern world is the place where and the means by which the public is created and has its being". This line shows that the media are an indispensible agent of development in any nation given there in valuable contribution to our governance as a watch dog and partner in progress with the arms of government. This paper is described the positive and important role of media in our Indian democracy.

Media places a crucial role in shaping a healthy democracy. It is the backbone of a democracy which makes us aware of various social, poltical and economic activities happening around the world. Media is just like a mirror, which shows, or strives us the base of truth and harsh reality of life.

As the largest democracy, India is considered a role model for a large no. of developing countries. We have a state and central government elected by the people. We have a government which is run by our own elected representatives, known as members of legislative assembly (MLAs) in the state and the members of parliament (MPs) at the centre.

Modern democratic government has the following components:

1. **A legislative:** State assemblies and parliament responsible for framing laws and decide the way we run our affairs.
2. **An executive:** The President, prime minister and council of ministers the Governer, and the CM etc. who run the country.
3. **A judiciary:** The Supreme Court and high court, decide laws and the constitutional provisions are followed by the elected government.

These institutions run the government of the country for the welfare and development of all the people. In a democracy the people should know what the three institution namely the legislative, the executive and the judiciary are doing for the welfare of the people. The main role of the media is to act as a bridge between the people and government and also media is a key role in democratic governance has been recognised since the late seventeenth century and remains the fundamental principle of modern day democratic theory and practice. So, that media can be considered as the fourth institution and also referred to as the fourth branch of government because of the power they and the right they exercise.

The Role of Media in Democracy

The role of the media in democracy must include the following:

1. Media provide a forum through which the governed could then react to government policies and activities.
2. Media assist in the articulation and pursuit of the nation's interest.
3. Media helps strengthen the economic, social and political fabric of the nation.
4. Media provide informed criticism and viable alternatives to public policies.
5. Media functions as an agent of modernisation.
6. Media provide such analysis as would enable the people to secure and adequate understanding and background to events.

To achieve these ends, the media must be seen and must itself perform as an agent of development and nations building.

Impact of Media

The tremendous positive impact of the media on people is as follows:

1. It provides laws and information required by the people.
2. Media can educate the whole public in the society.
3. Media helps in democracy functions effectively. They inform the public about government policies and programmes and also tell them how these programs can be useful to them.
4. Media can entertain people.
5. Media can bring in positive social changes in society.
6. Media can act as an agent of change in development.
7. Media has brought people of the world closer to each other.
8. Media promotes trait and industry through advertisement.
9. Media can also help in the political at democratic processes of the country.

10. Media has also helpful to make our society in a democracy by placing emphasis on issues that at one point in time could have been considered strictly private such as child birth, homosexuality, child care, domestic violence and sexual harrashment.

Functions and Responsibilities of the Media:

Media is a tremendous source of information for individuals as well as society. Let us see how the media perform their functions to bring about the changes.

1. **Media have made the world smaller and closer:**

The spirit of media has resulted in bringing people across the world closer. We also heard the term "global village". It means that the whole world is shrinking and becoming a village. Wherever we go to any part of the world, we see the products such as soft drinks, television, washing machine and refrigerator, and the same other types of advertisement. Similarly the world wide web and internet have brought people and countries much closer.

2. **Media is source of information:**

A truely democratic society requires citizen participation, if they do their jobs well; the media keeps citizens engaged in the business of governance and prompt to take action. Media is highlighting the people problems in front of the government and taking feedback from the government upon social and safety issues of the nation in terms of nation's welfare.

As a tool for information dissemination, the media aid the public in making inform choices, such as who to vote for and which policies should be endorsed and which oppose. Ideally newspaper and the public affairs programmes on radio and television should inform, educate and engage the public.

3. **Media promotes distribution of goods:**

Media are used by the consumers industry to inform people about their products and services through advertising. Without advertising, the public not know about various products and services (banking, insurance, hospital etc.) which are available in the market as well as their prices. Thus, media help the industries and consumers.

4. **Media's role creation of public opinion in democracy:**

In an uneducated democracy public opinion has to be generated and some agency is requiring to do work. An instrument of mass communication can serve the requirement of effective mobilisation of national opinion. This is the only way for a democracy can survive.

5. Media constitute powerful socialisation:

Media constitute powerful socialisation arenas for young people in contemporary society. The fact that media are embedded in most parts of young people everyday's life. It also place an important role in political socialisation or more precisely in the development in civic identities, political orientations, values, skills and patterns of political participation in the period from adolescence to young adult hood.

6. Leadership role of media in democracy:

The media don't only agitate or draw attention to the bad policies of the government but also draws support for the positive initiative of government in India. The efforts of the press are leading to incredible government policy and the other government programmes. The media support for the fight against corruption by exposing the highly placed politicians and government officials in todays government are indication of its leadership role in democracy.

7. Media as a watch dog in democracy:

The canine metaphor of the media as a watch dog is an indication of its watchful role in any government. The media not only serve as a watchdog but guides the government towards change.

With in this contest, this paper examines the role of media have played well in the socio-political and socio-economic reengineering of structures in a country faced with enormous problems as an emergent democracy.

CONCLUSION

After analysing the role of media in our democratic society, we here come to the conclusion that all these years since its establish the media has revolved the progress and development of our country. All its contribution is seen in a fully fledged democratic Indian society. Now media is creating a tremendous interest in promoting democratic values and principals. If this continues this process, India can fulfills its dream to be developing nation by 2020.

References

1. "Democracy"-Encyclopedia of Britannica.
2. Defination- BBC History of democracy (History learning site: democracy)
3. *Role of media in a democracy* an essay of UPSC examination (IAS).
4. Dutta, Somya, Social Rasponsibility of Indian Democracy, *Global Media Jaurnal,* Indian edition, July 2011.

22

Issue of Street Children: Role of Government and NGOs and Coverage by Media

Dr. Ambrish Saxena and ***Rajshree Chatterjee***

22.1 STREET CHILDREN: THE INDIAN SCENARIO

Street children are a worldwide phenomenon and the number of these children has been increasing. These are the runaway children who struggle for their survival. In India, the situation is grimmer than other countries. So, there is a need of conducting study on their status, and also the role of media in this regard.

22.1.1 *DEFINING STREET CHILDREN*

"*Street children*" is a term often used to describe both *market children* (who work in the streets and markets of cities selling or begging, and live with their families) and homeless children (who work, live and sleep in the streets, often lacking any contact with their families). At highest risk is the latter group. Murder, consistent abuse and inhumane treatment are the "norm" for these children, whose ages range from six to 18. They often resort to petty theft and prostitution for survival. They are extremely vulnerable to sexually transmitted diseases including HIV/AIDS.

UNICEF has defined three types of street children: Street-Living, Street-Working, and Street-Family.

Street Living Children: Children who ran away from their families and live alone on the streets.

Street Working Children: children who spend most of their time on the streets, fending for themselves, but returning home on a regular basis.

Children from Street Families: children who live on the streets with their families.

22.1.2 STUDYING PROBLEM OF STREET CHILDREN

The research methodology of this paper is based on content analysis and secondary data reference has been made like news reports of the online paper *The Hindu* and some other news reports. The parameters of the selection of news reports are the role and responsibility of NGOs and government.

22.1.3 STREET CHILDREN IN INDIA

India is home to the world's largest population of street children, estimated at 18 million. Street children are the one who run away from home or the one who stay with their family in the streets because of poor conditions. However, it further create problems like child labour, prostitution and are subject to malnutrition, hunger, health problems, abuse, theft, sexual and physical exploitation and harassment by authorities.

The maximum percentage of street children work like rag picking, vending, taking care of animals, assisting in shops, hotels, restaurants and domestic labor as a common means of earning a livelihood in order to feed themselves. The street children, who are at such a tender age, are forced to work and they never get the chance to get formal education of any kind. In India, still the male offspring is always the desired choice for parents and in some cases the girl child is forced to leave the house and they live on their own these actions lead to prostitution and these girls are often use for trafficking as well.

Another area of concern is the poor health of the street children, as half of all the children in India are malnourished, and this percentage is even higher in case of street children. Because of the unhygienic conditions, poor health and improper medical facility they are prone to all kinds of life threatening diseases, which results in higher mortality rate.

Street children in India may be homeless because their family is homeless through poverty or migration, or because they have been abandoned, orphaned or have run away. The children sleeping around the railway station, streets and near garbage areas are at high risk of suffering addiction, abuse and illness.

The government has taken initiatives in this regard to ensure the welfare of such children, and so have many NGOs. However, unless the masses start to see the problem as a serious one, all these would be rendered ineffective.

Estimates claim that Delhi's streets house between 100,000 and 500,000 of these children. Their fragile future hangs even more precariously on the edge, now more than ever- with the Commonwealth Games around the corner the Government has identified 18 'zero-tolerance zones' for beggars, a majority of who are children.

Working street children are most vulnerable to exploitation and abuse. Employers force these children to work for long hours, without food, without providing any safety equipment, and for very low wages as the children are not aware of their rights. Studies have shown that boys and girls on the street are particularly vulnerable to sexual abuse by strangers, adult street dwellers and at times by the police too.

Using the statistics of Consortium of Street Children, a sample survey of street children was done to understand their living conditions. Thirty-nine per cent of the street children slept in slums, 46 per cent in open, or public places and only four per cent slept in shelters provided by non-governmental organisations, or the government. Nearly 22 per cent of those surveyed said they used drugs, largely tobacco and pan masala.

Only a small percentage of children had access to some form of identity proof. Considering that most street children are from the poorest communities who have largely migrated to urbane centres as a survival strategy, they should be given some identity proof that the government accepts as an entitlement document and allows then get admitted in schools.

- UNICEF's estimate of 11 million street children in India is considered to be a conservative figure. The Indian Embassy has estimated that there are 314,700 street children in metros such as Bombay, Calcutta, Madras, Kanpur, Bangalore and Hyderabad and around 100,000 in Delhi alone.
- A survey among 100 street children at the New Delhi Railway Station in India revealed that 86 per cent of boys in the age group 14-18 years were sexually active; however a very low number of them knew about safe sex protection and condom usage. Not one of them reported having ever used a condom.

A study in 2007 in India found the following:

- 65.9% of the street children lived with their families on the streets. Out of these children, 51.84 per cent slept on the footpaths, 17.48% slept in night shelters and 30.67 per cent slept in other places including under flyovers and bridges, railway platforms, bus stops, parks, market places.
- The overall incidence of physical abuse among street children, either by family members or by others or both, was 66.8 per cent across the states. Out of this, 54.62 per cent were boys and 45.38 per cent were girls.

- On a study in India, out of the total number of child respondents reporting being forced to touch private parts of the body, 17.73 per cent were street children. 22.77 per cent reported having been sexually assaulted.

The difference in their future makes the issue relevant now, it is time for society to understand what the Delhi Government's efforts are for these children, time for our Government to analyse how well they are doing what they are supposed to be doing and whether what they are doing is enough.

22.2. STREET CHILDREN: CAUSES AND IMPLICATIONS

22.2.1 MAJOR CAUSES FOR EMERGENCE OF STREET CHILDREN

- Broken families/poor and large families/ step parent
- Migrant/ dislocated families living in slum/streets
- Migrant families suffered due famines/natural disaster
- Family conflict
- Physically abused
- Out classed by society
- Refugees
- Orphan
- Deterioration of morals
- Out of schools
- Sexually abused
- Forced to work (in farms, factories, stalls, household and hotels etc.)

22.2.2 IMPLICATIONS ON THE CHILD

- Loss of childhood
- Sexual/ physical abuse
- Destructive mind
- May be used for unlawful activities like terrorism
- Malnutrition and unhygienic appearance
- Drug/Inhalant addict
- Deterioration of values and morals
- Pick pocketing, thefts
- Loss of personal development/ No or less education background
- Health hazards, especially HIV/AIDS
- Police torture and atrocities
- Join labour market with physical, mental and psychological hazards

- Abused by criminals for trafficking of drugs, sex and other unlawful activities.

22.3. CHILD RIGHTS: CONSTITUTIONAL AND LEGAL STATUS IN INDIA

22.3.1 CHILD RIGHTS AS PER INDIAN CONSTITUTION

The Constitution of India has over two hundred statutes that address the child, directly, or indirectly. The fundament right that would make the state responsible for ensuring the care and protection of street children is not intended for children only – It is the Fundamental Right to Life and Personal Liberty, applying to all people, including children. Article 21 of the Constitution, The Right to Life and Personal Liberty, states 'No person shall be deprived of his life or personal liberty except according to procedure established by law.'

The Supreme Court has held time and again that 'life' implies more than just mere existence.

In 1978, the Supreme Court first found in the case of *Maneka Gandhi vs. Union of India* that the right to life provisions must be interpreted as the right to live with dignity.

In 1981, the Supreme Court, interpreting the Right to Life and Personal Liberty in the *Francis C. Mullin vs. Administrator, Union Territory of Delhi* case stated- "We think that the right to life includes the right to live with human dignity and all that goes along with it, namely, the bare necessities of life such as adequate nutrition, clothing and shelter over the head and facilities for reading, writing and expressing oneself in diverse forms, freely moving about and mixing and commingling with fellow human beings."

In the *Bandhua Mukti Morchas vs. Union of India and others,* the Supreme Court again stated- "It is the fundamental right of every one in this country, assured under the interpretation given to Article 21 by this Court in *Francis Mullen's Case,* to live with human dignity, free from exploitation. This right to live with human dignity enshrined in Article 21 derives its life breath from the Directive Principles of State Policy and particularly clauses (e) and (f) of Article 39 and Articles 41 and 42 and at the least, therefore, it must include protection of the health and strength of workers, men and women, and of the tender age of children against abuse, opportunities and facilities for children to develop in a healthy manner and in conditions of freedom and dignity, educational facilities, just and humane conditions of work and maternity relief."

The above judicial interpretations of the Right to Life and Personal Liberty by the Supreme Court imply that children on the street have a fundamental right to ask the State for shelter, food and clothing and also have a right to live without being harassed and exploited.

Article 15 of the Constitution is with regard to 'Prohibition of discrimination on grounds of religion, race, caste, sex, or place of birth' implying and agreeing with the text in article 14 about equality of people before the law.

But clause (3) of Article 15 states that "Nothing in this article shall prevent the State for making any special provision for women and children"; recognising children as a category of people requiring special consideration in our laws. It allows for 'positive discrimination' 16 of children allowing the government to make specials laws for them.

Acts can be passed in Parliament with special reference to children, drawing relevance from Article 15, clause (3). The evolution of these Acts in India is discussed below.

22.3.2 CHILD RIGHTS AS PER LAWS IN INDIA

The Children Act, 1960 was the first major Act in India dealing with street children, initially passed for Union Territories, defined street children as 'neglected' children (including a child found without having any home or settled place of abode or any ostensible means of subsistence or is found destitute, whether he is an orphan or not). Although the Act seemed to be concentrate more towards delinquent children it set the precedent for instruction regarding care of neglected children. The Children Act of 1960 was the first perspective the government took for rehabilitating street children-through institutionalisation; setting a precedent of sorts, for the perspective has not changed majorly in the last 50 years.

The National Policy on Children was formed in 1974. The Policy, recognising that India was a signatory to the UN Declaration of the Rights of the Child, 1959 lays emphasis on child welfare. The following points would apply to street children:

- To ensure equality of opportunity, special assistance shall be provided to all children belong to the weaker sections of the society, such as children belonging to the Scheduled Castes and Scheduled Tribes and those belonging to the economically weaker sections, both in urban and rural areas.
- Children who are socially handicapped, who have become delinquent or have been forced to take to begging or are otherwise in distress, shall be provided facilities of education, training and rehabilitation and will be helped to become useful citizens.

- Children shall be protected against neglect, cruelty and exploitation.

The policy directed the government to give priority to programs relating to 'maintenance, education and training of orphan and destitute children.' The document focused on child welfare, giving no insight on work to be done on protection of child rights as asked for in the Declaration of the Rights of the Child. Also, the policy gave directions for formulation of laws in 'suitable time', thereby implying no timeframe for their formulation.

Even with a policy in place, India still lacked a central act for uniform laws throughout the country for the rehabilitation of street children. A central act could not be created as the subject fell in the State List of the Constitution. It was brought into the Union List and the Juvenile Justice Act, 1986 was passed by Parliament.

In trying to be in accordance with the various agreements signed in the UN about children, particularly the UN Convention on the Rights of the Child, India replaced the Juvenile Justice Act, 1986 with the Juvenile Justice (Care and Protection) Act in 2000.

It was replaced by the Juvenile Justice (Care and Protection Children) Act in 2000.

The Act, which is applicable to the whole of India except the state of Jammu and Kashmir, includes street children in the category of 'children in need of care and protection.'

The Act lays down methods for rehabilitating street children which constitute sending them to children homes, shelter homes. It states that restoration of the child shall be the primary objective of the homes, implying that child should be restored to his/her parents or adopted parents as the case may be.

The Act also has emphasised the role of Non-Governmental Organisation (NGOs) in the process of care for street children.

22.3.3 ISSUE OF CHILD RIGHTS IN DELHI

To give full effect to the provisions of the Act, Juvenile Justice (Care and Protection) Rules, 2007 have been framed by the Centre. Under section 68 of the Act, every State Government has been empowered to frame their own Rules, and until the same are framed by the State Government, the Rules of 2007 would apply.

The Delhi Government has not passed Juvenile Justice Rules to implement the Juvenile Justice (Care and Protection) Act specific to Delhi, so it follows the Juvenile Justice (Care and Protection) Rules laid down by the Central Government. The Delhi Juvenile Justice Rules, 2009 are being prepared.

The duty of implementing the Juvenile Justice (Care and Protection of Children) Act in Delhi lies with the Department of Women and Child Development of the Delhi Government. It was formed on 14th November, 2007 when the Department of Social Welfare was bifurcated into the Department of Social Welfare and the Department of Women and Child Development. The Delhi Government has divided Delhi into four districts to administer these rules. There are four Child Welfare Committees and four District Level Officers in Delhi.

The Child Welfare Committees are quasi-judiciary bodies that have 'the final authority to dispose of cases for the care, protection, treatment, development and the rehabilitation of the children as well as to provide for their basic needs and protection of human rights. The Committees comprise five members (at least one woman) who function as a bench of magistrates. The Committee members are not paid; ensuring people passionate about are a part of the committee.

Street Children can be brought before the Committee by any police officer or the special juvenile police, any public servant, registered NGOs, a social worker or the child himself.

An inquiry is ordered to determine the support system/parents of the child. The inquiry, by a social worker or a child welfare officer has to be completed within four months of the committee ordering it. If the child is found to have 'no family or ostensible support' the child is kept in a children's home. During the period of inquiry however and for a year after if the child is found to have no family or support he/she may be kept in a temporary institution called a shelter home.

The District Level Officers are responsible for inspection of the children and various homes to ensure they conform to the various standards mentioned in the Juvenile Justice Rules.

22.4. ORGANISATIONS WORKING FOR STREET CHILDREN

NGO's have a potential to innovate, to produce and deliver in large scale, it is the most distinctive contribution that Government and Non Government Organisations plays towards the social development and child rights protection. NGO's and Government organisations play a crucial role in development of state provision for social services. Here we will discuss in detail about the various Government and NGO working for the rights, welfare and development of street children in Delhi.

22.4.1 GOVERNMENT ORGANISATIONS

22.4.1.1 *National Child Labour Project (NCLP):* National Policy on Child

Labour was formulated in 1987. The Policy seeks to adopt a gradual and sequential approach with a focus on rehabilitation of children working in hazardous occupations and processes in the first instance. The Action Plan outlined in the Policy for tackling this problem is as follows: Legislative Action Plan, Focusing of General Developmental Programmes for Benefiting Child Labour, Project Based Plan of Action.

22.4.1.2 *Ministry of Women and Child Welfare*: The Department of Women and Child Development was set up in the year 1985 as a part of the Ministry of Human Resource Development to give the much needed impetus to the holistic development of women and children. With effect from 30.01.2006, the Department has been upgraded to a Ministry.

22.4.1.3 *National Human Rights Commission*: The National Human Rights Commission (NHRC) of India is an autonomous statutory body established on 12 October, 1993, under the provisions of The Protection of Human Rights Act, 1993 (TPHRA).

22.4.1.4 *National Commission for Protection of Child Rights*: The National Commission for Protection of Child Rights (NCPCR) was set up in March 2007 under the Commission for Protection of Child Rights Act, 2005, an Act of Parliament (December 2005). The Commission's Mandate is to ensure that all Laws, Policies, Programmes, and Administrative Mechanisms are in consonance with the Child Rights perspective as enshrined in the Constitution of India and also the UN Convention on the Rights of the Child. The Child is defined as a person in the 0 to 18 years age group.

22.4.2 NON GOVERNMENT ORGANISATION

22.4.2.1 *Global March Against Child Labour*: Global March Against Child Labour is an international movement dedicated to giving every child a chance to live and grow without the burden of exploitative work. Global March is a movement to mobilise worldwide efforts to protect and promote the rights of all children, especially the right to receive a free, meaningful education and to be free from economic exploitation and from performing any work. The Global March Against Child Labour is a global movement against child labour. It has partners in over 150 countries and is based in New Delhi, lobby governments and the United Nations, provide training or education on child rights, research child rights, undertake legal casework on behalf of children, work directly with children, work in partnership with organisations, work with media and press. child labour and working children, children and education, children and participation, children and the media, children in armed conflict, gender and girls, rights based programming.

22.4.2.2 *Bonded Labour Liberation Front (BMM) Bandhua Mukti Morcha*: The main aim is to identify adult bonded labour, child bonded labour/child labour, in the various sectors of the economy, liberate them from slavery and follow up their rehabilitation by the government under the laws of the country, lobby governments and the United Nations, undertake legal casework on behalf of children, work with media and the press, children working and living on the street, individual cases of violations, sexual exploitation of children.

22. 4.2.3 *Child Labour Action Network (CLAN)*: The Child Labour Action Network's aim is to contribute to the creation of a society in which all children have equal opportunities for development and that they grow as responsible citizens with a view of co-existence, sustainable development and social justice leading to peace for all, lobby governments and the United Nations, provide training or education on child rights, research child rights, work in partnership with organisations, work with media and press. child labour and working children, children and education, children and health, children and the media, children in armed conflict, children in conflict with the law, children working and living on the street, reporting to and monitoring the CRC, sexual exploitation of children

22.4.2.4 *Foundation for Legal Aid, Environment and Social Action (FELSA)*: FLESA is a non-profit organisation comprised of legal experts, students, and human right activists. The organisation works mainly for the cause of protection of rights of women, children, prisoners, and persons with disabilities. It reaches to the grass-roots movement through its legal aid and advice programmes, lobbies governments and the United Nations, provides training or education on child rights, researches child rights, undertakes legal casework on behalf of children, works directly with children, works in partnership with organisation on child labour and working children, children and education, children and health, children without parental care, children working and living on the street, environment and habitat, sexual exploitation of children.

22.4.2.5 *Grace Action India (GRACE)*: GRACE tuns programmes on education, including for the street children and working children, disabled children, preparatory school for slum and street children, bible club for slum children, adult education for drop out children from school and labour children, multi-religious education, vocational training and social development, provide training or education on child rights, work directly with children, work in partnership with organisations, child labour and working children, children and education, children and health, children living with Hiv/Aids, children with disabilities, children working and living on the street, rights based programming.

22.4.2.6 *HAQ Centre for Child Rights*: HAQ seeks to recognise, protect and promote child rights, and believes that there is a need for realisation of human rights of children through policy, law and action, in particular works with the rights to survival, childhood and equal opportunity, lobbies governments and the United Nations, provides training or education on child rights, researches child rights, undertakes legal casework on behalf of children, works in partnership with organisations, works with media and press, child labour and working children, children and education, children and participation, children and the media, children and violence, children in armed conflict, children in conflict with the law, children without parental care, children working and living on the street, environment and habitat, gender and girls, individual cases of violations, minority or indigenous children, reporting to and monitoring the CRC, rights based programming, sexual exploitation of children

22.4.2.7 *Plan International – India*: Plan has programmes in 61 countries. It began its work in India in 1979, and it is one of the largest international NGOs working in the country. Plan India now works in 11 states in India through numerous partners. Plan reaches out to vulnerable children in remote areas and facilitates development processes that result in increased security for children, their families and communities, funds other organisations, lobbies governments and the United Nations, provides training or education on child rights, researches child rights, works directly with children, works in partnership with organisations, works with media and press, child labour and working children, children and education, children and health, children and participation, children and the media, children in conflict with the law, children living with HIV/AIDS, children with disabilities, children without parental care, children working and living on the street, reporting to and monitoring the CRC, sexual exploitation of children.

22.4.2.8 *Salaam Baalak Trust: Salaam Baalak* Trust provides support for street and working children in inner cities, providing education, basic literacy and schooling, full care facilities for the young (up to 12 years), drop-in shelters, nutrition, health care, family planning, Aids awareness, Tb prevention, counselling, banking facilities and remedial drama. The main aim is to rehabilitate the street child either by returning them home or finding an alternative means of income off the streets. Primary areas of work: Education, Nutrition, Health Care, Family Planning, Aids Awareness, Tb Prevention, Counselling, Remedial Drama.

22.4.2.9 *Social and Development Research and Action Group (SADRAG)*: This organisation conducts action research in development issues in the context of changing economic and socio-cultural variables. The issues would broadly pertain to gender, environment, health, education and micro-credit. It addresses development issues in rural as well as urban areas, study the socio-cultural construct of 'gender' as prevalent and practiced in Indian society, work directly with children. child labour and working children, children and education, children and health, children and participation, children working and living on the street, gender and girls, and rights based programming

22.4.2.10 *CRY: Child Rights and You*: Cry's role is that of an enabler, a catalyst between two groups of people-development organisations and individuals working at grassroots-level with marginalised children, their families and communities. For the past 29 years, CRY has been supporting grassroots-level NGOs that work with children and communities to ensure that all Indian children get the following four basic rights guaranteed to them by the United Nations Charter of Child Rights, 1992.

Right to Survival – to life, health, nutrition, name, nationality
Right to Protection - from exploitation, abuse, and neglect
Right to Development - to education, care, leisure and recreation
Right to Participation - to expression, information, thought, and religion

22.4.2.11 *India Alliance for Child Rights*: This organisation conducts policy advocacy, building Ngo and citizen's coalitions, information sharing on Crc, organise consultations and lobbying, reports to the Committee on the Rights of the Child, contributes to the elaboration of the Npa, does lobbying with governments and the United Nations and reports to and monitors the Crc.

22.4.2.12 *Indian Committee of Youth Organisations (ICYO)*: ICYO is a network organisation working in many areas and particularly in the field of child abuse and exploitation, funds other organisations, provide training or education on child rights, works directly with children, works in partnership with organisations. Focus area: Sexual exploitation of children.

22.5. WORKING PATTERN BETWEEN GOVERNMENT AND NGOs

The Delhi Government gives financial assistance to recognised Ngos to run Children Homes. But the recognition of Ngo Homes by the government is an issue in itself. Children Homes not recognised by the Juvenile Justice Act are illegal but Ngos claim recognition of Homes by the Government, impose upon them co-ordination with the government which involves lengthy bureaucratic procedures which are detrimental to the running of the Home. The Child Welfare Committee on the other hand claims that Ngos were 'stubborn' and had to learn to work within the ambit of the law. Besides this, there is no visible sharing of statistical information between both parties. Research seems to be conducted independently though recently, the Dil Se

Campaign started in 2005 was collaboration between the Ngo sector and the government.

It started in June 2005, with the objective of developing a scaleable intervention model that upholds the dignity and inclusive rights of the urban poor, specifically for children who live and work on the streets. *Dil Se* is not about short-term solutions; it is about building capacity in all sectors of society to help ensure that the most vulnerable urban street children have nutritious food, protection, health care, and proper education. Led by Sarva Shiksha Abhiyan (SSA) Delhi, Government of Delhi, the *Dil Se* Campaign is a joint endeavour with the Center for Equity Studies (CES) and Aman Biradari. The state is primarily responsible for our most vulnerable citizens; therefore, Aman Biradari has tried to avoid funding-dependent projects. In partnership with the Delhi Government and the community at large, this Campaign strives to create a community that is sensitive and responsive to the needs of children who live on the streets. Policy level advocacy and coordination with concerned government departments (such as Health, Education, and Welfare) will be a priority. The *Dil Se* Campaign has the potential of establishing a sustainable model of care and affection – transforming the lives of our city's most vulnerable children and bringing these children into the care of their local community.

22.6. ROLE OF MEDIA IN REVEALING LIFE OF STREET CHILDREN

Media plays an important role in raising public awareness of child rights. It also plays a vital role in protection, prevention and awareness of child rights. The role of media does not ends here, it also influences behavior and generates public opinion. Here we will discuss about the news reports which have mentioned the role of Ngos and government organisations in Delhi.

22.6.1 NEWS REPORT PUBLISHED IN THE HINDU ON APRIL 29, 2011:

The report reveals that the National capital is home to over 50,000 street children – constituting 0.4 per cent of Delhi's population and one per cent of the total number of children here – a latest study has claimed. North Delhi has the highest concentration of street children at 10,091 of a total figure of 50,923 estimated to be living in the city.

The study, the first of its kind, on the census of street children in Delhi covering all nine districts of the State, considered three categories of children for their enumeration. The first street-living children, who have run away from their families and lived alone on streets; the second being street-working children, who spend most of their time on the streets but returned home on a regular basis; and the last category is children on street families who lived on the streets with their families.

The study-done between July 12 and August 28, 2010 — has revealed that one out of every five (20.3 per cent) of the street children was involved in rag picking, This was followed by street vending (15.18 per cent), begging (15 per cent), working on road side repair shops (12.19 per cent), dhabas/hotels (6.24 per cent) and those employed in manufacturing units comprise a mere 1.22 per cent.

Conducted by Save the Children, a non-governmental organisation working for children's rights and the Institute for Human Development, the study is important on two counts as it determines the number of street children and details their living conditions, and also lays out clear recommendations on how to deal with the problem of such large number of children on the streets.

22.6.2 REPORT WRITTEN BY MADHUR TANKHA, IN THE HINDU ON MAY 18, 2007:

By all accounts the Capital's street children are vulnerable to all forms of exploitation and abuse. And their daily lives are likely to be far removed from the childhood envisaged in the UN Convention on the Rights of the Child.

As a result, these children suffer from sexually transmitted diseases, drug abuse and crime resulting in a deep sense of insecurity and emotional conflict. These findings are based on a recent survey conducted by Plan India in association with the Indian Alliance of Child Rights, Bal Sahyog, Ngo forum and YWCA as part of registration of children living in difficult circumstances.

While Delhi's official report on registration of births and deaths suggests that it has 100 per cent registration, the worrisome fact is that it is home to a number of unregistered children of sex workers, unwed or under-age mothers, Scheduled Castes and Schedules Tribes and girl children.

According to the voluminous report, 658 of the 1,065 children surveyed were born in Delhi and 407 in Bihar, Uttar Pradesh, Rajasthan, Assam, Jharkhand, Maharashtra and West Bengal. Each Ngo took a few children to the registration authorities and they experienced that registering children of less than one year did not face much of a problem. But proof of permanent address was demanded even though street children of older age, particularly without family, move continuously from one location to another. Police verification was asked for and there were expenses involved for registration fee including penalties.

The findings present a bleak picture of the quest for an identity for these children. The moot question is how the birth registration system should operate between street children and the registration authority.

22.6.3 REPORT BY RASHME SEHGAL, IN INFOCHANGE NEWS AND FEATURES, JANUARY 2004:

Ten children's organisations, 20 photographers, 12 translators and the staff of Youthreach have worked for three years to put together a volume that records the prose, poetry, pain and desires of street children across India in their own words.

Every day, all across India, an estimated 50 children escape the intolerable circumstances of their homes to begin lives on the streets. These kids become prey to all kinds of anti-social elements including drug peddlers and extortionist gangs who use them as messengers. Young girls are particularly vulnerable.

Delhi-based NGO Youthreach, founded in 1997, has been working to galvanise the private sector to reach out to these disadvantaged children. They have used publications, e-mail message, theatre and power point presentations to increase awareness about the lives of street kids. They have just published a book titled *If I Were Rain*, in which the children speak about their own lives in the hostile terrain of railway stations and on the streets. They discuss the survival strategies they are forced to adopt, including young girls disguising themselves as boys to escape sexual harassment.

Youthreach points out that 10 million Indian children are surviving on the streets and several million are living in the slums that have cropped up in all our urban centres. This book tries to bring home to India's upper classes the world these children occupy. It aims to show that despite their disadvantages, these kids are intuitive, compassionate, loving and creative people.

22.6.4 IN A NEWS REPORT PUBLISHED BY NEWS PORTAL WWW.OUTLOOKINDIA.COM:

This report with heading "*Roofless childhood" gives the statistics of the street children in India. It says that* there are 51,000 street children in Delhi; 20 per cent are girls. 70 per cent are on the street despite having a home in Delhi. 50.5 per cent are illiterate. 87 per cent earn a living—20 per cent as ragpickers, 15.8 per cent as street vendors, 15 per cent by begging. Over 50 per cent have suffered verbal, physical or sexual abuse. Fewer than 20 per cent have ID cards or birth certificates, and so they miss out on government schemes.

Little boys with painted moustaches perform acrobatics and beg for a reward, kids are seen dodging between vehicles to sell their wares, girls with siblings in their arms seeking alms is a common enough vignettes at the crossroads in Delhi, as in many other cities of India. Just like the sight of innumerable children working in roadside eateries and industrial units. Between feeling upset and wanting to help these children enjoy a normal life, including going to school, many of us wonder about their hard lives. In a first-of-its-kind census, Save the Children, an Ngo, in association with the Institute for Human Development, Delhi, has now tried to supplement the quantitative data with qualitative data on some 51,000 children, below 18, living and eking out a livelihood on the streets of Delhi.

The survey, 'Surviving the Streets', conducted in all nine districts of Delhi state in July-August 2010, reveals that an astonishing 70 per cent of street children have to fend for themselves though their parents, siblings or other relatives also live in the city. Only around 10 per cent were found to be totally cut off from their homes and villages. The largest chunk (61 per cent) was in the 7-14 years age group, while 23 per cent were in the 15-18 years bracket.

Most of the children are engaged in ragpicking (20.3 per cent) followed by vending (15.18 per cent), begging (15 per cent), working in roadside stalls or repair shops (12.19 per cent), dhabas (6.24 per cent) and manufacturing units (1.22 per cent). It is difficult to ascertain the number working in industrial units, as these kids are hardly able to get out of the hell-holes they work in. Earning on an average about Rs 2,240 per month, over 57 per cent of the street children visit their homes periodically and hand over about half their earnings to parents, relatives, gang leaders and even the police. Despite staying and moving about in groups, over 50 per cent spoke of some kind of abuse—verbal, physical and even sexual, sometimes at the hands of policemen.

22.6.5 DELHI GOVT'S INITIATIVES, DMRC BUILDS HOME FOR STREET CHILDREN BY AMBIKA PANDIT, TNN FEB 15, 2010

Eight-year-old Rahul can't forget the day when his school bag, uniform and books were stolen from near the Hanuman Mandir in Connaught Place. For this street kid, it was like his only hope of a better life being snatched away. But the incident now seems just like a bad dream, as he prepares to enrol in a school again after Holi.

What changed it all for Rahul- and 89 other street children - was getting shelter at Arman, a children's home built by Delhi Metro Rail Corporation and being run by the Ngo, Salaam Baalak Trust. The state-of-art shelter-cum-protection home, which turned functional in January, is built on DMRC land next to pillar number 65 on Metro line 1 near Tis Hazari station.

The three-storeyed red-brick *Bal Greeh* has well furnished dormitories for 120 inmates, large classrooms, an activity hall with Lcd TV, an amphitheatre and a computer room, among other facilities. DMRC said the shelter is chairman E. Sreedharan's way of giving homeless children a better life.

For Salaam Baalak Trust, the home has come as much needed space for qualitative development. While the building and all infrastructure was given by DMRC, the NGO is responsible for running the home for providing care and protection, education, training and extra-curricular activities. The building has been let out by DMRC on a five-year lease to begin with and Metro officials would be visiting it regularly. In fact, with the home located along the metro line, DMRC also plans to take the kids for a ride soon.

Salaam Balak Trust said the procedures relating to running a children's home were in the process of being completed.

When *TOI* visited the home on Saturday, a large driveway led to a spacious reception where the notice board listed the various activities underway. DMRC Arman is already home to 90 children, teenagers and youth. Rahul was playing with other children in a large dormitory on the ground floor. Bunker beds with colourful mattresses and blankets neatly lined the large room overlooking the greens outside.

The ground floor dormitory is home to children who don't live here permanently but come for short-term stay, or just for the night, through the NGO's contact centres in various areas. Honey, an inmate, feels the drop-in centre-cum-night shelter is a delight. "*Yahaan sab kuch achchha hai. Padhai hai, TV hai, khelne ko hai or sone ke liye bhi achchhi jagah hai,*" she said.

The corridor along the dormitory leads to an activity hall where teenage boys were seen watching a movie on an Lcd TV. A staircase along the hall leads to another dormitory and classrooms on the first and second floor with similar facilities. Many of the inmates are runaway kids, others have been rescued from extreme poverty on the streets and still others who have families but due to poverty they have been put under the care of the Ngo.

If the small children are happy with the mix of play and study, big boys like Satnam, who is doing his graduation from Delhi University and a multi-media course under the Ngo, find the peace and tranquillity of the campus very encouraging.

Rajinder Kumar, a runaway child who has been associated with Salaam Baalak for 10 years now and is currently studying in class X, pointed that the facilities at Arman had given them new dreams and the will to work hard to achieve them.

22.7. RECOMMENDATION

- Government laws should be revised.
- NGO should influence Government and try to incorporate their opinions into Governments policies and programmes made for children.
- Media should be used to spread awareness.
- School teachers need to be trained to handle misbehaving students through guidance and counselling.

- Education should be imparted to the children by the Government and voluntary agencies to enlighten their minds and their growth opportunities.
- Education and enrolment in formal schools should be encouraged.
- Education and Vocational skills should be developed for self support.
- Counselling should be held at contact points, providing basic needs like medical aid, food, shelter, washing facility and basic education.
- Counselling of parents should be undertaken.
- 24 hour drop in centre and shelter homes should be set up.
- Stringent laws should be enacted to completely and child abuse and trafficking of children.

22.8. CONCLUSION

Ngos and government agencies should work in rural area to prevent family breakups and migration of families due to poor economic conditions and strengthening a gender focus to reach out to girls and should work to stop child trafficking and child abuse. Ngos should also work on issue based programmes with the government to reach refugees, victims of riots and sexual abuse to ensure the full implementation of policy, legislation and child friendly services for children.

References

1. Salaam Baalak Trust, 'Health Program' [online]. Available at: http://www.salaambaalaktrust.com/health.asp, [Accessed 11 July 2009].
2. Kacker, L, et al (2007), Study on Child Abuse: India 2007, pp. 38-39, Ministry of Women and Child.
3. Development, Government of India, [Online] Available at: http://wcd.nic.in/childabuse.pdf. [Accessed 19 July 2009].
4. (2003, August). India together: Salaam, dilli!. Retrieved July 11, 2009, Web site: http://www.indiatogether.org/2003/aug/chi-sbt.htm.
5. Railway Children, 'Our work in India', [online]. Available at http://www.railwaychildren.org.uk/asia.asp.
6. http://www.indianexpress.com/news/from-feb-dial-1098-to-rescue-child-beggars/410380.
7. 3. Declaration of the rights of the child:facts, discussion forum, and encyclopaedia article. Retrieved June 25, 2009, Web site: http://www.absoluteastronomy.com/topics/Declaration of the Rights of the Child.
8. (2009, May 13). Child welfare not an issue for 80 percent candidates: NGO. Retrieved June 10, 2009, Web site: http://www.thaindian.com/newsportal/politics/child-welfare-not-an-issue-for-80-percent-candidatesngo_100191944.html.
9. (2005, October 17). The pathetic reality of street children in nepal. Retrieved July 8, 2009, Web site: http://www.globalpolitician.com/21288-nepal.
10. Retrieved June 5, 2009, from Convention on the Rights of the Child Web site: http://www2.ohchr.org/english/law/crc.htm.
11. Maneka gandhi vs union of india on 25 january, 1978. Retrieved June 24, 2009, Web site: http://www.indiankanoon.org/doc/1766147/.

12. Saran, Vineet (2008). Child in need of care and protection: Their welfare and rehabilitation. JTRI Journal, XXIX, Retrieved June 24, 2009, from http://www.ijtr.nic.in/webjournal/2.htm.
13. Agnihotri P. Street boys of Delhi: A study of their family and demographic characteristics. Indian J Med Sci [serial online] 2001 [cited 2009 Jun 26];55:543-8. Available from: http://www.indianjmedsci.org/text.asp?2001/55/10/543/12037.
14. Working Group on Development of Children for the Eleventh Five Year Plan (2007-2012) Vol. I.
15. http://articles.timesofindia.indiatimes.com/2010-02-15/delhi/28115241_1_street-children-dormitory-e-sreedharan.

23

Race and Ethnicity of Tribal in Print Media Content

Umesh Kumar and ***Minu Sharma***

Introduction

There is much evidence which bears indirectly on the reflection of social diversity in media content. So called "bad News" is often thought more news worthy than good news and ethnic minority members are differentially more like to be identified in the negative content, even if cast as victim (Hartman and Husband, 1974; Van Dijk, 1991). Process of stereotyping in the mass production of fiction also lead to patterns of this kinds (Berelson and salter, 1946). In general expectations of large discrepancies between fictional (or news) world and statical real worlds have been confirmed, indicating a general failure of media by such criteria to reflect the diversity of world at all faithfully.

Ethnicity refers to selected cultural and sometimes physical characteristics used to classify people into groups or categories considered to be significantly different from others. Commonly recognised American ethnic groups include American Indians, Latinos, Chinese, African Americans, European Americans etc. In some cases, ethnicity involves merely a loose group identity with little or no cultural traditions in common. This is the case with many Irish and German Americans. In contrast, some ethnic groups are coherent sub-cultures with a shared language and body of tradition. Newly arrived immigrant groups often fit this pattern.

It is important not to confuse the term minority with ethnic group. Ethnic groups may be either a minority or a majority in a population. Whether a group is a minority or a majority also is not an absolute fact but depends on the perspective. For instance, in some towns along the southern border of the U.S., people of Mexican ancestry are the overwhelming majority population and control most of the important social and political institutions but are still defined by state and national governments as a minority. In small homogenous societies, such as those of hunters and gatherers and pastoralists, there is essentially only one ethnic group and no minorities.

For many people, ethnic categorisation implies a connection between biological inheritance and culture. They believe that biological inheritance determines much of cultural identity. If this were true, for instance, African American cultural traits, such as "black English", would stem from genetic inheritance. We now know that this is not true—biological race and culture are not the same thing. The pioneering English anthropologist Edward Tylormay have been the first scientist to understand this fact and to state it in print. In 1871, he wrote that cultural traits are entirely learned. Subsequently, a baby can be placed into another culture shortly after birth and can be thoroughly enculturated to that culture, regardless of their skin color, body shape, and other presumed racial features. For example, both women in the photographs on the right are genetically African, but they do not speak the same language nor do they share any other significant cultural patterns due to the fact that they were brought up in very different societies. The African American woman is far more similar culturally to her European American neighbors than to the West African woman from Senegal.

A **race** is a biological subspecies, or variety of a species, consisting of a more or less distinct population with anatomical traits that distinguish it clearly from other races. This biologist's definition does not fit the reality of human genetic variation today. We are an extremely homogenous species genetically. As a matter of fact, all humans today are 99.9 per cent genetically identical, and most of the variation that does occur is in the difference between males and females and our unique personal traits. This homogeneity is very unusual in the animal kingdom. Even our closest biological relatives, the chimpanzees have 2-3 times more genetic variation than people. Orangutans have 8-10 times more variation.

It is now clear that our human "races" are primarily cultural creations, not biological realities. The commonly held belief in the existence of human biological races is based on the false assumption that anatomical traits, such as skin color and specific facial characteristics, cluster together in single distinct groups of people. They do not. There are no clearly distinct "black", "white", or other races.

The popularly held view of human races ignores the fact that anatomical traits supposedly identifying a particular race are often found extensively in other populations as well. This is due to the fact that similar natural selection factors in different parts of the world often result in the evolution of similar adaptations. For instance, intense sunlight in tropical latitudes has selected for darker skin color as a protection from intense ultraviolet radiation. As a result, the dark brown skin color characteristic of sub-Saharan Africans is also found among unrelated populations in the Indian subcontinent, Australia, New Guinea, and elsewhere in the Southwest Pacific.

SC & ST population of Madhya Pradesh is present of total population of the state Mandla, Seoni, Chhindwara, Khandwa, Badwani, Khargon, Bhalaghat, Dindori, Jhabua and Alirajpur etc. districts population is mainly *Aadivasi*. Their belief and culture is different from other peoples. Media is a medim which promote the diversity of culture of the world. The main purpose of the study is to determine how media represent aadivasi population on and their culture.

Objectives of Research

The purpose of research is to discover answer to question through the application of scientific procedures. The main aim of research is to find out the truth which is hidden and which has not been discovered as yet. The research objectives as falling into a number of following broad groupings:

1. To gain familiarity with a phenomenon or to achieve to new insight into it;
2. To portray accurately the characteristics of a particular individual, situation, or a group;
3. To determine the frequency with which something occurs are with which it is associated with something else;
4. To test a hypothesis of a causal relationship between variables.

These are the objectives of this research:

1. To study the coverage of *Aadivasi* culture in the media;
2. Representation of *Aadivasi* population in Media;
3. To study the strategies of media to promote the *Aadivasi* culture; and
4. Socio-political coverage of *Aadivasi* population;

Research Methodology

Research is a common parlance refers to a search for knowledge. Once can also define research as a scientific and systematic search for pertinent information on a specific topic. Infact research is an art of scientific investigation. The Advance learner's Dictionary of current English lays down the meaning of research as "A careful investigation or inquiry specially through search for new facts in any branch of knowledge." Redman and Mory define research as a systematised effort to gain new knowledge.

Content analysis consists of analysing the contents documentary material such as books, magazines, newspapers and the contents of all other verbal materials which can be either spoken or printed, content analysis is measurement through proportion content analysis measures pervasiveness and that is some times and index of the intensity of the force. The analysis of content is a central activity whenever one is concerned with the study of the nature of the verbal materials. A review of research in any area, for instance, involves the analysis of the content of the research article that have been published. The analysis may be at a relatively simple level or may be a subtle one.

It is at a simple level when we pursue it on the basis of certain characteristics of the document or verbal materials that can be identified and counted. It is a subtle when researcher makes a study of the attitude, say of the press towards education by feature writers.

Relevence of the study: Tribal population is more than other states in Madhya Pradesh. MP government has introduce too many policies for tribal conservation of their art, culture, Language and dialects. Khandwa is a tribal district of Madhya Pradesh so it is important to learn how much print media provides space to these castes.

Literature review: Berelson and Salters (1946) have done a research on American magazine. The research design was paradigmatic: norms for the representation of minorities in the magazine stories were derived from population statistic and applied to the fictional content which was treated as if it too had a 'population; made up of the individual story characters. For instance, the American black population was then around 10 per cent and 70 per cent of American were accountable as white, native American. Findings showed black to have 2 per cent of role in magazine content, while 90 per cent went to Americans.

Limitation

Quantative analysis of Data

Total News Stories and Photo Publish in Newspapers

Name of the newspaper	*News publish from 1st December to 15 December*	*News Publish from 1st January to 15th January*	*No. of photos publish*
Nai Dunia	18	4	13
Dainik Bhaskar	23	3	7
Hindustan Times	19	4	19

1. In *Khandwa* New Delhi based newspaper can not be accessed, so the newspaper is published from Indore is used in the study.

2. only 15 days newspaper have been selected for the study.
3. Electricity is also a limitation of this study.

During the first half of study period *Nai Dunia* published 18 stories and in second half published only four stories related to tribal. At the same time Dainik bhaskar published 23 and three stories and Hindustan published 19 and four stories. Nai Dunia published 13 photos, Dainik Bhaskar published 7 and Hindustan published maximum 19 photos.

Source and Place of the Story

Name of the newspaper	*source*		*Place*			
	Reporter	*Agency*	*Rural*	*State*	*National*	*Inter-national*
Nai Dunia	18	4	14	2	6	0
Dainik Bhaskar	24	2	7	14	5	0
Hindustan Times	17	6	10	8	5	0

Nai dunia published 18 stories covered by their own reporters and 4 by agency. Place of stories are 14 from rural and 2 from state and 6 based on national news. On the other hand *Dainik bhaskar* publish 24 stories covered by their reporters and 2 from the agency. 7 stories are from rural, 14 from state and 5 stories are national. *Hindustan Times* publish 17 stories reported by their own reporters and 6 from agency. 10 stories are based on rural, 8 are state and 5 are national news.

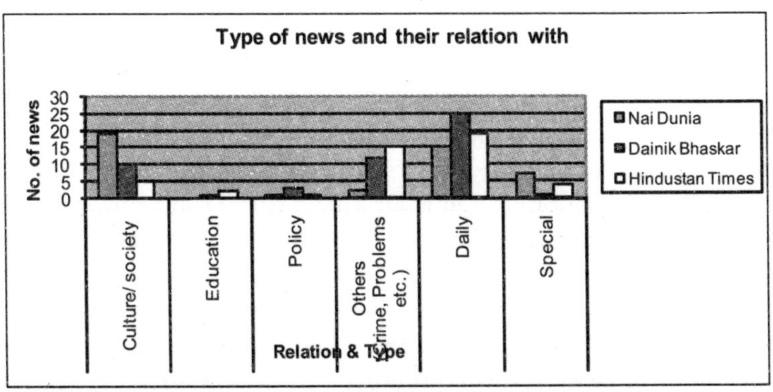

Name of the Newspaper	*Related to*				*Type of news*	
	Cultural/ society	*Edu- cation*	*Policy*	*Others (Crime, Problems etc.)*	*Daily*	*Special*
Nai Dunia	19	0	1	2	15	7
Dainik Bhaskar	10	1	3	12	25	1
Hindustan Times	5	2	1	15	19	4

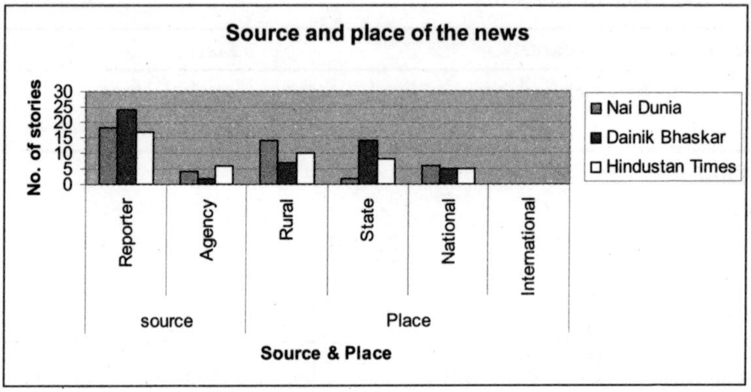

Nai Dunia published 19 stories related to culture, one related to policy and 2 others. There are 15 daily news and 7 special package of news. *Dainik Bhaskar* published 10 cultural, one education, 3 policy related and 12 others type of news. DB reports 25 daily news and 1 one is special. *Hindustan Times* publish 5 cultural, 2 education one policy related and 15 are other type of news. There are 19 daily and 4 special news in the newspaper.

Quantative analisys of Data

During the 1st half of study period *Dainik Bhaskar* published only 23 stories related to the tribal. 5 news are related to *Nimad Utsav*, 2 news is related to health problem in tribal, 3 news are related to crime and accident, 3 news are related to policy and others are related to society, development, electricity crisis, migration etc. On 1st December 2011 Dainik Bhaskar publish two based on tribal related to *Nimad Utsav* and *Korku* community radio. On 2nd December 2011 one story is publish on tribal song in this newspaper. Health is a problem in the tribal area. Only two stories are based on heath problem, one is on Malaria and another is letter to Prime Minister on heath matter. In crime news sexuality, murder and thieves are covered by the newspaper. Joint Family of a tribal family is also find place in the newspaper. The story is of a house where three generation take pension. Migration is also find place in the newspaper. Peoples of tribal area migrating from their native land to cities because of lack of employment. Electricity is a factor which is denoted as development. Electric supply is banded in the tribal majority district Jhabua. In some tribal area electric cut is too much. Near about four hours electricity supply is in these area. Although government has announced that one hundred farmers of the trible area will get free electiricty. But the truth is that the electricity comes after 72 hours or more than that. Marriage culture related news also find place in the newspaper. In some tribal areas marriage will held on DEVUTHNI GYARAS. Aadivasi Ekta Parishad's meeting related to this news has placed in some newspapers.

After the study of this paper we found that only those news which related to the tribal culture got place in this. Apart of this news related to the other matter not covered in the *Dainik Bhaskar*.

During the 2nd half of the period of this study *Dainik Bhaskar* publish only three news related to the tribal art and culture and their problems. Totoal space provided to these reports is 0.02 per cent of the newspaper. Although two reports are publish on the front page and one on the last page of the newspaper. This shows that matters related to the tribal are important but coverage is too less.

It means when a big function or tragedy acquire place in tribal area, media pay's attention on that. Except days media keep silent on tribal matters.

First story is related to the film named *Tantya Bheel.* Headline of the story is "PAHLE FIRANGIO (BRITISERS) KO BHAGAYEGI TANTYA BHEEL" The cast of the film is near about one corer rupees. First shot of this film is from the native land of Tantya bheel. Director and hero of the film is Mukesh R. Choukse. This film is based on the life of great sociologist Tantya bheel.

Second story of the DB is related to crime. This is a national news and source the this news is agency. Headline of the story is "NIRITYA MAMLAE ME CASE DARJ" (case filed on dance matter). This story is from port Blaire. Port Blaire police filed F.I.R. against the unknown people in the case of nude dance of tribal women. The story is publish as a daily news. Two column space on the front page is given to this. Third story is follow up of this story and publish on the last page in three columns. After nude dance by JARAWA *aadivasi* government passed order to bring them in main stream. The constitution of India provide right against exploitation, but due to illiteracy it take place here and there.

Newspaper neglect the problems related to tribal. *Dainik Bhaskar* have never publish any news during the 2nd half of the study period related to Education, Health, Social Problem etc. Only cultural and crime news are reported in these days.

Qualitative Analysis of Nai Dunia

When we talk about social responsibilities of *Nai Dunia*, we found that this newspaper cover tribal related news by their own reporters. Maximum news are covered by their own reporters but they concentrate only on the social and cultural activities.

Nai Dunia publish an editorial on tribal issue. Although untouchability have been prohibited by Indian constitute but it acquire place here and there. *Nai Dunia* say that nowadays government should make that type of policies that provide an open area for all castes of Indian society. In the mean time this newspaper raised an issue related to the sexual harassment of the tribal girl aged 14 years. Two advertisement also find place in this newspaper. One is related to employment and another is based on training programme. Maximum stories are from rural area.

An news on proposed film on famous social activist and freedom fighter "*Tantya Bheel*" also find place which shows that Nai Dunia is promoting not only main stream leader but also those who have been forgotten from Indian history. The first KORKU community radio has launched in Madhya Pradesh for the cultural upliftment of *Korku Janjati*. Popular fair Antyodaye Mela of Madhya Pradesh government was held in the month of November have also covered by this newspaper.

Nai Dunia published four news and one advertisement during the second half of the study. One is related to culture, another is historical and crime based. *Nai Dunia* provided 0.03 per cent space of newspaper during this period. *Nai Dunia* published only special news related to the tribal.

First story of the newspaper is related to the culture of *Barela Aadiwasi*. Headline of the story is "*January Me Dewali*" (*Deepawali* in January). Report says that *Barela Aadiwasi* celebrate *deepawali* in the month of January. This story is publish in four column with border. The story is a rural story. This story do not give any reason why these *aadiwasi* celebrate *deewali* in the month of January. Without any historical background it can not be happen.

Two stories are related to crime. Some illegal elements of the society make nude video of *Jarawa Janjati*. The video is uploaded on *youtube*. After that a huge problem started in the area and whole country. Video have been removed from *youtube*.

Qualitative Analysis of Hindustan Times

During the study of *Hindustan Times* we found that all news are covered by their own reporters. There are a different type of news like political, economic, food crisis, crime, violence and sexual harassment protest and development issues related to the tribal are covered in this paper. This news paper publish special news on food crisis and tribal art and culture with data and figures. A Sunday special news based on violence and social issues. One story of crime was publish on front page with the heading of "Worden's son arrested for raping hostler". A photo covered five column space with caption was publish on migration of tribal. As we know that food crisis is the biggest issue for India, Hindustan Times publish two special reports with photo on this problem related to tribal. In our study we found that *Nai Dunia* and *Dainik Bhaskar* published those news which were related to culture and social problems but the leading English newspaper *Hindustan Times* has covered development related news as we know that in Barwani electricity crisis is too much and this newspaper cover the problem of tribal people's need of electricity for irrigation.

Findings and Recommendation

1. Apart of the *Hindustan Times*, others newspaper do not provide space for the tribal news on the front page.
2. The news based on the cultural and social aspect of the tribal are basically covered and other aspects are neglected by them.
3. Only *Nai Dunia* published, an editorial based on tribal problem but others do not pay attention on this.
4. Coverage of tribal is less than other news although the population of tribal in near about 20 per cent in India. When any big incident happened like *Jarawa* case in Port Blaire find place in newspaper.
5. Newspaper should pay attention on all classes of the Indian society.
6. Our educational institutes should promote that type of syllabus which reflect tribal's culture and their issues.
7. Research institute should do research on the tribal.

References

- Ninan, Sevanti, Headlines from the Heartland-Reinventing the Hindi public sphere, Sage publication, New Delhi.
- Kothari, C.R., Research Methodology- methods and techniques (second revised edition), New age international publication, Delhi.
- Mcquail, Denis, Media Performance Sage Publication, Los Angles.
- Kumar, Keval j., Mass Communication in India Jaico Publication House, New Delhi.
- Kumar, Ranjit, Research Methodology: Step by Step Research, Sage Publication, New Delhi.

24

Bipolar Disorder: Health Issues, Social Changes and Role of Media

Pradeep Kumar, Priyanka Singh, Abid Rizvi and ***Prashanta Kumar Pal***

Introduction

Bipolar disorder, also known as manic-depressive illness, is a brain disorder that causes unusual shifts in mood, energy, activity levels, and the ability to carry out day-to-day tasks. Symptoms of bipolar disorder are severe. They are different from the normal ups and downs that everyone goes through from time to time. Bipolar disorder symptoms can result in damaged relationships, poor job or school performance, and even suicide. But bipolar disorder can be treated, and people with this illness can lead full and productive lives. Bipolar disorder often develops in a person's late teens or early adult years. At least half of all cases start before age 25. Some people have their first symptoms during childhood, while others may develop symptoms late in life. Bipolar disorder is not easy to spot when it starts. The symptoms may seem like separate problems, not recognised as parts of a larger problem. Some people suffer for years before they are properly diagnosed and treated. Like diabetes or heart disease, bipolar disorder is a long-term illness that must be carefully managed throughout a person's life.

Bipolar disorder or bipolar affective disorder, historically known as manic–depressive disorder, is a psychiatric diagnosis that describes a category of mood disorders defined by the presence of one or more episodes of abnormally elevated energy levels, cognition, and mood with or without one or more depressive episodes. The elevated moods are clinically referred to as mania or, if milder, hypomania. Individuals who experience manic episodes also commonly experience depressive episodes, or symptoms, or a mixed state in which features of both mania and depression are present at the same time. These events are usually separated by periods of "normal" mood; but, in some individuals, depression and mania may rapidly alternate, which is known as rapid cycling.

Severe manic episodes can sometimes lead to such psychotic symptoms as delusions and hallucinations. The disorder has been subdivided into bipolar I, bipolar II, cyclothymic, and other types, based on the nature and severity of mood episodes experienced; the range is often described as the bipolar spectrum.

SYMPTOMS OF BIPOLAR DISORDER

People with bipolar disorder experience unusually intense emotional states that occur in distinct periods called "mood episodes." An overly joyful or overexcited state is called a manic episode, and an extremely sad or hopeless state is called a depressive episode. Sometimes, a mood episode includes symptoms of both mania and depression. This is called a mixed state. People with bipolar disorder also may be explosive and irritable during a mood episode. Extreme changes in energy, activity, sleep, and behaviour go along with these changes in mood. It is possible for someone with bipolar disorder to experience a long-lasting period of unstable moods rather than discrete episodes of depression or mania. A person may be having an episode of bipolar disorder if he or she has a number of manic, or depressive symptoms for most of the day, nearly every day, for at least one or two weeks. Sometimes symptoms are so severe that the person cannot function normally at work, school, or home.

People with bipolar disorder experience unusually intense emotional states that occur in distinct.

SYMPTOMS OF MANIA OR A MANIC EPISODE INCLUDES]

Mood Changes:

- A long period of feeling "high," or an overly happy or outgoing mood.
- Extremely irritable mood, agitation, feeling "jumpy" or "wired."

Behavioural Changes:

- Talking very fast, jumping from one idea to another, having racing thoughts being easily distracted.
- Increasing goal-directed activities, such as taking on new projects.
- Being restless.
- Sleeping little.
- Having an unrealistic belief in one's abilities.
- Behaving impulsively and taking part in a lot of pleasurable, high-risk behaviours, such as spending sprees, impulsive sex, and impulsive business investments.

SYMPTOMS OF DEPRESSION [OR A DEPRESSIVE EPISODE INCLUDE]

Mood Changes:

- A long period of feeling worried or empty.
- Loss of interest in activities once enjoyed, including sex.

Behavioural Changes:

- Feeling tired, or "slowed down".
- Having problems concentrating, remembering, and making decisions.
- Being restless, or irritable.
- Changing eating, sleeping, or other habits.
- Thinking of death or suicide, or attempting suicide.

In addition to mania and depression, bipolar disorder can cause a range of moods, as shown on the scale.

One side of the scale includes severe depression, moderate depression, and mild low mood. Moderate depression may cause less extreme symptoms, and mild low mood is called dysthymia when it is chronic or long-term. In the middle of the scale is normal or balanced mood. At the other end of the scale are hypomania and severe mania. Some people with bipolar disorder experience hypomania. During hypomanic episodes, a person may have increased energy and activity levels that are not as severe as typical mania, or he, or she may have episodes that last less than a week and do not require emergency care. A person having a hypomanic episode may feel very good, be highly productive, and function well. This person may not feel that anything is wrong even as family and friends recognise the mood swings as possible bipolar disorder. Without proper treatment, however, people with hypomania may develop severe mania or depression. During a mixed state, symptoms often include agitation, trouble sleeping, major changes in appetite, and suicidal thinking. People in a mixed state may feel very sad or hopeless while feeling extremely energized. Sometimes, a person with severe episodes of mania, or depression has psychotic symptoms, too, such as hallucinations or delusions. The psychotic symptoms tend to reflect the person's extreme mood. For example, psychotic symptoms for a person having a manic episode may include believing he or she is famous, has a lot of money, or has special powers. In the same way, a person having a depressive episode may believe he or she is ruined and penniless, or has committed a crime. As a result, people with bipolar disorder who have psychotic symptoms are sometimes wrongly diagnosed as having schizophrenia, another severe mental illness that is linked with hallucinations and delusions. People with bipolar disorder may also have behavioural problems. They may

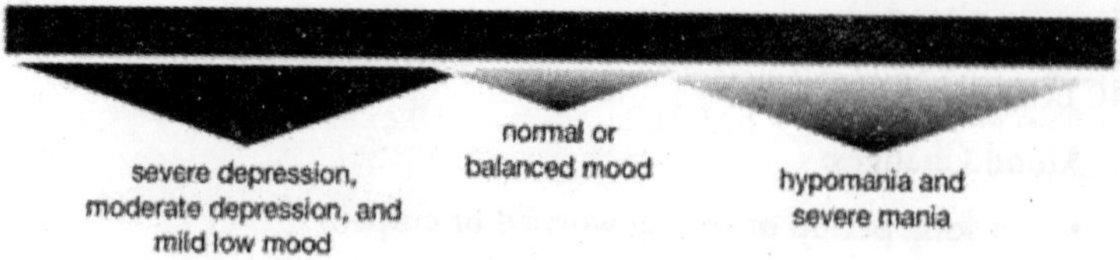

abuse alcohol or substances, have relationship problems, or perform poorly in school or at work. At first, it's not easy to recognise these problems as signs of a major mental illness.

THE EFFECTS OF BIPOLAR DISORDER

It may be very hard to take that first step to help yourself. It may take time, but you can get better with treatment.

- Talk to your doctor about treatment options and progress.
- Keep a regular routine, such as eating meals at the same time every day and going to sleep at the same time every night.
- Try to get enough sleep.
- Stay on your medication.
- Learn about warning signs signalling a shift into depression or mania.
- Expect your symptoms to improve gradually, not immediately.

STATISTICAL DATA AND BIPOLAR DISORDER

When it comes to children with Bipolar disorder and adolescents that have it, they will usually have one parent that has the disorder. This isn't always the case so you want to still watch for any symptoms of Bipolar in your children just in case. Children who have parents with this illness will have a risk of 15 per cent to 30 per cent. If both of the parents have it then the risk will be increased to 50 per cent to 75 per cent.

The Bipolar disease is more common in youth as it is in adults. Adolescents that are of the age of 14 to 18 were found to have had criteria for this disorder or for cyclothymia at some time in their life. The study found that this was true in one percent of youth. According to statistics there is 20 per cent of youth that deal with major depression that will get Bipolar within a five year time frame from the start of the depression. There are 3.4 million children and adolescents who have depression in the U.S. can experience early development of the Bipolar disorder. When Bipolar kids are having a manic episode they will be more likely to experience moods where they are irritable and they will often have outbursts that you are destructive. They can then change moods in the blink of an eye and be elated or euphoric. If they get depressed they can even start having physical problems that will cause them to complain about having a headache, stomachache, or being overly tired. They can also experience poor performance when at school, social isolation and sometimes they will even be extremely sensitive to rejection of any type, or failure.

Genetic Factors

When talking about biological causes, the first issue is whether bipolar disorder can be inherited. This question has been researched through multiple family, adoption and twin studies. In families of persons with bipolar disorder, first-degree relatives (parents, children, siblings) are more likely to have a mood disorder than the relatives of those who do not have bipolar disorder. Studies of twins indicate that if one twin has a mood disorder, an identical twin is about three times more likely than a fraternal twin to have a mood disorder as well.

In bipolar disorder specifically, the concordance rate (when both twins have the disorder) is 80 per cent for identical twins, as compared to only 16 per cent for fraternal twins. (Identical twins occur when one fertilised egg splits in two, so they share the same genetic material; fraternal twins come from separate fertilised eggs, so the mixtures of genetic material are different.) There is overwhelming evidence that bipolar disorder can be inherited and that there is a genetic vulnerability to developing the illness.

Stress Triggers

For mental, emotional and environmental issues, stressful life events are thought to be the main element in the development of bipolar disorder. These can range from a death in the family to the loss of a job, from the birth of a child to a move. It can be pretty much anything, but it cannot be precisely defined, since one person's stress may be another person's piece of cake. With that in mind, research has found that stressful life events can lead to the onset of symptoms in bipolar disorder. However, once the disorder is triggered and progresses, "it seems to develop a life of its own." Once the cycle begins, psychological and/or biological processes take over and keep the illness active.

When we look for the cause of bipolar disorder, the best explanation according to the research available at this time is what is termed the "Diathesis-Stress Model." The word dia-thesis means, in simplified terms, a physical condition that make a person more than usually susceptible to certain diseases.

Thus the Diathesis-Stress Model says that each person inherits certain physical vulnerabilities to problems that may or may not appear depending on what stresses occur in his or her life. Durand and Barlow define this model as a theory "that both an inherited tendency and specific stressful conditions are required to produce a disorder."

BIPOLAR DISORDER AND CHALENGES WITHIN SOCIETY

If one comes to know someone having bipolar disorder, it affects that person too. The first and most important thing one can do is help him or her get the right diagnosis and treatment. You may need to make the appointment and go with him or her to see the doctor. Encourage your loved one to stay in treatment. To help a friend or relative, you can:

- Offer emotional support, understanding, patience, and encouragement.
- Learn about bipolar disorder so you can understand what your friend or relative is experiencing.
- Talk to your friend or relative and listen carefully.
- Listen to feelings your friend or relative expresses–understand about situations that may trigger bipolar symptoms.
- Invite your friend or relative out for positive distractions, such as walks, outings, and other activities.
- Remind your friend or relative that, with time and treatment, he or she can get better.

Never ignore comments about your friend or relative harming him or herself. Always report such comments to his or her therapist or doctor.

Like other serious illnesses, bipolar disorder can be difficult for spouses, family members, friends, and other caregivers. Relatives and friends often have to cope with the person's serious behavioural problems, such as wild spending sprees during mania, extreme withdrawal during depression, poor work or school performance. These behaviours can have lasting consequences. Caregivers usually take care of the medical needs of their loved ones. The caregivers have to deal with how this affects their own health. The stress that caregivers are under may lead to missed work or lost free time, strained relationships with people who may not understand the situation, and physical and mental exhaustion. Stress from care giving can make it hard to cope with a loved one's bipolar symptoms. One study shows that if a caregiver is under a lot of stress, his, or her loved one has more trouble following the treatment plan, which increases the chance for a major bipolar episode. It is important that people caring for those with bipolar disorder also take care of themselves.

ROLE OF MASS MEDIA AND HEALTH PROMOTION

1. Media should aware the society about a particular problem or issue related to this disorder.
2. The media's characterisation of bipolar disorder helps educate the public in a positive manner or distort perceptions of illness.
3. The media can raise awareness of bipolar disorder through movies and TV programme.
4. Unfamiliar social surroundings may be unable to distinguish between actual bipolar symptoms and the film industry's tendency to take liberty with the facts.
5. The community mobilisation campaigns remove barriers to behaviour change.
6. The talk shows let listeners learn more.
7. The stories can help generate to buzz about the issues of bipolar disorder like *nukkar natak* (street plays) can be brought under video coverage for reaching out to larger masses in rural areas in a district.
8. Train partners around the world to tackle important issues in their community using a blend of Entertainment-Education (E-E) storytelling, interactive talk shows and Community Mobilisation Campaigns for bipolar and psyiacratic disorder.
9. Empowering hundreds of communities like regional radio channel and health channels by experts through peer-to-peer learning and knowledge sharing.
10. Society should be aware about bipolar disorder symptoms.

Disorder Awareness Day is part of Mental Health Awareness Week (1-7 October). It was created by the National Alliance on Mental Illness and Abbott Laboratories, in 1990, to increase awareness of bipolar disorder, promote early detection and accurate diagnosis, reduce stigma, and minimise the devastating impact on the 2.3 million Americans presently affected by the disorder. This day can be covered by media. The real gritty important details of Bipolar Disorder such as drug abuse, suicide attempts, and psychosis.

Through awareness projects in print or video etc., media canpositively influence patient, people around (at home and workplace) and legal structures for support for the cause of people affected with bipolar disorder directly, or indirectly. Effectiveness and success of media in awareness projects can surely be enhanced by use of vernacular languages, or local dialects. Programmes like talk shows, conferencing, reality shows, documentaries, can be specially designed for the purpose. Radio FM channels and community radio programmes can also play vital role and can be aimed towards the cause.

References

1. Dr. C. J. Yzermans, NIVEL, P.O. Box 1568, 3500 BN Utrecht, The Netherlands (e-mail: J.Yzermans@nivel.n!).
2. American Academy of Child and Adolescent Psychiatry, 3615 Wisconsin Avenue, NW, Washington, D.C.–20016-3007. Telephone: (202) 966-7300 Fax: (202) 966-2891 http://www.aacap.org.
3. American Psychiatric Association (APA), 1000 Wilson Boulevard, Suite 1825, Arlington, VA 22209-3901. (888) 35-PSYCH or (703) 907-7300. Email: apa@psych.org http://www.psych.org.
4. Depression and Bipolar Support Alliance, 730 N. Franklin Street, Suite 501, Chicago, Illinois 60654-7225. Telephone (800) 826-3632. Fax: (312) 642-7243.
5. Mental Health America (formerly National Mental Health Association), 2000 North Beauregard Street, 6th Floor, Alexandria, VA 22311. Telephone: (703) 684-7722 or (800) 969-6642. TTY: (800) 433-5959. Fax: (703) 684-5968. http://www.nmha.org.
6. "Bipolar Disorder," *Medline Plus*, January 19, 2009 [cited January 28, 2009]. http://www.nlm.nih.gov/medlineplus/bipolardisorder.html.
7. "Bipolar Disorder," National Institute of Mental Health, April 2, 2008 [cited January 28, 2009]. http://www. nimh.nih.gov/health/topics/bipolar-disorder/index.shtml.
8. Mondimore, Francis M., Bipolar Disorder: A Guide for Patients and Families, 2nd ed. Baltimore: Johns Hopkins University Press, 2006.
9. Bernstein, D. A., Clarke-Stewart, A., Penner, L.A., Roy, E. J., & Wickens, C.D. (2000). Psychology (5th ed.). Boston, MA: Houghton Mifflin Company.
10. Davis, S. F. & Palladino, J. J. (2000), Psychology (3rd ed.), Upper Saddle River, NJ: Prentice-Hall, Inc.
11. Durand, V. M. & Barlow, D. H. (2000), Abnormal Psychology: An Introduction, Scarborough, Ontario: Wadsworth.

25

Spiritual Journalism: A Ray of Hope Amidst the Present Crisis of Values

[Media Cultural Studies]

Dr. Sukhnandan Singh

Present Crisis of Values

Today we are living in a critical moments of the History, where the whole Humanity is at cross road. Old percepts are shattering and new ones evolving. Different ideologies are at clash with each other. The pace of change is so fast and furious that old traditions are losing their relevance and creating grave cultural void. Life values are wavering amidst this chaos of faith and doubts. The process had started in the last century well highlighted by Dharmveer Bharty–the values on which the whole civilisation was established are proving false. Result is awesome disintegration.[1]

As such contemporary society is in the grip of materialistic thinking and pleasure seeking life style. Instant gratification and monetary gain at any cost is the life goal of majority. Integral vision of life is missing. Life beyond petty selfishness and ego gratification is unthinkable to most. As such there is a grave degeneration in the core value system of the society. No wonder all the Pillars of Democracy are wavering. Legislative is already breathing its last breath. How can Executive under its infected shelter remain secure? Role of Judiciary is also questionable at times. The 4th pillar Press was expected to play its role as a Watch dog of society, but it is also seen busy in the rat race of TRP and monetary gains. So is the truth of other sectors of life and society.

Materialistic attitude has converted individual into a consumer. Nature has become a means of exploitation. Environmental pollution and ecological imbalance is its inevitable outcome, threatening the very existence of Earth and the life. Our obsession with science and consumerism has diverted our attentions away from our moral responsibilities toward each other. It is impossible for this moral void to be filled by consumerism or scientific theories and investigation. The state of society and humanity reveals a very gloomy and awesome picture. At the peak of material progress modern man has lost his true self and human values.

At the root of all moral degradation of humanity can be seen the materialistic and self centered value system replacing the idealistic view and way of life.[2] In order to regain moral responsibility we require a spiritual revival based on a shared transcendental reality bringing about an inclusive meaning and purpose. Only then can the mental and emotional well being of society begin to improve and heal.[3] Journalism as 4th pillar of democracy can play its decisive role in this direction.

Journalism: The 4th Pillar of Democracy, the Weapon of Change

For the healthy functioning of any society Journalism is an integral part of it. In the words of Jawaharlal Nehru, The press is one of the vital organs of modern life especially in a democracy. The press has tremendous powers and responsibilities. The three major objective of journalism are—1. To inform, 2. To educate and 3. To provide healthy entertainment to people.[4] As a watch dog of the society it is also called as the 4th pillar of democracy. To keep a vigilant eye on the functioning of the legislature, executive and judiciary are as such its prime functions. In the words of Gandhi Ji, The Press is called the Fourth Estate. It is definitely a power; Newspapers (TV & net) are a powerful influence. The true function of journalism is to educate the public mind. I am a journalist myself and shall appeal to fellow journalists to realise their responsibility and to carry on their work with no idea other than that of upholding the truth. Besides being an expression of culture, civilization and freedom, journalism is also a carrier of revolution.[5]

Journalism can be Defined as–[6]

1. telling true stories, well and accurately.
2. communicating information that will help people make sense of their world.
3. getting the story behind the story, avoiding the spin, finding the truth.
4. a public trust with citizens to investigate and expose wrongs and trumpet rights.
5. being part of a community, or a "universal reflex of citizenship."
6. adding "meaning, context" to facts.
7. gathering, analysing, and disseminating socially relevant information in a consistent, transparent, and honest way.

Guidelines for a responsible journalism are–[7]

1. Journalism's first obligation is to tell the truth.
2. Its first loyalty is to the citizens.

3. Its essence is discipline of verification.
4. Its practitioners must maintain an independence from those they cover.
5. It must serve as an independent monitor of power.
6. It must provide a forum for public criticism and compromise.
7. It must strive to make the news significant, interesting, and relevant.
8. It must keep the news comprehensive and proportional.
9. Its practitioners must be allowed to exercise their personal conscience.

These guidelines and definitions provide an insight into the nature of Journalism. So the basic elements of Journalism are the passion for Truth, social responsibility, a core value system and wider public interest.

No wonder "A good newspaper, I suppose, is a nation talking to itself."– *Arthur Miller.*

"The power is to set the agenda. What we print and what we don't print matter a lot." – *Katharine Graham.*

"Take away the newspaper—and this country of ours would become a scene of chaos. Without daily assurance of the exact facts—so far as we are able to know and publish them—the public imagination would run riot. Ten days without the daily newspaper and the strong pressure of worry and fear would throw the people of this country into mob hysteria—feeding upon rumors, alarms, terrified by bugbears and illusions. We have become the watchmen of the night and of a troubled day…" –*Harry Chandler*

"I still believe that if your aim is to change the world, journalism is a more immediate short-term weapon."– *Tom Stoppard*

Indian Journalism during Freedom struggle - was active very much in this role. The visionary leaders of that era used this powerful weapon for the liberation of Mother India. The stalwarts like – Rajaram Mohan Roy, Bhartenduji, Tilak, Sri Aurobindo, Malviyaji, Ganesh Shankar, Makhanlal, Prarhkar, Gandhiji etc. used this medium to educate, inspire and to awaken the public about the cultural past, self rule and political freedom. No wonder the command of nation at that time was more in the hands of Journalists than the politicians. Journalists of the period were fired with the missionary zeal to serve the nation and society. Declared Gandhi Ji - The true function of journalism is to educate the public mind, not to stock the public mind with wanted and unwanted impressions. The sole aim of journalism should be service. The press is a great power, but just as an unchained torrent of water submerges whole country sides and devastates crops, even so an uncontrolled pen serves but to destroy. It can be profitable only when exercised from within[8] Indian journalism of the era was driven by the committed and sensible journalists.

After independence the missionary zeal of Journalism gradually fades away. Its process of conversion from mission to business begins. With the advent of globalisation and liberalisation it becomes a business.

Indian Journalism itself at Cross-Road

The state of India's press – which played such a pivotal role during the fight for Independence from the British – is now at a crossroads. Today media is a big industry. In the rate race of TRP and monetary gains the basic values of profession are at stake and the responsible journalism is a rare thing to see. There is grave degradation of values and media is in dire need of revival.

The media in India has grown into an economic giant, with a business turnover which exceeds one percent of the country's Gross Domestic Product and matches the economic size of many individual Indian industries. It is considered the world's most dynamic media industry and one of the fastest growing anywhere. The media's worth is equivalent to half the value of India's famously successful computer software exports.

For the past two decades, India's media business has clocked double-digit growth annually, which clearly outpaces India's GDP growth rate, which has itself risen from about 5 per cent to almost 9 per cent in a year. [9]

In India a worrying trend as the media becomes a big industry is the tendency to tradeoff favors with the political class. The phenomenon of 'paid news' and revelations by Radia tapes confirm that the market forces are playing a dominant role in formulation of news content and even cover ups.[10] Real events, stories about everyday heroes and news that effects the common man is often relegated to the lower ranks. And, in this age of sensationalism very little grassroots work it to our front pages except a few publications.[11]

The Indian media now faces a serious crisis of credibility. If it does not reform itself, it will find its greatest asset getting rapidly devalued and eventually vanishing. Robbed of authenticity, reliability and credibility, the media will cease to matter to large numbers of people except as a source of cheap entertainment and titillation. Journalism will then cease to be all that makes it worthy and socially relevant: an honest, investigative, analytical, public-oriented and ethical pursuit. That would be a grave tragedy and a terrible disservice both to democracy and to the causes of enlightening and empowering the public.[12]

In this hour of overall crisis there is need to give a spiritual touch to Journalism and promote positive and spiritual journalism. This is also the psychological need of the peoples fed up with the materialistic life style and the traditional institute of religion.

Historic Background of Spiritual Journalism

The trend was inevitable in the 20th century, in which the people turned to spirituality from the traditional religion. During this period a feeling of disgust and even hatred had evolved in the mind of rational people for the dogmatic and fanatic mode of religion.[13] In West the trend of Spirituality begins from this silent revolt. In the form of new age spirituality this trend starts in the mid sixties and by nineties it becomes wide prevalent.[14] From newspapers to books, health care centers to self improvement centers are established under this wave.[15] In this way in the industrial and developed countries this fascination for spirituality increases within and outside the traditional religion.[16] According to a survey people there like to be called spiritual rather than being leveled as religious.[17] Spirituality is in, religion is out. According to one poll, 24 per cent of Americans define themselves as being "spiritual but not religious."

In India this was the period of liberalisation and globalisation. With this triggers the pace of materialism, physical luxuries and economic progress. And side by life becomes more hectic, stressful and anxietyprone. Shattered humanity in the grip of consumerist culture in search of inner peace and stability seeks spirituality as breather. Indian media cater to the need of its consumers and the spiritual journalism steps in the mainstream journalism of India. Regular column in daily *Jansatta* and *Navbharta* by the name *Dharma kshetra* and *aastha* and *Ekda* starts during this period. In this track other dailies also starts this column regularly, later on with special weekly supplement on religion and spirituality are added. Before describing the present trend of Spiritual Journalism, it would be relevant to clarify the much confusion about the terms Religion and spirituality.

Spirituality vs. Religion

Broader definition of Religon is the immanent virtues of a person that gives his existence meaning. These include virtues to be inculcated in life. As such ten characteristics of religion are given by scriptures, which in the contemporary context can be called as-Truth, Discrimination, Self restrain, Dutifulness, Discipline, Idealistic resolves, Love-affection, Valor-Hard work, Cooperation and Benevolence-magnanimity.[18]

According to Encyclopedia of Religion, religion means peak experience.[19] The ways to this experience can vary, called as Hindu, Muslim, Sikh, Christ, Jain, Buddha, Parsi etc. Different dimensions of religion can be - Traditionalism, Myth and Symbol, concept of salvation, sacred places and objects, sacred actions (Rituals), sacred writings, Sacred community and Sacred experience.[20] They can be further abridged into four dimensions[21]:

1. **Philosophy** – The rationale of the whole scope of each religion. It represents the essence, the principles of every religion. These principles find expression in Mythology.
2. **Mythology** – Lives of saints or heroes, demi-gods, or gods, or divine beings. The philosophy of religion as illustrated in the lives of divine or human teachers acknowledged by each religion.
3. **Symbology or Rituals** – It is ceremonial part of religion using different Symbols, which presents concrete examples to the beginners to grasp and understand the subtler aspects of truth, which comes under Mysticism.
4. **Mysticism or Spirituality**—It is direct experience of the higher reality. It is the essence of the religion, its culmination point.

Mostly the differences between religions are between the first three dimensions. The acts of intolerance, violence and fanaticism are mainly due to overtly stress over the superficial facts than the spiritual one.[22]

To Swami Vivekananda Religion is the manifestation of the Divinity already in man.[23] Religion is not in doctrines, in dogmas, nor in intellectual arguments; it is being and becoming, it is realisation.[24] Religion is the realisation of spirit as spirit.[25] Religion is a question of being and becoming.[26] All the religions, from the lowest fetishism to the highest absolutism, mean so many attempts of the human soul to grasp and realise the Infinite.[27] The essential thing in religion is making the heart pure; the Kingdom of Heaven is within us, but only the pure in heart can see the king.[28] There is no greater Dharma than this service of living being.[29] Service to these (poor, illiterate, ignorant and afflicted) alone is the highest religion.[30]

In the words of Acharya Pt. Sri Ram Sharma, religion can be outlined in three dimensions – Ethics, theistic Philosophy and Spirituality (which includes spiritual practice and rituals).[31] It is his firm conviction that by following the ethics and ritual of a religion one gradually gets the glimpse of his infinite potential, which becomes the basis of Theism (*Astika)*. It further leads to the realm of spirituality with transformation of lower nature. This Spirituality is the common meeting point of different religion. It can be defined as – the Deepest centre of the person and experience of ultimate reality.[32] It is faith on God, nobility and peak of Idealism.[33]

Thus Religion is a path to God. Spirituality is also a path to God. However they have differences in approach. "The essence of religion: Fear God and obey God. The quintessence of spirituality: Love God and become another God." Spirituality comes from a sense of mystery and an unprovable sense that we are connected to the universe. Religion is the organised and formal system that was created to help human beings understand and maintain their relationship to that mysterious sense of connection. In fact, Religion is given life by the spirituality of those practicing it.[34] Religion is spiritual and spirituality is religious. One tends to be more personal and private while the other tends to incorporate public rituals and organized doctrines. The lines between one and the other are not clear and distinct — they are all points on the spectrum of belief systems known as religion. Neither religion nor spirituality is better or worse than the other; people who try to pretend that such a difference does exist are only fooling themselves.[35]

Spirituality can refer to an ultimate or an alleged immaterial reality; an inner path enabling a person to discover the essence of his/her being; or the "deepest values and meanings by which people live." Spiritual practices, including meditation, prayer and contemplation, are intended to develop an individual's inner life; spiritual experience includes that of connectedness with a larger reality, yielding a more comprehensive self; with other individuals or the human community; with nature or the cosmos; or with the divine realm. Spirituality is often experienced as a source of inspiration or orientation in life. It can encompass belief in immaterial realities or experiences of the immanent or transcendent nature of the world.

Spirituality is something for adolescents who want freedom; *religion* is for adults who are willing to be bound fast.[36]

Religion and spirituality do conjure up differences, but at the same time they are just terms and words. Spirituality and religion can be interchangeable. The boundary between religion and spirituality is fluid. In fact religion has been a fertile ground for the sprouting of Spirituality. Through following their religion, great saints have attained the fruits and realisations of a mystical approach to God. This includes Christian mystics such as Teresa of Avila, St Francis of Assisi, and Sufi saints like Rumi, Hafiz and Attar. Each religion has produced spiritual seekers of the highest order.[37] Swami Vivekananda, the Hindu Monk thundering the Parliament of World Religion at Chicago in 1893 was a product of Sanatna Dharma. To Swami Vivekananda, Religion as a science, as a study is the greatest and healthiest exercise that the human mind can have. This pursuit of the Infinite, this struggle to grasp the Infinite, this effort to get beyond the limitations of the sense – out of matter, as it were –and to evolve the spiritual man – this striving day and night to make the Infinite one with our being – this struggle itself is the grandest and most glorious that man can make…It is the greatest motive power that moves the human mind. No other ideal can put us the same mass of energy as the spiritual. So far as human history goes, it is obvious to all of us that this has been the case and that its powers are not dead.[38]

Religion is the greatest motive power for realising the infinite energy which is the birthright and nature of every man. In building up character, in making for everything that is good and great, in bringing peace to others and peace to one's own self, religion is the highest motive power and, therefore, ought to be studied from that standpoint...Religion must be studied on a broader basis than formerly. All narrow, limited, fighting ideas of religion have to go. All sect ideas and tribal or national ideas of religion must be given up.[39]

Besides in the words of great Psychologist Jung, Religion has therapeutic effects because it preserves the parental images in the individual. This protects the individual against up rootedness. When traditions disappear consciousness becomes separate from instincts and loses its roots.[40]

Thus spirituality and religion both are the part of spiritual journalism. Whole consciousness being the area of spirituality, whole human existence, society earth and planet are the area of concern and study under spiritual journalism. Of course it has nothing to do with the petty, narrow and dogmatic claims of surface religion.

Importance of Spiritual Journalism

In the present state of overall value degradation and thought pollution the value of spiritual journalism can be well understood. When most of the space is filled with sensation, crime, politics and all types of negative news and views, a sacred space for positive and elevating spiritual content can be seen as a breather to the media and its consumer.

Importance of Spiritual journalism can be seen as[41]-

1. Propagation of Positive thoughts
2. Motivation to move in the Righteous path
3. Cleansing the environment of thought pollution
4. Inspiration to live a moral and disciplined life
5. As a peacemaker between the religious clashes
6. Freeing the society from religious dogmas and superstitions
7. Revealing the subtler dimensions of life
8. Helping to Resolving the burning issues of the era
9. Ray of hope amid the present crisis of morality and cultural pollution
10. Awakening the Nation with a feeling of Self dignity
11. Bridging the gap between different hearts in Globalised world.

This is not a mere Utopia. Many spiritual magazines are active in this direction with selfless dedication and working silently as the torch bearers of value based and missionary journalism.

Evolving trend in Spiritual Journalism and its Present State

Mainstream Journalism and Leading Newspapers – The trend of devoting spiritual columns in dailies starting in the last decade of 120th century has further evolved in 21st century with weekly spiritual pageds, which is on the process of further growth.

Daily	*Regular Spiritual Columns*	*Weekly Spiritual pages*
Amar Ujala	Antaryatra	Shradha
Dainik Jagran	Urja	Urja, Saptrang Dharma aur adhyatam
Dainik Hindustan	Mansa Vacha Karmna	Anant Adhyatam
Rashtriya Sahara	Satsang	Dharm darshan
Times of India	The Speaking tree	Speaking Tree (8 page magazine)
Hindustan Times	Inner Voice	————————
The Hindu	Religion	————————
Economics Times	Cosmic Uplink	————————

Unfortunately, in the Mainstream Magazines. Space devoted for spiritual content is by and large questionable. Magazines like – India today, outlook, kadambini, the week etc. gives coverage to it only when there is some controversy or big event. Magazine like Aha Jindagi and Navneet have space devoted for such interviews or articles named *Atma sambad and Chintan respectively.*

In fact the true torch bearer of Spiritual Journalism are Magazines working silently with selfless service and devotion far away from publicity and propaganda.

Some of noted Spiritual Magazines -

Spiritual Magazine	*Publisher*	*Founder-Patron*	*Since*
Praudha Bharta	Advaita Ashrama Kolcatta	Swami Vivekananda	1896
Kalyana	Geeta Press Gorakhpur	Sanatna Dharma	1926
Akhanda Jyoty	Akhand Jyoty Sansthan Mathura	Acharya Pt Sri Ram Sharma	1940
Life Positive	Megus media Pvt. Ltd.	Dr. Kartikeyan	1996

Swarna Hansa	Sri Aurobindo Ashrama Pudduchery	Sri Aurobindo	—
Sri Aurovinda Karmadhara	Sri Aurobindo Ashrama Delhi	Sri Aurobindo	—
Osho World	Osho World foundation	Acharya Rajneesh	—
Veda Amrit	Pioneer Books ltd Mumbai	Sanatna Dharma	—
Viveka Jyoty	Ramakrishan Vivekananda Ashrama Raipur	Sri Ramakrishna-Vivekananda	1972

Spiritual Journalism – A Ray of Hope

The importance of these magazines as carrier of positive thoughts and holy vibrations can be understood as a means of silent and sattvic changes in the society. It can be well seen under following points –

As Manuals of Spiritual Growth : The magazines like – *Kalyana, Akhanda Jyoty, Agnishikhā, Purodha, akhand anana and Parmartha* etc. are so reputed among the reader that they are prescribed and read like sacred scriptures. Special issues of *Kalyana* like - *Manas ank* and *shakti ank* are used as part of spiritual *sadhana* on daily basis and special occasions.[42] Same is true about *Akhanad Jyoty*, spiritual magazine published from *Akhand Jyoty Sansthan Mathura.* Its Special issues on – *Yoga sadhna. Shishya Sanjeevni, Sri Guru Geeta, Antarjagat ki Yatra ka Gyan Vigyan* are use as spiritual manual by its devoted readers. Same can be said regarding some other spiritual magazines, which are spiritual companion to the seekers.

Examples of Value based Journalism: These magazines are being published at a very reasonable price without any advertisements even in this era of corporate culture. Motivated by the selfless service of masses, these magazines as such are the light house of inspiration for the values based journalism. Some of the magazine indulge in cheap advertisements but they don't have deep credibility among the readers and nor they have serious impact.[43]

Agents of Personal and Social Refinement – Due to powerful rational base and spiritual force spiritual magazenes have inspiring many big and small creative movements. *Akhand Jyoty* published from Mathura having millions of reader is working for the cultural and spiritual upliftment of society with *Yug Nirman Andolan. Kalyana* has been catalyst in spreading the spiritual message of *Sanatana Dharma* in millions of houses. People are inspired to lead a pure and *satvik* lifestyle by these magazines. These magazines have done great work by spreading noble thoughts and *sanskaras* in so many families. Besides spiritual magazine like – *Jata Ram Jyoty, Gujraty Kalyan, Jan Kayan, Akhand Ananda, Ananda Sandesh, Mahaprabhu Darshan, Guru Sarvbhom, Ramdarshan, Tatvadeep, Akhand Prabha, Akahand Sacchidananda Sandesh, Veda Savita* etc. have promoted small movements and inspires readers on spiritual path.[44]

Spiritual Journalism can be the Dawn of New Era: The vision of contemporary mystic and philosopher Acharya Rajneesh is worth noting - "Although politically we are free, psychologically we are still slaves. Journalism is a product of the West, and we are imitating whatever is being done there; it is not our creation. The West does not believe in any spirituality, and it is suffering great anguish and great anxiety because of it…Why it is significant to include the spiritual dimension in the teaching of journalism. Spiritualism is the very meaning of life. Without a spirit, a man is only a corpse. And without spiritualism, anything — education, journalism… they are only corpses, they stink…Although politically you are free, psychologically you are not free. Journalism has to attain freedom from the West and it has to give an authentic, original shape to itself. And you will be surprised that if you can manage to introduce a spiritual dimension to journalism, the West is going to imitate you sooner or later — because there is a great hunger, a great thirst….And spiritualism does not mean any kind of fanaticism. Spiritualism does not mean that you have to preach Hinduism, that you have to preach Jainism, or you have to preach Mohammedanism. Spiritualism simply means you have to spread the basic fundamentals of all religions, which are the same."[45]

"The time is ripe, and journalism can become the beginning of a new era…Spirituality means giving importance to something which is a permanent value, which gives life, light and guidance forever, which is sanatan, which is eternal. Eternal values constitute spirituality; momentary values constitute politics. Politics and religion are just polar opposites….One of the greatest revolutions in journalism will be, if we can create in this country a different kind of journalism— which is not dominated by politicians, but is inspired by its wise people…It should be one of the basic functions of journalism to bring the wise people and their wisdom before the masses, into the light.[46]"

Potential Challenges: To establish spiritual journalism and make it a weapon of positive change in society is a challenging task. The major challenges facing are –

1. **Still a Neglected Beat** - Despite being concerned to a big group, this is so far a neglected area in main stream Journalism. Mostly it is covered when

there is some scandal, big event or fair-festival.[47] On the regular column base most of English dailies are still giving hardly any space for it. In this aspect space given by *The Times of India* through *Speaking Tree* column and weekly magazine is commendable. In the view of experts, observing the bulk of Spiritual–religious magazines being published, even from business point of view they cannot be neglected altogether.[48] There potential is immense.

2. **Need to update with the Trend** – In this era of package there is need for the traditional magazines to update their lay out design and printing Quality. Also the tradition needs to be defined with the rational and scientific approach of the modern era.[49] Thus the spiritual convictions must be ready to face the litmus test of Science.

3. **Challenge of forging Spiritual Journalists** – This is perhaps the most challenging task. Because the journalist working for spiritual journalism must be properly trained with the basics of religion and spirituality. Firstly, there is no such training school or curriculum. Even if a school is established, to get such spiritual aspirants as media student is not an easy task. The crowd of youths aspiring media in search of glamour, money and prestige have nothing to do with spiritual journalism. Further the teacher to prepare spiritual journalists of competence need to be highly evolved acharyas of Character and high conduct.

Conclusion

Seeing the present crisis of value across the nation and globe there is needed to take multipronged steps in all directions. Revival of Mainstream Journalism on the spiritual track can be one such effective step. Present crisis of value is due to degeneration of thought force. Spirituality is one potent means to avert the present crisis of value. Shattered individual, fragmented society and agitating nation can be integrated only by the Spirituality. The idealistic vision of society looking to be a distant dream can be a reality of tomorrow on the basis of such efforts.[50] There is dire need to give the positive and uplifting material maximum space in media. Also a new breed of Journalist fired with the spirit of Self refinement and Service is needed. In the words of Acharya Sri Rram Sharma, "Amongst Newspapers/magazines published today none have missionary zeal nor do they have any program of serious nature. Henceforth in large numbers such newspapers/magazines must be published which instead of looking upon journalism merely as a profession to eke out huge amounts of cash should be imbibed as a mission and must throw true light on every aspect of human life".[51] The Least effort in this direction would be a great service to the ailing humanity and the Nation at cross road.

References

1. Bharty, Dr. Dharmveer, Manav mulya aur Sahitya, pp.134-135.
2. Pandya, Dr. Pranav, Akhand Jyoti, year 60, issue 3, p. 30.
3. http://www.irishadvocacynetwork.com/Jim%20Walsh.htm.
4. Naqvi, Hena, Journalism and Mass Communication, Upkar Publication, p. 1.
5. Tiwari, Dr. Arjun, Jansanchar smagra, Upkar publication, p. 50.
6. http://savethemedia.com/2009/04/06/so-what-is-journalism/.
7. Kovach Bill, The Element of Journalism.
8. http://www.asthabharati.org/Dia_July%20010/my.htm.
9. http://www.chillibreeze.com/articles_various/Journalism-trends.asp.
10. http://www.audiencescapes.org/india-media-crossroads-diversity-environment-Nira-Radia-development.
11. http://www.chillibreeze.com/articles_various/Journalism-trends.asp.
12. http://www.thesundayindian.com/en/story/indian-media-in-crisis-of-credibility/14766/.
13. Encyclopedia of Religion, Vol. 11, Mcmillan Pub. Co., NY, 2005, p. 720.
14. *Ibid.*
15. *Ibid.*, pp. 363-364.
16. *Ibid.*, p. 369.
17. Robert Withnow and Wade Clark Rod–Spiritual Market Place.
18. Acharya, Pt Shree Ram Sharma, *Dharm ka tatvadarshan evm marm*, CW-53, pp. 4.1-4.14.
19. Encyclopedia of Religion, Vol. 1, McMillan Pub. Co., NY, 1987, p. 286.
20. Encyclopedia of Religion, Vol. 11, McMillan Pub. Co., NY, 2005, pp. 7696-7700.
21. Complete Works – Vol. IV, p. 374, Vol. VI, p. 6, Vol. II p. 377.
22. S. Radhakrishnan – Religion in the Changing World, George Allen & Co, 1967, p. 70.
23. *Ibid.*, Vol. IV, p. 358.
24. *Ibid.*, Vol. II, p. 43.
25. *Ibid.*, Vol. I, p. 469.
26. *Ibid.*, Vol. IV, p. 216.
27. *Ibid.*, Vol. I, p. 17.
28. *Ibid.*, Vol. VIII, p. 8.
29. *Ibid.*, Vol. VI, p. 502.
30. *Ibid.*, Vol. VI, p. 288.
31. Acharya, Pt Shree Ram Sharma, *Akhand Jyoti*, June 1992, p. 23.
32. Encyclopedia of Religion, Vol. 11, McMillan Pub. Co., NY, 2005, p. 719.

33. Acharya, Pt Shree Ram Sharma, *Vigyan aur adhyatam: parspar purak, cw-28*, p. 5.13.
34. http://www.care-givers.com/pages/inspiration spiritvsreligion.html.
35. http://atheism.about.com/od/religionnonreligion/a/spirituality_2.htm.
36. http://witness2christ.blogspot.in/2011/12/are-you-spiritual-or-religious.html.
37. http://www.biographyonline.net/spiritual/articles/religion_vs_spirituality.html.
38. The Complete Works of Swami Vivekananda, Vol. II, p. 66.
39. *Ibid.*
40. Jung, Psychotherapy in the present, CW-16.
41. Aloke, Dr. TDS, Adhyatmik Patrakarita, Media Prabandahan, Suryaprabha Prakashan, pp. 54-56, 2009.
42. Jyotirmay, in Press, Prahar Aur Pratirodh by Gyanendra Rawat, p. 134.
43. *Ibid.*, pp. 134-135.
44. *Ibid.*, pp. 135.
45. Media Vimarsh, Year 1, issue 4, June-August, 2007.
46. *Ibid.*
47. Gautam, Roop Chand, Media aur Sanskriti, Sri Natraj Publication, p. 135, 2008.
48. *Ibid.*, p. 134.
49. Vedik, Ved Pratap, Hindi Patrakarita ke Vividh Ayam, p. 412.
50. Acharya, Pt Shree Ram Sharma, *Akhand Jyoti*, year 25, issue 2, p. 7.
51. Acharya, Shriram Sharma, *Akhand Jyoti*, June 1963, p. 44.

26

The Role of Media in Safeguarding Democracy – with Special Reference to Puducherry State

K. Kulasekarn, Dr. P. Rajendran

Introduction

This paper is analysing the role of media in safeguarding democracy with special reference to Puducherry State. India is the largest democratic country in the world, and media has a vital role in safeguarding the democracy. The role of the Media has been recognised as Fourth Estate and also as a forum for public discussion. The primary role of media is to deliver the news to the public and also to gather and report news that is true, fair, honest, accurate, non-biased and non-critical. The media also informs us about what is going on, in and around the world. It also helps to, investigate events and deliver information to a large number of diversified audiences. Media not only play an investigative role or cover entertainment, but also helps to safeguard the democracy, by way of informing the current democratic situations. The constitution of India does not specifically mention the freedom of press. Freedom of press is implied from the Article 19 (1) (a) of the Constitution of India. Thus the press is subject to the restrictions that are providing under the Article 19(2) of the Constitution of India.

In recent times, the media in Puducherry State has been subject to criticism for the manner in which they have disregarded their obligation to social responsibilities. Dangerous business practices in the field of media have also affected the fabric of Indian democracy. Though media has successfully played the role of a watchdog of the government activities, it has aided in participatory communication. The media also can play a positive role in democracy, if there is an enabling environment that allows them to do so. The biggest debate, as far as the characteristic of democracy in the nation goes, is the renewed debate between 'parliamentary democracy' and 'people's democracy'. In this paper, the tendency of media in Puducherry state, enactment of law and constitution body, media coverage and reporting on democracy and literature will be reviewed. This paper also attempts to gauge the influence of media reports on the corruption, human rights, social reforms and the unethical governance.

Hypothesis

This paper tries to review the role of media in safeguarding democracy with special reference to the Puducherry State. The paper tries to examine the following:

(1) Present trends and potential roles of media in Puducherry State,

(2) how the Government and constitutional body control the media in Puducherry and India,

(3) Role of the media in safeguarding Democracy in Puducherry, and

(4) Analysis of coverage of media with reference to Democracy in Puducherry.

This study also includes the interview conducted with media reporters to incorporate contextual information about their experiences and their level of involvement in safeguarding the democracy. While this study uses surveys, reporters are specifically chosen from the available population. The data was collected by interview and collected information from dailies and periodical published from Puducherry State.

Media and its Role in Democracy

As defined by Abraham, the common definition of democracy is 'the government of the people, by the people and for the people'. The word *"democracy"* is a term that comes from Greek and it is made up with two other words '*demos* = People' and '*kratein* = to govern, to rule'. "Democracy" can then be literally translated by the following terms: Government of the People or Government of the Majority. Democracy in its purest or most ideal form would be a society in which all adult citizens have an equal say in the decisions that affect their lives. Democracy is a form of government in which all citizens have an equal say in the decisions that affect their lives. Ideally, this includes equal participation in the proposal, development and passage of legislation into law. It can also encompass social, economic and cultural conditions that enable the free and equal practice of political self-determination.

According to some theories of democracy, popular sovereignty is the founding principle of such a system. However, the democratic principle has also been expressed as "the freedom to call something into being which did not exist before, which was not given… and which therefore, strictly speaking, could not be known". While there is no specific, universally accepted definition of 'democracy', equality and freedom have both been identified as important characteristics of democracy since ancient times. These principles are reflected in all citizens being equal before the law and having equal access to legislative processes. For example, in a representative democracy, every vote in India has equal weight, no unreasonable restrictions can apply to anyone seeking to become a representative, and the freedom of its citizens is secured by legitimised rights and liberties which are generally protected by a constitution.

The media in Puducherry and India are functioning for preserving the health democracy. Every citizen needs food, clothing, healthcare and shelter for his physical survival. Similarly communication is regarded as an indispensable factor for the social welfare of people. In this twenty first century every individual is keen to be updated with the latest developments in all walks of life. It is here where the Media comes into the picture which aims to reach out to a very large audience. It carries out its functions through advertising, marketing, propaganda, public relations and political communication.

Media is now considered as an effective tool for advocating business and social concerns. But what role does media and information play in a democratic society need to be examined as there is still a dispute regarding the significance and magnitude of media in Indian society. This is a fundamental principal established that the freedom of speech and of the press which is secured by the constitution does not confer on absolute right to seek or publish without responsibility ever one may choose.

In Indian media is always misused by political parties for the purpose of misrepresentation many politicians particularly in Puducherry State where they have started private channel either on their name or on their relatives. *AJK TV., G TV, Sun TV, Jay TV, and Kalainar TV,* etc. are good examples. The face of Puducherry media has been fast changing with the growth of the Internet, the phenomenal rise of satellite and cable networks, the continuing growth of regional press, despite various challenges and the blurring of lines between news and entertainment. But there is a sort of 'crises' in the present media due to processes of commercialisation, democratisation, and commoditisation. It is also often remarked that the quality of 'serious' political journalism is steadily declining, with a dilution in its substantive political content to the detriment of the democratic process. An opposite view asserts not that there is too little serious politics in the media, but too much. This is seen as a kind of information overload that bores audiences and diminishes public interest resulting it will safeguarding the democracy with their support.

Press Freedom and Legal Validity for Safeguarding Democracy

The Press Freedom is very importance role in the constitution of India for safeguarding Democracy of our Nation. For example, in a landmark judgment of the case *Maneka Gandhi v. Union of India, the Supreme Court held that 'the freedom of speech and expression has no geographical limitation and it carries with it the right of a citizen to gather information and to exchange thought with others not only in India but abroad also.'* The constitution of India does not specifically mention the freedom of press. Freedom of press is implied from the Article 19 (1) (a) of the Constitution of India. Thus the press is subject to the restrictions that are providing under the Article 19 (2) of the Constitution. Before Independence, there was no constitutional or statutory provision to protect the freedom of press. As observed by the Privy Council in Channing Arnold V. King Emperor: (*The freedom of the journalist is an ordinary part of the freedom of the subject and to whatever length, the subject in general may go, so also may the journalist, but apart from statute law his privilege is no other and no higher. The range of his assertions, his criticisms or his comments is as wide as and no wider than that of any other subject*).

The Preamble of the Indian Constitution ensures to all its citizens the liberty of expression. Freedom of the press has been included as part of freedom of speech and expression. The heart of the Article 19 (1) says: "Everyone has the right to freedom of opinion and expression, this right includes freedom to hold opinions without interference and to seek, receive and impart information and ideas through any media and regardless of frontiers." In *Romesh Thapar* v. *State of Madras*, Patanjali Shastri observed: "Freedom of speech and of the press laid at the foundation of all democratic organisations, for without free political discussion no public education, so essential for the proper functioning of the process of popular government, is possible." The Supreme Court observed in *Union of India v. Assn. for Democratic Reforms*: "One sided information, disinformation, misinformation and non information, all equally create an uninformed citizenry which makes democracy a farce. Freedom of speech and expression includes right to impart and receive information which includes freedom to hold opinions".

In *Indian Express v. Union of India*, it has been held that the press plays a very significant role in the democratic machinery. The courts have duty to uphold the freedom of press and invalidate all laws and administrative actions that abridge that freedom. Freedom of press has three essential elements. They are: 1. Freedom of access to all sources of information, 2. Freedom of publication, and 3. Freedom of circulation. In Puducherry State, the press has not been able to exercise its freedom to express the popular views. Democracy and media are the two essential components of Indian life. It has accomplished the task of transforming the lives of the people. But to what extent has Indian lives progressed and what advancement has the nation achieved is a matter of concern. Like every coin which has two sides the effects of media in Indian democracy has brought in serious advantages as well as disadvantages. We need to understand the role and functions of media in Puducherry State and the significance of media in democracy. There is a need to analyse media and democracy in relation with each other to comprehend the impact of these core aspects.

In the context, the media is having full power for safeguarding the democracy in India including Puducherry. It is highly focused various issues about the role of democratic and related activities often occurred in Puducherry State so as to safeguard the Democracy in India and Puducherry. Today, the various print and electronic Medias are focusing various issues for the healthy democracy to their audience. Either Government of India or Puducherry has not enacted any act to safeguard the Media because the Article 19 (1) (a) of the Constitutional India is giving freedom of writing and speech. Freedom of speech and expression, which are enable an individual to participate in public activities. The phrase, "freedom of press" has not been used in Article 19, but freedom of expression includes freedom of press. Reasonable restrictions can

be imposed in the interest of public order, security of State, decency or morality. It is a sufficient legal provision to safeguard the media and it will also safeguard the democracy by their voice.

Perception of Public about Media for Safeguarding Democracy

The Puducherry is a small union territory but numbers of the media is increasing day by day. Most of the print media in Puducherry have published the real story of democracy about the corruption, human rights issues, white collar crime and present trend of the politics for creating awareness among their audience for safeguarding democracy. Some of the Media has focused the fact of the corruption of various departments after obtaining information through Right to Information Act. The Department of Information and Publicity is the apex body and also nodal department for the print and electronic media. This Department is taking all welfare and controls of Media and issuing Media Persons identity card so as to take them press coverage freely in the jurisdiction of Puducherry. At the same time, the citizen in Puducherry will give complaint against the press to the Press Council of India when the print media publish the story against the rights of the public and violating the natural justice. Government of Pondicherry has a policy that protects the rights of the press to be free. Free from political or corporate influence. Free from any restraint. Free to carry out sting operations. Free to report anything that they deem worthy and various issues of democracy.

The media in Puducherry is published various story and news about the issues of democracy. Mainly the democracy is affected from the coverage and publishing story while it corrupted and on bias. Some time, least of media is published the false new and story which is paid news. Paid news means that news published after received money from a party and some news will be published for money. Mostly the media in Puducherry has published news story with corruption and on bias or against the corruption. Corruption is simply, use of public office for private profit. Thus, it is injustice, particularly in a democracy. So, exposing corruption through sting operation carried forward by media is an essential instrument to contain corruption. This will definitely empower democratic machinery for the upholding justice in its own right.

A democratic society permits freedom of speech and expression. We Indians have the freedom to think, freedom to write, freedom to discuss with others, freedom to explain, freedom to criticise and freedom to dissent. Democracy demands the fulfillment of every citizen's right to expression. Nowadays, media provides a platform for every individual to exercise his right of being heard. Innovative talk shows and public discussions organised by the media is now playing a major role in the enforcement of the right of freedom of speech and expression guaranteed as provided in the constitution of India.

Media in Puducherry has tried every possible means to satisfy the democratic ideals. For example, during Puducherry Legislative Assembly Election of Puducherry State in 2011, voters are educated and informed to the point where they are able to understand the most important political issues. During all these years the Puducherry media has successfully performed the following functions:

- Supporting democracy issues and informative programs so that people can make quick decisions for safeguarding the democracy.
- Cultivating alternative media, so that multiple voices and opinions will be heard.
- Mobilising popular participation in the transition process for making health democracy.
- Multiplying the impact of transition activities by disseminating information on successful local peace and participatory efforts in the issues of democracy.

Compared to the Tamilnadu, the freedoms that the press in Puducherry has could easily venture towards the right to slander. Media and democracy in Puducherry have been intertwined for a long, long time. While other state exercises freedom of the press, the reason that the setup of the Puducherry democracy's relationship with the media is so strong is because the media played a big role in helping Puducherry Government achieve their achievement. While the existence of a free press is one of the prerequisites of a democracy, the issues based media that we have in today's date is doing a job that can be certified as good enough. Access to information is essential to the health of democracy for at least two reasons. They can be analysed as follows:

(a) Media ensures health democracy that citizens make responsible, informed choices rather than acting out of ignorance or misinformation.

(b) Information serves as a checking function by ensuring that elected representatives uphold their oaths of office and carry out the wishes of those who elected them.

Analysis the Coverage of Media on the Issues of Health Democracy

The Puducherry State is a small Union Territory, but the numbers of media is upward day to day. A basic issue in the discussion of the role of the media in Puducherry and today's society is whether they do reflect social reality in a broad sense, or whether they filter out the view of reality which they see fit to be made public. Some media in Puducherry are focusing the issues of reality even it democracy or not, and some of the Media is downward in coverage of issue of democracy and it will publish the story for entertainment. In this context, it will constrained for this question is that the media do both, depending on the way we define reality. The media is a vital source of important information for people on the issues of democracy, primarily in the form of news that may affect them. People can be forewarned of problems and issues, so they can make better choices about their future including safeguard of democracy.

Every human being is entitled to enjoy certain rights which ensure good living. In a democracy all citizens enjoy equal rights. The Constitution of India guarantees those rights in the form of Fundamental Rights. Fundamental Rights are one of the important features of the Indian Constitution. Fundamental Rights are justifiable and are protected by the judiciary. The six fundamental rights recognised by the constitution are: (1) Right to equality, including equality before law, (2) Right to freedom which includes speech and expression, (3) Right against exploitation, (4) Right to freedom of religion, (5) Cultural and Educational rights, (6) Right to constitutional remedies. In case of violation of any of these rights one can move to the court of law for their protection. While the rights are given as guarantees to the people, the duties are obligations which every citizen is expected to perform.

Print Media

Printing Media in Puducherry State is functioning as powerful tool bringing out the issues of democracy. The challenges in democracy report in Puducherry State are in very critical position so as to bring out the real information to the public. As of now 143 Newspapers and periodical are being published from Puducherry. The people of Puducherry are reading the dailies and periodical in which the trend of political issues what are going on today. We have taken the following dailies and periodical have been taken for this study, which are: 1. *Dailies; Dinamalar, Dinathandhi, Malai Boomi, Malai Malai, the Hindu, and the Indian Express*. 2. Weekly; *Namadhu Manasatchi, Pondy Express, Pondy Times, and Puducherry Vision*, 3. Bimonthly; *World Union Goodwill, and Union Territory Independent*, and 4. Monthly; *Chozha Nadu, Pudhuvai Muzhakkam, and Puducherry Report*.

Mostly, the *Dinamalar*, and *Dinathanthy* were focused the rights against exploitation, and Right to constitutional remedies, but daily of *The Hindu* and *Indian Express* were focused the Right to freedom of religion, and Cultural and Educational rights. The periodical like weekly and Bimonthly mentioned above were focused about the rights against the exploitation and freedom of religions. The Monthly was focused about the rights of exploitation and cultural. But, the daily has not created the awareness about the freedom of religions. If the Tamil (regional language) focused the democracy issues against the exploitation and freedom of religions it will more appropriate for health democracy. The print media if supposed focused the democracy on equality it will most appropriate to Puducherry for better development. The various print media were covered the issues of safeguarding democracy in Puducherry State are analyzed and discussed in following paragraphs.

Mr. N. Rangasamy has formed a new political party namely All India N.R. Congress and he started this political party before two months from Assembly Election of Puducherry. The *Dinamalar* daily on 09.02.2011 has highlighted and focused the above issues of political democracy in the angle of the inefficient administration of the existing rolling party under the Government of Mr. V. Vaithilingalm, and why Mr. N. Rangasamy, enormous leader, has been dismissed by the Congress party. Further, it was appeared in the times of India newspaper and *Dinamalar* daily on 24.08.2011 that the Lok Adalat hosted by the Union Territory of Puducherry Legal Services Authority settled 23 cases and recovered Rs. 7.95 lakh from defaulters at Nettapakkam village of Puducherry State. The *Lok Adalat* of Puducherry the hosted for Indian Overseas Bank, 47 cases was settled and Rs. 18.51 lakh was recovered from the defaulter. So the media ensures the health democracy against exploitation.

During this study, some media have not covered this issue of democracy and publish article on bias. But some of the media was totally covered the news and issues of democracy and awareness about the election and powers of votes. This issue was created awareness among the voters of the Puducherry during Puducherry Legislative Assembly General Election during 2011. After analysed the coverage of Media, the voters of the Puducherry had decided that Mr. N. Rangasamy is a right person to make good government in the Puducherry. So, the reality of the story of present politics will make equality in safeguard the democracy.

In Puducherry, one incident was reported in the Arobindo Asharm, Puducherry that, one named Parvathisha was raped and murdered with her family members with the help of her husband. The accused parties have been supported indirectly by many high level politician of state and national level. Even though, the Supreme Court had dismissed the anticipatory bail petition of the accused due to the agitation of local peoples of Puducherry and real story covered by the media of local and national. In the above case, the media have taken their rights of freedom of expression and publish real story so as to create awareness among the public.

Credit goes to media campaign in several high profile cases like corruption in Pondicherry University in evolution of answered paper for MBBS and Engineering Examination, and various rights to votes, when every citizen of Puducherry who believes in justice received an opportunity to send their messages through cell phone, letter to the Editors of various electronic media, opinion columns, Editorial etc. Such messages were published in the *Dinamalar* on 23.09.2010 to evoke response and awareness among the people about their rights and duties and to sustain the dignity of common Indian.

Table 1: Safeguarding in the Issue of Democracy has been Focused by the Print Media

Sl.No.	*Dailies and periodicals*	*Focused and covered the issues of various types of democracy (in percentage)*				
		Equality	*Freedom of speech*	*Against exploitation*	*Religion, Cultural and Educational*	*Constitutional remedies*
1.	*Dailies*	20	20	15	30	15
2.	*Weekly*	15	15	20	30	20
3.	*Monthly*	15	15	15	35	20
4.	*Fortnightly*	25	25	20	15	15

Another one issues has appeared in the magazine namely Union Territory Independent (December 18-31, 2011) has published story entitled 'Non-cooperation'. It was focused that Puducherry is not getting adequate central funds and due to lack of funds development related to people are getting affected. The Union Territory Independent has blamed the Puducherry MP, who despite being influential in Delhi, not helping the Puducherry Government in its initiative to get central funds. This story is creating awareness among the public of Puducherry about lack of fund position. Based on result and discussion, the following has been constrained about the issues of the constitutional rights covered by the print media for safeguarding the democracy and which is place in Table 1.

Electronic Media

The some T.V. (private) named *Sun TV, Raj TV, Kalignar TV, and Zee Tamil TV* and also Pothigai T.V. (Government); some cable T.V. (private) named *AMN TV, Eye's TV, AJK TV, Sky Sat, Supreme TV, X4 TV,* and also FM (Private) and AIR (Government) were selected for this study. The Electronic Media of the above are covering and focused the news stories on the issues of safeguarding democracy in Puducherry. During this study, the private TV channel has mostly covered the issues against exploitation, cultural and constitutional remedies, which is discussed in the following paragraphs. Further, the cable TVs have focused the news story on bias and not cover the full story because most of parties established their channel for their own welfare. Moreover, the FM has not cover the any rights besides the AIR focused the issue of constitutional and cultural rights.

In Puducherry, the electronic media is starting their activities for safeguarding the democracy with visual shot. Some TV channel are covered the issues of democracy so as to create the awareness among the public of Puducherry State. The talk shows like "We, the People" provided the platform to hail justice and the whole country including the Puducherry was united to appreciate the judgment. "Nijan" (True) in Sun TV, *Sitharikapattavai* (imagination) in Jaya TV, *Nambinal Nambungal*" (may be believed) in Zee Tamil and "*Nadanthadu Enna*?" (what happened) in Jaya TV have the main theme of the various TV channel of Tamil Nadu and Puducherry which was the creating awareness about the various crimes of political, economic, social democracy so as to safeguarding the democracy.

The electronic media is focusing the all issue related with the democracy and bringing it to their door step. Thus the every citizen in Puducherry knows the real factor of the story what is going now in the Pondicherry. The X4 TV, 24 news channels has focused a story about a murder at Yanam of Puducherry State which was delayed by the Police for investigation and also creates awareness about dread for free life. Due to the awareness of the TV Channel, the people have got information about the violation of democracy and so they have struggled for constitutional remedies and free life without fear. So, the people of the Puducherry have called for strike on 02.02.2012 requesting constitutional remedies and it was successfully completed strike for making health democracy.

The role of government is vital in a democracy, and it is the media that not just inform us of their actions, but analyse and give opinions on their significance. Abuses by governments and others can be revealed, so the media becomes an important balancing factor to enable good government. Hence there is often a spectrum of the news media, including different 'camps' that generally reflect the different political points of view of politicians and the electorate. Many issues lack an absolute 'right' or 'wrong', but instead have a range of opinions catered for by the media. The down side of this is that objectivity can be submerged under a slant. However, most of these news outlets are commercial operations; they are there to make money.

During this study, the *Pothigai* TV (Public) has not focused the issues against exploitation equality rights but it has mostly cover the new story on cultural and education. The local electronic media has made the voice of the common man significant for the Pondicherry as a whole. When there was enactment of the Domestic Violence Act, 2005, there was wide ranging round of applause throughout the country. Based on result and discussion, the following has been constrained about the various issues of the rights covered by the electronic media for safeguarding the democracy and which is place in the Table. 2.

Table 2: Safeguarding in the Issue of Democracy has been Focused by the Electronic Media

Sl.No.	*Electro Media like T.V. and Radio*		Focused and covered the issues of various types of democracy (in percentage)				
			Equality	*Freedom of speech*	*Against exploitation*	*Religion, Cultural and Educational*	*Constitutional remedies*
1.	*T.V.*	*Public*	25	15	15	30	15
2.		*Private*	15	20	25	25	20
3.	*Radio*	*Public*	15	20	20	20	25
4.		*Private*	20	15	25	25	20
5.	*Cable T.V.*	*Private*	25	20	15	20	20

Other Media

Other media may be called the media other then print and electronic media and new media also called as other media. Now, the new media like website, e.mail, sms, and mms are also powerful tools for safeguarding the democracy. We have selected some website like Govt. of Puducherry Official website, and Puducherry online news for this study. The other media mostly cover against exploitation and Freedom of speech, etc. For example, during the Puducherry Legislative Assembly Election in 2011, the most of the political party sent their SMS to all mobile of the Public as "you may forward this sms to your five friends and then you will be recharged of Rs. 100 for your mobile". Now, every political party and media has hoisted their own website with the issues of democracy so as to creating awareness among their audience. The posters and banners were also fixed in various public places with the information about the issues of safeguarding the democracy. The effective coverage of the other media was analyzed and discussed in the Table. 3.

Table. 3: Safeguarding in the Issue of Democracy has been Focused by other Media

Sl.No.	Dailies and periodicals	Focused and covered the issues of various types of democracy (in percentage)				
		Equality	*Freedom of speech*	*Against exploitation*	*Religion, Cultural & Educational*	*Constitutional remedies*
1.	*Internet*	20	15	25	20	20
2.	*Wall Posters*	15	25	25	15	20
3.	*Hording & Banners*	20	25	20	20	15
4.	*Pamphlet & Pit notice*	15	25	25	15	20

In Puducherry, the various Media like print media (dailies and periodicals), electronic media (TV and Radio) and other media (Internet, posters, hoardings, etc.) are covering issues of democracy occurring in the local areas so as to create the awareness among them. It has been analysed and discussed in the angle of the coverage and focused by the media on the issues of democracy. During this study, the electronic media is focused and telecasting the news and story of democracy issues in prime level and next is print media and other media is in last position. The chart of the overall picture indicating awareness for safeguarding democracy is placed in the Chart 1.

Chart -1

Conclusion

Despite so many constraints, Puducherry news media played a brave and praiseworthy role in upholding democratic values in the country whether it was during the time of misappropriation of tsunami fund or autocratic democratic regime. Therefore, a patriotic government and media owners must realize the potential of media freedom for a democratic society and take necessary measures to lessen civil, political and economics controls over media.

The self regulatory mechanism across media organisations need to be strong enough to stop anomalies whenever they occur. Constitutional body like Press Council of India needs to be vigilant to stem the rot. Big media conglomerates are a serious threat. To counter this problem pluralistic media organisations which are financially viable need to be encouraged.

Media is like a watchdog in a democracy that keeps government active. From being just an informer it has become an integral part of our daily lives.

With the passage of time it has become a more matured and a more responsible entity. The present media revolution has helped people in making an informed decisions and this has led to beginning of a new era in a democracy.

All these years, since its establishment the media has worked for the progress and development of our country. All its activities were concentrated to see a fully fledged democratic Indian society. But observations also prove the fact that media nowadays prefer to sensationalise news. Media is losing interest in promoting democratic values and principles. Media corporations are now concerned about improving the financial position of their organisations. If this continues Puducherry can never fulfill its dream to be a developed nation by 2020.

References

1. Takis Fotopoulos, Dependent Development: the Greek case, Athens: Exantas, 1985.
2. Milton Friedman and Rose Friedman, Free to Choose, London: Penguin, 1979.
3. Karl Polanyi, The Great Transformation, Beacon Press, Boston, 1957.
4. Michael Taylor, Community, Anarchy and Liberty, Cambridge University Press, 1982.
5. Will Hutton, The State to Come, London, Vintage, 1997.
6. James Robertson, Beyond the Dependency Culture, Adamantine Press, 1998.
7. Noam Chomsky, 'On freedom of press and culture :an interview'.
8. World Bank, World Development Report, 1997.
9. Noam Chomsky, Domestic Constituencies, Z Magazine, May 1998.
10. The data about the film industry, Film and Television Handbbok, 1993.
11. Niklas Luhmann, Die realitat der massenmedien, Westdeutscher Verlag, Wiesbaden, 1997.
12. Edward S. Herman and Noam Chomsky, Manufacturing Consent, New York, 1988.
13. Pierre Bourdieu, On Television and Journalism, London:Pluto Press, 1996.
14. Maurizio Passerin d' Entreves, Hannah Arendt and the Idea of Citizenship, 2001.
15. Takis Fotopoulos, Towards An Inclusive Democracy, Yale University Press, 1988.
16. FICCI and PricewaterhouseCoopers, Indian Entertainment and Media Industry, 2006.
17. Retrieved from http://www.pwc.com/.
18. Flew, T., Democracy, participation and convergent media: contemporary online news, 2009.
19. Kumar, E., Journalism in Indian Communication, Politics and Culture, 2005.
20. Habermas, J., Information and democracy. Webster, 2006.
21. Jebaraj, P., Opinion: The spotlight is on the media, 2010.
22. McQuail, D. McQuail's Mass Communication Theory, Vistaar, Publications, 2005.
23. Panikkar, N. K., Opinion: Media and the public sphere, 2004.
24. Parceiro. S., The Role of Media in Democracy: A Strategic Approach, 2008.
25. Humanity and Social Sciences Journal, Retrieved from http://www.idosi.org/ hssj/ hssj3(1)08/2.pdf.

Index

D

E

F

K

L

M

N

R

S